Social Interaction in Learning and Instruction

The Meaning of Discourse for the Construction of Knowledge

ADVANCES IN LEARNING AND INSTRUCTION SERIES

Series Editors:
Andreas Demetriou, Erik De Corte, Stella Vosniadou and Heinz Mandl

Published

VAN SOMEREN, REIMANN, BOSHUIZEN & DE JONG
Learning with Multiple Representations

DILLENBOURG
Collaborative Learning: Cognitive and Computational Approaches

SCHNOTZ, VOSNIADOU & CARRETERO
New Perspectives on Conceptual Change

BLISS, SÄLJÖ & LIGHT
Learning Sites: Social and Technological Resources for Learning

KAYSER & VOSNIADOU
Modelling Changes in Understanding: Case Studies in Physical Reasoning

Forthcoming title

ROUET, LEVONEN & BIARDEAU
Multimedia Learning: Cognitive and Instructional Issues

GARRISON & ARCHER
A Transactional Perspective on Teaching and Learning

Other titles of interest

REIMANN & SPADA
Learning in Humans and Machines: Towards an Interdisciplinary Learning Science

Computer Assisted Learning: Proceedings of the CAL series of biennial Symposia 1989, 1991, 1993, 1995 and 1997 (five volumes).

Related Journals – sample copies available on request

Learning and Instruction
International Journal of Educational Research
Computers and Education
Computers and Human Behavior

Social Interaction in Learning and Instruction

The Meaning of Discourse for the Construction of Knowledge

edited by

Helen Cowie and Geerdina van der Aalsvoort

 Earli

2000

PERGAMON
An imprint of Elsevier Science
Amsterdam – Lausanne – New York – Oxford – Shannon – Singapore – Tokyo

ELSEVIER SCIENCE Ltd
The Boulevard, Langford Lane
Kidlington, Oxford OX5 1GB, UK

First edition 2000

Library of Congress Cataloging in Publication Data
A catalog record from the Library of Congress has been applied for.

British Library Cataloguing in Publication Data
A catalogue record from the British Library has been applied for.

ISBN: 0 08 043597 1

⊗ The paper used in this publication meets the requirements of ANSI/NISO Z39.48-1992 (Permanence of Paper).
Printed in The Netherlands.

3/3/03

Contents

Acknowledgement

Producing this book would not have been possible without the support of the European Science Foundation, Strasbourg. The European Science Foundation is an association of 62 major national funding agencies devoted to basic scientific research in 21 countries. The ESF assists its Member Organisations in two main ways: by bringing scientists together in its Scientific Programmes, Networks and European Research Conferences, to work on topics of common interest; and through the joint study of issues of strategic importance in European science policy. The scientific work sponsored by the ESF includes basic research in the natural and technical sciences, the medical and biosciences, the humanities and social sciences. The ESF maintains close relations with other scientific institutions within and outside Europe. Through its activities, the ESF adds value by cooperation and coordination across national frontiers and endeavours, offers expert scientific advice on strategic issues, and provides the European forum for fundamental science. This book is one of the outcomes of the ESF Scientific Programme on "Learning in Humans and Machines".

Contributors

Geerdina M. van der Aalsvoort
University of Leiden
Department of Special Education
Wassenaarsewegg 52
2333 AK Leiden
The Netherlands

Carla van Boxtel
University of Utrecht
Department of Educaitonal Sciences
Heidelberglaan 2
3584 CS Utrecht
The Netherlands

Raymond A.J. Brown
The Graduate School of Education
The University of Queensland
Brisbanee
Queensland 4072
Australia

Helen Cowie
School of Psychology and Counselling
Roehampton Institute London
West Hill
London SW15 3SN
UK

Ed Elbers
Faculty of Social Sciences
Utrecht University
P.O. Box 80140
3508 TC Utrecht
The Netherlands

Eveline Gebhardt
University of Amsterdam
Department of Education
Wibaustraat 4
NL-1091 GM Amsterdam
The Netherlands

Michèle Grossen
University of Lausanne
Lausanne
Switzerland

Frits J.H. Harinck
University of Leiden
Department of Special Education
Wassenaarseweg 52
2333 AK Leiden
The Netherlands

Judith Ireson
Psychology and Special Needs Group
Ireson Institute of Education
University of London
25 Woburn Square
London WC1H 0AA
UK

Gabrielle Ivinson
School of Education
The Open University
Walton Hall
Milton Keynes
MK7 6AA
UK

Gellof Kanselaar
University of Utrecht
Department of Educaitional Sciences
Heidelberglaas 2
3584 CS Utrecht
The Netherlands

Kristiina Kumpulainen
University of Oulu
Faculty of Education
PO Box 222
FIN-90571 Oulu
Finland

Paul P.M. Leseman
University of Amsterdam
Department of Education
Wibautstraat 4
NL-1091 GM Amsterdam
The Netherlands

Jos van der Linden
University of Utrecht
Department of Educaitonal Sciences
Heidelberglaan2
3584 CS Utrecht
The Netherlands

Neil Mercer
Centre for Language and Communications
School of Education
The Open University
Walton Hall
Milton Kenes
MK7 6AA
UK

Mika Mutanen
University of Oulu
Faculty of Educaiton
PO Box 222
FIN-90571 Oulu
Finland

Paul Naylor
School of Pscyhology and Counselling
University of Surrey Roehampton
West Hill
London SW15 3SN
UK

Peter D. Renshaw
The Graduate School of Education
The University of Queensland
Brisbane
Queensland 4072
Australia

Sylvia Rojas-Drummond
Faculty of Psychology
Graduate Division
National Autonomous University of Mexico
  (UNAM)
A.P. 22-836
Tlalpan 14000 DT
Mexico

Linda Rollenberg
University of Amsterdam
Department of Pedagogy
Wibautstraat 4
1091 GM Amsterdam
The Netherlands

Leen Streefland†
Freudenthal Institute for Mathematice
  Education
Utrecht University
Tiberdreef 4
3561 GG Utrecht
The Netherlands

Rupert Wegerif
Centre for Language and Communications
School of Education
The Open University
Walton Hall
Milton Keynes
MK7 6AA
UK

†Leen Streefland died on April 29, 1998.

1

Introduction

Helen Cowie and Geerdina M. van der Aalsvoort

The idea for this book grew out of the activities of the EARLI Special Interest Group, Social Interaction in Learning and Instruction. An experts' meeting at the University of Leiden in April 1998 provided a forum for discussion of issues – theoretical and applied – in the domain of the social context of learning. This edited book arose from that meeting.

In Chapter 2 Van der Aalsvoort and Harinck discuss methodological approaches and problems regarding the study of social interaction. Taking the bio-ecological model of Bronfenbrenner and Ceci (1994) as their main theoretical framework, they claim that *social interaction* links learning and instruction and affects effective functioning. They provide an overview of different models and discuss the potential of these approaches for investigating social interaction in the classroom in the context of teaching and learning processes. They conclude by suggesting criteria for evaluating studies that use discourse to illuminate learning outcomes.

In Chapter 3, Grossen starts from the assumption that cognition is a situated activity rooted in social practices. Here she explores the relationship between institutions and cognition in three ways: (i) the framing of institutions upon the individual's actions and competence in teaching-learning situations, as well as in test situations; (ii) the relationships between institutions and the representations which individuals have of a body of knowledge; (iii) the intertwining of institutions and social identities. She argues that institutions both determine, and are constructed through, inter-individual interactions, and suggests that there is a close relationship between cultural innovation and reproduction, and between inter- and intra-subjectivity.

In Chapter 4, Elbers and Streefland argue that we need to know how children view themselves as learners for an understanding of how children learn and co-operate. The introduction of a new mathematics curriculum in one classroom, in which the pupils worked as a community of inquiry, compelled teachers and pupils to create new forms and expressions for their co-operation. The pupils, aged between 11 and 13 years, and their teachers had to negotiate new roles in the classroom. The authors claim that these new discursive means created new identities amongst the members of this community of inquiry.

In Chapter 5 Brown and Renshaw explore classroom practices in the upper primary school. They use a sociocultural perspective as a tool to generate new practices and to reflect critically on change as it has occurred. One pedagogical strategy that they use is "collective argumentation" and they include a principle of "consensus" and a principle of "recontextualisation". Consensus requires that all members of the group understand the agreed approach to solving the problem. Interactively it requires that all members of the group contribute to the co-construction of arguments in support of the solution process, and can articulate the arguments in their own words. The "recontextualisation" principle involves children re-presenting the co-constructed argument to the other members of the class for validation. Communicating to class members outside the group challenges students to rephrase their ideas in terms familiar to the class, to defend their thinking from criticism, and perhaps to reassess the validity of their thinking.

In Chapter 6 Ivinson also claims that the curriculum can be understood as a social representation both as a whole and in its parts. Teachers' social representations of the curriculum, exemplified in classroom practice and discourse, provide the resources from which children internalise the curriculum. Children re-construct the curriculum as an active process that depends on the development of their own socio-cognitive resources and on the structure provided in specific classrooms. In her chapter she investigates how children in classrooms with three different types of curriculum organisation represent the curriculum and how these change over time. Ethnographic investigations were employed to compile a typology of recognition and realisation rules used to map the range and type of curriculum structure in each classroom. Children's representations of the curriculum were investigated through specially designed psychological instruments. The chapter focuses on the findings from one of these, a modified version of Kelly's repertory grid, which yielded both quantitative and qualitative data.

The case study presented in Chapter 7 by Naylor and Cowie illustrates the collaborative learning that takes place when young people in partnership with an adult team are trained in the skills of peer support. They claim that group learning environments, if properly structured, encourage questioning, evaluating and constructive criticism, leading to a restructuring of knowledge and understanding. It is not just the encounter that brings about change, but the internalisation of this joint intellectual activity. They suggest that it is not only "expert adults" who construct children's social and cognitive learning experiences. The implication is that Vygotskian ideas about social learning and scaffolding are to be generalised to all learners, adults and children alike, and it includes the likelihood that "expert children" can scaffold adults' learning.

In Chapter 8 Leseman, Rollenberg and Gebhardt present a study in which they examined four-year-old kindergartners' free play from the perspective of cognitive co-construction with respect to effects of social and individual factors. It was argued that co-construction processes in social interaction could be seen as the creation of an intersubjective zone of proximal development, but that the cognitive-educational potential of this ZPD would depend upon *what* was actually constructed in the social process based on the research literature into family socialisation. The four-year-old children who were studied in free play situations did play interactively most of the time and, within their interactive play, appeared to collaborate quite well as was reflected by the large proportion of shared verbal and nonverbal actions.

In Chapter 9, Ireson examines the aspects of educational settings that influence interactions between teacher-child dyads. She contrasts two settings: a construction activity in a pre-school playgroup and individual teaching of reading in a primary school. The first study gives examples of the part played by both adults and young children in an open-ended activity. Ireson concludes that the adults' participation in the activity was influenced by the perceptions of the cultural setting of the playgroup and their pedagogical beliefs about educational provision. In the second study, Ireson considers the links between teachers' perceptions of programme goals and the ways in which they structure the activity. She concludes that the complex process of structuring and engaging in educational activities needs to be viewed in a wider pedagogical and social context than has been traditionally presented.

Kumpulainen and Mutanen introduce a descriptive system of analysis for investigating the situated dynamics of peer group interaction in Chapter 10. The method takes a dynamic and process-oriented perspective on peer interaction, which is seen as socially and situationally developed in students' evolving interactions. The authors find the mechanisms of social and cognitive dimensions of peer group activity of particular importance. Their method of analysis has emerged as a result of a number of studies they have conducted of primary-aged students' classroom interactions on various educational tasks in Greece, Britain, and in Finland. The main goal in these studies has been to investigate the nature of students' social interaction, particularly verbal interaction in different learning situations.

In Chapter 11, Van Boxtel, Van der Linden and Kanselaar describe and illustrate indicators of deep processing activities in a collaborative learning environment. They claim that deep processing is needed to achieve and extend conceptual understanding. They present the results of an experiment that was designed to investigate the effects of some task characteristics on the appearance of deep processing in student interaction. According to Van Boxtel et al. conceptual understanding implies that a person can communicate the meaning of a certain concept, relate the concept to other concepts within the domain and use the concept adequately in explaining an object or phenomenon in a scientific way or in performing an action.

In Chapter 12, Wegerif and Mercer use analysis of the talk of children to explore the changes in language use that occur as children work together on a reasoning task. The authors combine the idea that reasoning is embodied in social practice with a neo-Vygotskian view of individual cognitive development. They describe a study in which children were encouraged to use "exploratory talk", a kind of talk in which reasoning is made explicit, and the effects of this experience on their ability to solve a reasoning task. They found that the individual scores of children who had been encouraged to use exploratory talk improved significantly in comparison with a control group. In analysing the children's talk, the authors not only explored effective group work but also elaborated on the relationship between social interaction and individual reasoning.

In the Chapter 13, Rojas-Drummond summarises two strands of research on the nature of guided participation taking place in Mexican pre-school and primary classrooms (including interactive and discursive practices between adults and students), and on the relationship between guided participation and the construction of students' knowledge in several domains. This research has been greatly influenced by a sociocultural perspective. A consistent pattern emerged when results were taken together: particular styles of guided participation characterised by social-constructivist, scaffolded practices between adults and children were associated with a more competent and independent performance in activities when compared with more conventional, directive, transmissional practices.

In Chapter 14, Van der Aalsvoort, Cowie and Mercer overview the contributions through a template that interrogates issues of content and methodology. They conclude by suggesting new perspectives regarding the use of discourse to study the construction of knowledge.

2

Studying Social Interaction in Instruction and Learning: Methodological Approaches and Problems

Geerdina M. van der Aalsvoort and Frits J.H. Harinck

Introduction

Contributions to the study of learning and instruction related to social interaction have been made from a number of areas such as mother–child interaction, teacher–child dyads and psychotherapy. In this contribution, we will discuss methodological approaches and problems regarding the study of social interaction with respect to its meaning for learning and instruction. We will start with a short review of approaches, and discuss their potential for investigating social interaction in the classroom in relationship to teaching and learning processes. Moreover, we will highlight the need for complementary approaches in this respect.

The bio-ecological model is our main theoretical framework to understand social interaction in relationship to learning and instruction regarding developmental outcome (Bronfenbrenner & Ceci, 1994; Ceci et al., 1997). This relationship consists of specific types of environmental resources, e.g. interactions that are called proximal processes. The effectiveness of learning and instruction is understood through studying these proximal processes. The method of studying learning and instruction thus needs to include both individual as well as social processes that occur during teaching and learning. This point of view requires the study of social interaction as a means and as a contributor to learning outcomes. The interdependence between social and individual processes is recognized in the constructivist approach with respect to the construction of knowledge (Vosnadiou, 1996; Salomon & Perkins, 1998; Palincsar, 1998).

We define social interaction for the purpose of this chapter as an ability to engage with others as persons and specifically to be equipped to engage in mutual influence over others as a fundamental capacity. There occurs a contingent reciprocal coordination of actions reactions, and emotional expressions over time from the partners in the interaction (Dallos, 1992).

In the following paragraphs we start out with describing the main paradigms that form the background of studying social interaction in the classroom. We proceed by explaining methods that are used in each of these paradigms in order to investigate social interaction in relationship to instruction and learning processes. We conclude our contribution by discussing the state of the art of each method with respect to investigating social interaction from a multi method approach.

Basic Paradigms in the Study of Social Interaction

Paradigms are systems of inquiry with particular underlying ontological, epistemological and axiological assumptions (Hoshmand & Martin, 1995, p. 12). Paradigms that are most influential for social interaction research are briefly reviewed in this section. We will first briefly review the empirical and the ethno-methodological paradigm as these have been foremost in their influence on social interaction research. In the last decades two other approaches have gained influence, the linguistic approach and multi method pluralism. These approaches will also be included in the review.

(a) In the *empirical tradition*, a number of related philosophical approaches converge, like positivism, neo-positivism and critical rationalism. In this tradition (e.g. Guba & Lincoln, 1983) reality is seen as a single observable reality, existing outside the researcher. It is the researcher's task to observe and describe this reality in order to produce knowledge with a firm empirical basis. Theories have no or limited value, until the researcher confronts them with empirical reality (testing of hypotheses).

Hypotheses are propositions that are derived from a theory and that describe causal relations between two or more elements of the theory. These elements are translated into variables that can be measured in empirical reality. Objectivity in the measurement (or at least intersubjective agreement) is highly important, as the results of the testing procedure should be independent from the researchers. For the same reason interaction between researcher and subjects studies are kept on a minimum level and restricted to research needs. The empirical researcher may be considered as an external expert, gaining knowledge by objective procedures. Only theories that survive successive testing of derived hypotheses are considered valuable. Furthermore, a theory is considered more valuable as it has larger scope and contains laws with a higher degree of generalizability (nomothetic laws). The empirical researcher generally selects a small part of reality for research and theory testing (analytic point of view). According to the empirical tradition, this part can be studied isolated of its context.

The experiment has traditionally been a favourite research tool in the empirical tradition. However, a growing disappointment with its possibilities has led to a number of new approaches, e.g. quasi-experiment, correlational design, time series analysis. Nowadays few empirical researchers believe in the more rigid assumptions of the empirical tradition. Particularly positivism has been almost completely abandoned (Cronbach, 1975).

(b) The *ethno-methodological paradigm* includes orientations like symbolic interactionism, hermeneutics, grounded theory, ethnography and phenomenology (Creswell, 1998). As opposed to the empirical tradition, ethno-methodologists do not believe in a single observable reality or in general laws. Their world is a multiple meaningful world, guided by rules and patterns that are dependent on the context and persons studied. Human beings in the ethno-methodological paradigm are seen as giving meaning to their environment instead of obeying causal laws.

Research is not primarily directed at observing behaviour but at learning the "insiders point of view".

In order to understand this point of view "one has to go where people live, participate in their activities, asking questions, eating strange foods and learning a new language, watching ceremonies, taking field notes, washing clothes, writing letters home, observing play, interviewing informants ..." Rather than "studying people" ethnography means "learning from people" (Spradley, 1979, p. 3).

Generally, ethno-methodologists do not use a structured approach in their inquiry. Participant observation and non-structured interviewing are favourite research tools. Moreover, written documents may be used if available.

(c) The *linguistic approach* may elicit doubts whether it is a paradigm such as the empirical and the ethno-methodological tradition. However, its influence on social interaction research is substantial and warrants an inclusion in this section. In this approach, reality is studied as language, e.g. meaningful utterances used in social communication, written products containing such communication. According to Edwards and Westgate (1994, p. 13) investigating classroom talk is needed "in order to understand more clearly how language is used and organized in various modes of teaching and learning".

Linguistic approaches have attributed both to theoretical views concerning language uses and to techniques, used for coding and analysis of language. Two sentences with an identical semantic content may refer to totally different meanings because of differences in intonation, pitch, pauses, or nonverbal cues like eye gaze, spatial organization of speakers or body movements. Linguistic tools assist researchers to interpret these differences in a valid way.

On a theoretical level, the linguistic tradition has drawn attention to the role of non-linguistic factors in talk. Differences between syntax and "language-in-use" gradually were included in interpreting language between teachers and students in order to understand social and cognitive factors. "Language-in-use" consists of discourse types. These types are related to speaker characteristics such as social status, age, sex, and race. Moreover, the situation where language is used and the partners involved are relevant cues to interpret discourse.

Finally, rules in classroom talk evolve during classroom talk by way of reciprocal and spiral processes that elicit in-depth meaning to the partners in conversation. Shortly in modern linguistics: "Individual speakers are deemed to operate not with a language, but with wide linguistic repertoire, developed through need and experience, and appropriately deployed as they move between and within the social networks they belong to ... Meanings conveyed in talk may be far more extensive and complex than might appear from the words that are used" (Grice, in Edwards & Westgate, 1994, p. 22).

(d) *Multi method pluralism approach*. On a philosophical level, it is easy to differentiate the paradigms mentioned before. For many years, its followers have strictly adhered to the rules of their paradigms, battling the opponents of competing paradigms. In the seventies however, controversies gradually weakened and researchers got progressively interested in the tools of alternative paradigms

(Miles & Huberman, 1984, pp. 19–20; Patton, 1986, pp. 210–213). This development is called the multi method pluralism approach, referring to a combination of tools from different methodologies in order to gain more fully an understanding of phenomena studied.

This pluralistic approach, also called "paradigm of choices", is currently the dominant paradigm in social sciences. Mishler states that "in fact it is harder to find any methodologists solidly encamped in one epistemology or the other. Increasingly 'quantitative' methodologists, operating from a logical positivist stance, are using naturalistic and phenomenological approaches to complement tests, surveys and structured interviews. On the other hand an increasing number of ethnographers and qualitative researchers are using predesigned conceptual frameworks and prestructured instrumentation. Few logical positivists will now dispute the validity and explanatory importance of subjective data and few phenomenologists practice pure hermeneutics" (Mishler, in Miles & Huberman, 1984, p. 20).

Methods in Studying Social Interaction

In this section, four different approaches of social interaction analysis will be presented. These approaches can be roughly connected with the first three paradigms discussed in the preceding section. However, they all have their share in methodological pluralism. In fact, it is difficult to present pure examples of an approach. Each approach is introduced with a description of its main characteristics. Next, an example is presented to put flesh on the bones and to illustrate strength and weaknesses.

Systematic Observation and Use of Sequential Analysis

Introduction
Systematic observation is one of the main tools in the empirical tradition. The focus is on observable, moment to moment interactions and elaborate category systems have been constructed for a detailed coding of such behaviours. A wide variety of scientific fields already exist in which methodological issues have been discussed as well as resolved following the tradition of systematic observation. For examples we refer to Flanders (1967) and Kerry (in Edwards & Westgate 1994, p. 91) for classroom interaction, to Bales (1968) for group discussions, to Erkens (1997) and Littleton and Light (1999) for interactions with computers, and to Kiesler (1973) and Kazdin (1992) for psychotherapeutic interaction. Generally, these systems encompass a broad range of behaviour categories for all interaction partners. A number of powerful techniques have been developed for the analysis of interaction and behaviour sequences (e.g. Wampold, 1995; Bakeman & Gottman, 1997). We will shortly review some of its basic principles.

A major point of reference in this approach is the behaviour stream. Social processes are conceived as a system of two or more individuals. Each of these individuals is constantly emitting small behavioural acts and this sequence of behaviours is called behaviour stream. A behaviour stream can be seen as a chain of small behavioural acts, e.g. a sentence or a meaningful motor movement. Actual behaviours show great diversity but the researcher codes "states", each behaviour acts as one of a small number of behaviour categories. In this way, a behaviour stream is reduced to a large number of subsequent states in which the interaction partners proceed. The states may be time based, or based on logical units (utterances) and episodes (Hoogsteder, Maier & Elbers, 1996). Analysis of interaction from this perspective means searching relationships between the individual behaviour streams. The following principles are useful in this approach:

- *contingency*: State A and B are contingent if the presence of one of the states (e.g. A) will increase the probability that the interaction partner will show state B. An example is that a teacher asking his students "to suggest problem-solutions", increases the chance that they will 'come up with solutions".
- *basic and transitional probability*. In order to know whether the probability for a certain state increases, it is necessary to know its "natural probability" or base rate. The base rate for state B is defined as the number of units coded as "B" divided by the number of units observed. The base rate for state B is compared with its "transitional probability". To discover a sequential relationship between A and B given state A, the transitional probability is defined as the number of times that state B is shown after the partner was in state A, divided by the number of times the partner was in state A.
- *self-dependency and other dependency*. Much behaviour shown is not primarily related to partner's behaviour, but to the own preceding behaviours. Although interaction analysis generally will focus on partner-dependent relationships, it is possible to test for self-dependent relationships by studying the sequence of states in an individual behaviour stream. If self-dependency fully dominates other-dependency, one can doubt if partners really interact.

Systematic observation techniques have been heavily criticized given the strict assumptions and the degree of reduction present in the tools discussed (e.g. Shotter, 1990; Karasavvidis, Pieters & Plomp, 1998). Still one should be careful to abandon this approach. Firstly many interaction modes (for example the more structured types of classroom interaction) fit well within the moment to moment interaction paradigm, particularly when the focus is not on the content or intentions of the behaviour shown, but on its form and short-term function. Moreover, researchers in this tradition have struggled with the limitations of their tools and sometimes found solutions to enhance their scope within the tradition of systematic observation. In the example below, some of these developments will be shown.

Example of a systematic observation study

The example is derived from an observational study on interaction in play therapy (Harinck, 1986; Harinck & Hellendoorn, 1987). Although this topic is somewhat beside the area of social learning the study seems suitable to illustrate the possibilities of the method and a number of limitations. The study focuses on children receiving Imagery Interaction Play Therapy (IIPT)[1]. The data consist of 60 videotaped play therapy sessions, representing different therapy stages with 15 children. All videotapes are scored on form, content and style. We will discuss the analysis of form, the focus of the study. Form aspects were scored every 5 seconds with an observation system that was composed of 34 categories. The system was rooted in phenomenological play theory but the individual categories were derived from a content analysis of transcripts from play-therapy sessions. Although there were little differences between child and therapist categories, both systems were sufficiently similar to bypass these differences. Examples of categories were non-play categories (exploration of playroom; asking for help; giving information); play categories (naming play material; functional play action; expressing play emotion).

A first problem arose in the construction of the category system. IIPT can not be understood completely from verbal utterances only. Non linguistic verbal behaviour, such as speech speed and voice intonation as well as gestures and gross motor movements, plays an additional but important role. We constructed multimode categories: both verbal and non-verbal behaviour cues were used in the process of coding. The category "shows emotion in play-context", for example, is scored in each of the following occasions: child says: "The doll is angry"; child's voice sounds "angry"; child shows aggressive movements, e.g. a toy soldier is stamping another soldier. Moreover, priority rules were given for conflicting circumstances such as motor behaviour contradicting verbal behaviour.

A second problem to be solved was the role of context information. Observers were asked to score a unit in its context, referring to the behaviours preceding it and if necessary the next behaviour unit. Although this approach is not the default one in the empirical tradition, we found it virtually impossible to score isolated units in the context of play therapy where many utterances or behaviours were understood as a reaction to preceding behaviours.

A third problem that we encountered was that within a session several types of interactions occurred. These were the formal context at the beginning and the end of a play-session (e.g. saying goodbye, making arrangements for the next sessions, explaining what the child is coming to do here); the context of talk when child and therapist exchange information and express feelings, and the context of playing together (e.g. selecting materials, functional play, make believe play). Each of these types or modes of interaction has its own rules, and requires specific observation categories: the categories are related to interaction context.

After the scoring (about 50,000 time intervals were coded) we started with simple frequency counts and sequential analyses. The results are mentioned only briefly here. According to our expectation, high frequencies were found for all the play categories,

---

[1] IIPT is a phenomenological form of play therapy with a strong emphasis on working through emotional problems in the disguised form of symbolic play. It is assumed that the working through of the problems in symbolic form has healing properties, and that talking about the problems with the child in this context is considered as less important. The therapist is supposed to join in the child's play, thereby facilitating, modelling and supporting the child's own way of expressing himself.

for both child and therapist. Moreover, talk is rare during play, except for "play-talk". When the child plays and the therapist is interrupting his play activities for some moments, he will prefer "giving simple attention" instead of "talk" as a general rule. We also checked for self-dependency and other-dependency, using log linear analyses. We found that self-dependency was the major determinant of shown behaviour for child and therapist, revealing that the behaviour of each participant was most strongly related to his own preceding behaviour. But there was also evidence for "other-dependency": child behaviour was related to preceding therapist behaviour and vice versa. Other-dependency was stronger for therapists than for children. Moreover, other-dependency was strongest during make-believe play, the central therapeutic medium according to IIPT.

A fourth problem arose regarding the limitation of sequential analysis as it isolates behaviour from its context. We were interested in how the therapist reacts on the child showing behaviour A, and lumped together all the instances where the child showed A in order to study the next reaction of the therapist. This procedure has two disadvantages. Firstly the focus is on two behaviour unit-chains and the studied interaction is a very short-term interaction, a 10-second interval. Next, it would be more interesting to study behaviour sequences in a short meaningful episode of 5 or 10 minutes. For example: a play-theme within one session including selecting materials, arranging them, introducing imaginative elements, and then a fully developed imaginative play. We expected that play categories are hierarchical: generally play-preparation will be at the start of a theme (selecting and arranging materials), sometimes followed by functional play (play activities with few imaginative elements; riding with the toy), and ideally leading to fully developed imaginative play.

We discovered that a simple plotting of scores on a time axis was very helpful to analyse behaviour streams during short episodes. An example of this approach is presented in Figure 1. In this figure, time (5-second intervals) is plotted horizontally. The 37 behaviour categories are plotted vertically. For convenience non-occurring categories have been omitted in the figure. The names of individual categories are not given but the broad categories to which they belong are presented at the left. In the figure the therapist-behaviour scores are marked by "rectangles", the child's codes by "ovals" and "dollar signs" in the case of equal child and therapist codes.

About 10 minutes of a single therapy session (90 intervals) have been plotted in Figure 1. The child and the therapist are involved in mutual imaginative play activities in the beginning. At interval 315 there is a transition to functional play and play preparation, and the therapist reacts with more "simple attention". At interval 360 imaginative play begins to reappear. For the therapists this is reason to change his "simple attention" into a more active playing together.

Rating Scales

Introduction

Rating scales are another tool in the empirical tradition for studying interaction. These scales can be used for scoring the behaviour of the individual partners, or for

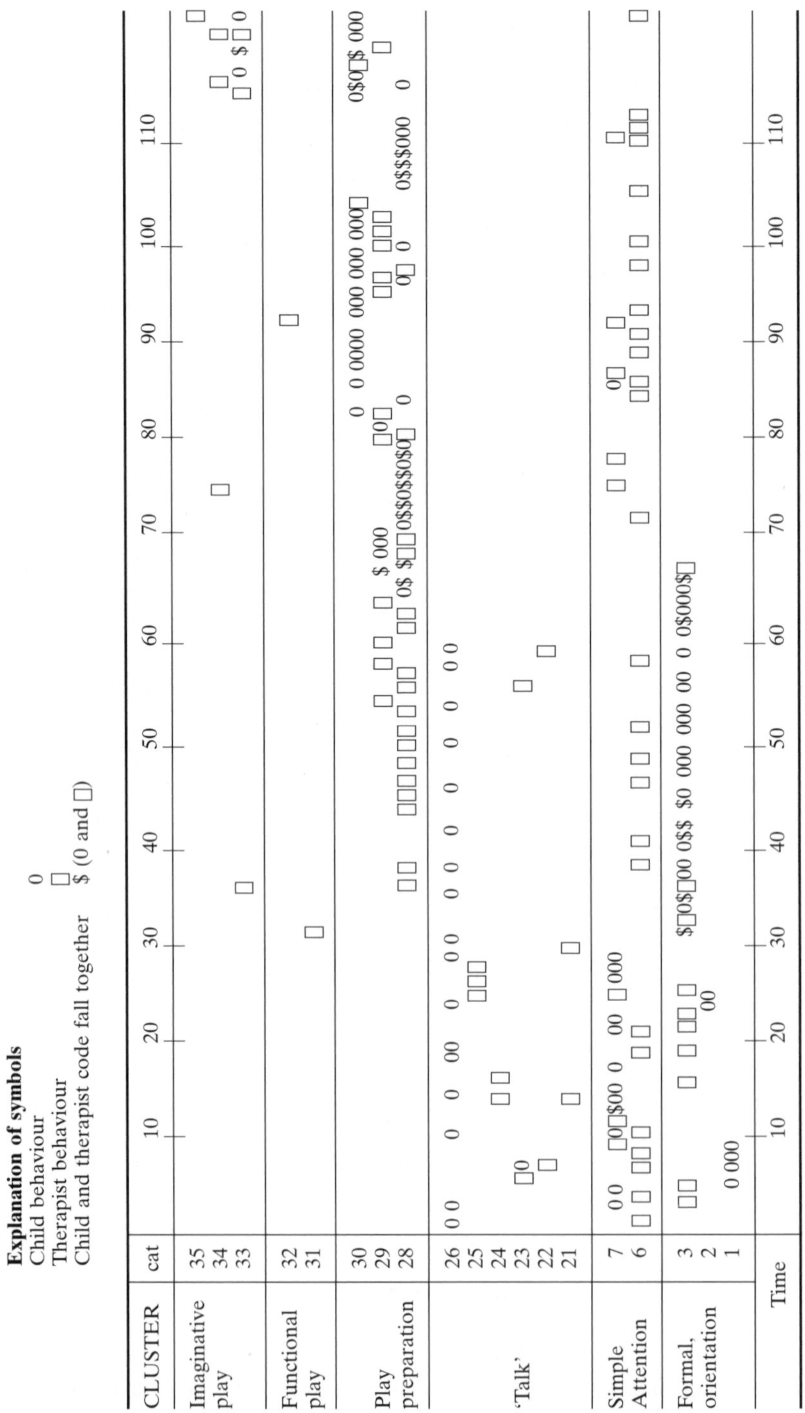

Explanation of symbols
Child behaviour   0
Therapist behaviour   ☐
Child and therapist code fall together $ (0 and ☐)

Figure 1 Plot of child and therapist behaviour in play therapy.

a direct rating of interaction characteristics. Rating scales do have several advantages compared with systematic observation (Hill, 1995). The method is less time consuming, not confined by grammatical structures, and by certain modalities of interaction. Rating scales may be used for molar behaviours that do not fit well into small scoring units. Moreover rating scales may be used more easily for high inference concepts, such as "empathy" and "feeling supported".

A regular practice in psychotherapy research (e.g. Orlinsky & Howard, 1975) has been rating interaction patterns. Moreover, it is used in qualifying pedagogical appropriateness, such as Early Childhood Environment Rating Scales designed by Harms and Clifford (1980). This instrument rates pedagogical quality regarding appropriateness of caregiving, and activities in the institution, containing 37 items that regard seven categories on daily individual care, language and thinking experiences, activities regarding fine and gross motor skills, creative activities, social development, and adult facilities. Such an instrument may be included in order to rate the quality of the social interaction context, since social learning also depends on a minimum quality of communication in the institutions that are involved in intervention studies. A recent study with young retarded students and their pre-school teachers revealed that the effectiveness of improving social interaction quality during tasks by video feedback was significantly related to the quality of the institution that participated in the study (Van der Aalsvoort, Meesters & Ruijssenaars, 1998).

Erickson, Sroufe and Egeland (1985) designed scales to rate social support from mothers to their child during tasks in order to evaluate mother's behaviour according to supportive presence; respect for autonomy; structure and limit setting; hostility and quality of instruction. Although Chen (1999) suggests that social support as a construct is hard to measure as it contains multiple dimensions, Riksen-Walraven, Smeekens and Stapert (1999) showed a strong stability of this behaviour with mothers interacting with their children.

The rating scales mentioned before are designed to overcome the disadvantages of losing context information during measuring social interaction quality. Effective functioning is supposed to be the result of social learning that may differ among children according to child and or environmental related characteristics. The method is however more global as moment to moment variations are averaged out, and special measures are required to reach sufficient inter-scorer reliability.

Example of a rating scale study (combined with systematic observation)
The following example shows how a combination of molecular analysis and rating scales may be combined in order to strengthen the findings regarding the quality of parent–child interaction. Bus, Belsky, Van IJzendoorn and Crnic (1997) carried out a longitudinal study with four observation moments when children were 12, 13, 18 and 20 months old, regarding interactions between parents and their children during book reading. On two observation moments 5-minutes book-reading sessions took place and were recorded. In the other observation moments attachment levels were assessed using the Strange Situation procedure. The

book-reading sessions were coded on the micro level, and on a more global level of overall interaction quality. For the microanalysis a detailed coding (frequency counts) of child and parent behaviour was conducted in order to describe situational variability. Behaviour categories were derived from a priori observations of a sample of sessions.[2]

Interaction is a contextual phenomenon according to Bus and her associates. Two context factors were included in the study: parent (father or mother) and attachment (secure, insecure resistant and insecure avoidant). The authors assumed that interaction quality was related to quality of attachment. After the frequency count, overall interaction quality was rated with a 7-point scale. The more the parent evoked child initiatives, shadowed the child's interests, and was flexible toward child's initiatives, the higher interaction quality was scored.[3]

A regression analysis was conducted in a preliminary analysis with the overall rating quality as dependent variable and the behaviour categories as predictor variables. The multiple correlation of approximately 0.82 for mother–child and 0.79 for father–child dyads reveals that rating and behaviour categories have much in common. All scores on book reading (both frequency counts and ratings) were compared for children with different attachment classifications to test for context influences in the main analyses. Type of attachment was strongly related to scores on book reading, ratings as well as behaviour categories. The "insecure avoidant" dyads had lower scores than "secure" and "insecure resistant" dyads on the overall quality ratings. More specific differences were found in the analysis of behaviour categories as well as between "secure" and "insecure resistant" dyads. Bus et al. (1997) included a part of one of the protocols of the task in order to discuss the findings more closely with respect to book reading. A combination of measures such as in this study strengthens the results as both quantitative and qualitative statements are included. This multi-method approach overcomes the relatively weak interpretation that results in case just one instrument had been used.

Ethnographic approach

Introduction
Ethno-methodological approaches have played a major role in social learning research, particularly ethnography. Ethnographic researchers participate for extended periods in the daily life of his subjects, in order to understand the way they interpret their situation and the rules that guide their interaction with others (insiders point of view). In order to understand this point of view, ethnographers

---

[2]Examples of parent behaviour categories are: pointing at details, questioning, giving positive or negative feedback. Examples of child behaviour categories are: initiating (pointing at a picture), labelling, aggression toward the parent.
[3]Verbal cues were added to the scale to clarify the meaning of interaction quality, and in order to increase scoring reliability.

make use of multiple data sources, particularly participant observation, talk and taking notes. Generally a wealth of qualitative data is gathered and in the analysis of this data little reduction occurs and often individual cases can be recognized (idiographic patterns, thick description).

Example of an ethnography

Gutierrez, Larson and Kreuter (1995) studied literacy instruction in a classroom from an urban middle school in the United States. The presented data are part of a larger study. The main purpose of the study was to show how instruction is organized and in which way the socially constructed relationships in the classroom influence learning processes. The study combines ethnographic data in order to understand the classroom, qualitative findings that reveal how particular classroom communities evolve, and discourse analysis by describing "scripts" of one of the students called "Nora" who is in conflict with the teacher. Gutierrez, Larson and Kreuter (1995) refer to scripts in order to describe how appropriate socialisation proceeds.

Classroom scripts are characterized by a range of social, spatial, and language or discourse patterns, constructed by the participants in the course of everyday classroom activity. There may be multiple scripts, and the most dominant one is the teacher script. The teacher script is highly traditional[4] in the Gutierrez study. Most students comply with teacher-script and many of its rules have become implicit and covert. However, within the small limits the teacher permits, several students develop their own counter-scripts, for example with mildly sarcastic reactions to teacher statements. Nora's counter-scripts however have a much more petulant and resisting character. In her script, delaying tactics and giving priority to private matters above teacher requests play an important role. She is also an expert in asking the wrong questions, for example, discussing teacher requests instead of giving the correct answer. The teacher generally tries to ignore Nora's counter-script, to force her back in the dominant script, but now and then Nora effectively succeeds in blocking the teacher script.

The Gutierrez study gives a number of results that would have been not easily reached within the empirical tradition, particularly the discovery of classroom scripts and its major characteristics. The qualitative orientation of the study shows in two ways. Firstly the characteristics of each script are not systematically derived from, but illustrated with data. It is not certain for example whether contra-evidence exists and in what amount. Questions such as whether the teacher always uses the dominant script, and what elements of her script are most prevailing are not answered in the study.

---

[4]The main characteristics of the teacher-script are clarified with several examples, that are derived from field notes and observations. Control is in the hand of the teacher; rigid structuring of activity and talk; little possibility for pupil-initiatives; rigid monitoring of talk, movement and writing, ignoring/repressing task irrelevant behaviour; teacher tasks: giving directions, clarifying instructions and administering discipline.

Discourse Analysis

Introduction

Hicks (1995) states that learning is considered as social meaning construction. It occurs through repeated participation in meaningful social activity. This means that communication is socially situated and sustains social positionings. That is the main reason why discourse should be analysed. Discourse analysts have a number of things in common with ethno-methodology, such as interest in underlying rules, the search for meaning, and interpretation of observations in order to find the insider's point of view.

There are also a number of differences. The most important one is the focus on language, its structure as well as its functions used by specific groups in specific situations. Language is seen as a highly specific and dynamic tool in human interaction or so called communicative practices. Discourse analysts are eager to compare language-use studied in a certain setting with the use in related settings, e.g. how children's language at home differs from language in school. As a consequence, less interest goes to non-verbal processes, as data gathering tools generally are limited to a detailed coding of ongoing speech, such as syntactic characteristics. Pauses, segmentation of utterances, and volume however may be included.

Another difference with ethnography is the focus on systematic observation and the use of category systems. Discourse analysts often prefer data-gathering tools from an empirical tradition, but their techniques of analysis and interpretation reflect a qualitative orientation. Finally, discourse analysis takes a less inductive stance than their ethnographic colleagues do. Generally, some conceptual notes precede the data collection, e.g. conceptions of power balancing or indoctrination. Typical ethnographic tools like interviewing participants and participating in activities have limited value for the discourse analyst. Sometimes a detailed written protocol may completely replace extensive participant observations in real life situations.

Example of a discourse analysis

Elbers and Streefland (1997) describe the try-out of a new curriculum for mathematics in 7th grade. This curriculum differs from regular instruction as it is based on social learning principles. Students are given responsibility for their own learning by functioning as a group of researchers. This requires developing new perspectives on student roles and responsibilities in the classroom, and applying discursive means in teamwork. Discourse analysis is a means to investigate how students learn to view themselves as learners from the inside point of view, the so-called ethnographic perspective.[5]

As in ethnographic research, the main power of discourse analyses is that it may show that certain phenomena exist and that it may clarify their attributes (e.g. type of indoctrinating techniques used). This is the area of concept (typology) formulation and highly relevant in the context of theory building. However, the scope and range of results cannot be easily deduced from most discourse analytic studies, as the transcripts generally are not systematically sampled from a specified population of classroom interaction occurrences.

Discussion

In the preceding sections major paradigms were presented that have been influential in the research on social interaction in relationship to instruction and learning. These paradigms have led to a number of different methodological approaches to study social interaction. The typical characteristics of these approaches were clarified in the examples presented in the previous section. We conclude this section by discussing methodological issues regarding social interaction studies.

Once again we stress the interdependence between social and individual processes that are involved in the construction of knowledge implying that social interaction requires to be studied as a means, and as a contributor to learning outcomes. Social interaction is a means to individually and socially shared thinking processes (Grossen & Perret-Clermont, 1994; Grossen et al., 1997). A method is called for that includes both individual as well as social interaction measures in order to draw conclusions from the instruction and learning processes that have been investigated. The main consequences of this point of view are that specific contribution of child and of environmental characteristics as well as understanding tasks as integrated and situation dependent systems must be included (Palincsar, 1998; Salomon & Perkins, 1998; Sfard, 1998).

The three methodological approaches that we described in the former sections all contain valid assumptions regarding the meaning of social interaction processes for the construction of knowledge, but they all have specific advantages and drawbacks. Interpretative methodologies such as ethno-methodology and discourse analysis fit easily with respect to discovering patterns in ongoing interaction and incorporating context elements including dynamic aspects of context. These procedures are probably superior to systematic observation procedures within the context of discovery. At the same time empiricist approaches are superior in "rigor" of design and in context of verification. Such stereotypes are too crude and simple for careful assessment of strength, and weaknesses of different methods. Each approach has different strengths and weaknesses, and the nature of the research question will determine what method (or combination of methods) fits best.

Social learning researchers need a set of quality standards for the judgement of scientific methods available, in order to generate methodological decisions. Such

---

[5]Elbers and Streefland (1997) use participant observation and on-going classroom talk that is recorded by audio and videotapes. Subsequent analyses are confined to transcripts of the audio recordings however, and interviewing the participants, a common practice in ethnographic study, has been left out completely.

standards should apply to the choice of the research question, the process of data gathering, the analyses conducted and the conclusions drawn. In the empiricist tradition standards have been in use for many years, for example: quality of sample (size, random), internal and external validity of the research design, objectivity of data gathering and analysis and statistical power of the study. One may question whether these criteria hold equally well for studies in an ethno-methodological or a discourse tradition. Whilst proponents of such alternative paradigms were originally not strongly interested in quality standards, the last two decades have shown a change in interest. Authors like Guba and Lincoln (1981), Miles and Huberman (1984), Howe and Eisenhardt (1990), Creswell (1998), and Gee and Green (1998) have proposed alternative standards. We have derived a set of eight basic quality standards from the authors mentioned before for social learning researchers. These standards will be presented in the next section. Moreover we will try to link these standards with the main methods that were presented and discussed in this chapter.

A priori *theoretical conception*. A sound theoretical conception on social learning should guide the research question and precede data gathering. Moreover, data should be gathered concerning relevant parameters of the social learning process. Finally hypotheses concerning these processes should be clearly stated. Both systematic observation researchers and ethno-methodologists are vulnerable on this point, regularly preferring a more inductive line of reasoning.

Prolonged engagement and persistent observation of relevant practice. Insider perspectives of social learning processes, and prolonged engagement in practice may be helpful, particularly when the focus is to understand underlying rules. This is particularly true when rules are covered (tacit rules) or do vary strongly with different context. Moreover prolonged engagement makes it easier to develop a relationship with the persons studied. This may improve the quality of the data gathered, and reduce researcher bias. Both linguistic and empiricist traditions may fall short on this criterion. Empiricist researchers generally do not participate for a long time in field settings, while linguist researchers by their focus on language may be inclined to focus on audiotapes or written transcripts of social learning practice.

Importance of context. Social learning researchers, whatever the paradigm, have to find ways to incorporate context elements. For systematic observation researchers, such adaptations do not come easily but several developments are under way. These may include: analysing sequential data that are derived from short meaningful episodes; model testing approaches in which interactional patterns and background factors are included, such as personality characteristics of the subjects, and description of type of lesson. As the contextual nature of social learning is fundamental to the approach of discourse analysts, they will easily incorporate such elements in their research design.

Importance of non-verbal signs. Social learning researchers should be careful to restrict social interaction to the words spoken by the interacting partners. Both nonverbal elements of the language (pitch, speed, rhythm) and nonvocal elements (eye gaze, spatial organization, and kinesics) may be important. Particularly in situations where the linguistic code is difficult to unravel (implicit) or where nonverbal elements play an important role (e.g. young children, intellectually disabled individuals) nonverbal as well as non-vocal elements add necessary information. Note that a detailed coding of verbal and nonverbal data is not always necessary. Simple notes on nonverbal discourse may be just as fruitful as a more detailed and more technical type of coding.

Multiple data sources and informants. We advocate for the use of multiple data sources, e.g. written documents, observation and questioning techniques. The exclusive use of texts (audiotapes, written excerpts), as in discourse analysis, may easily lead to conclusions that are an artifact of the used data source. Additional talk with participants seems required when the insiders point of view is at stake or when the principles of discourse are covered or implicit (silent language). This may be done during data gathering (triangulation) of after the first analyses (member check). Moreover we advocate the collection of quantitative and qualitative data. It is hard to discover patterns of discourse, and conceptions of social identities without qualitative analysis (thick description). Relations of discourse patterns with context factors (e.g. age of child, school climate, type of curriculum) ask for quantitative testing of hypotheses as well. The contribution of Ivinson (see Chapter 6 of this book) illustrates how such techniques can be combined in a single study. Using multiple data sources is a favourite tool in ethnomethodological studies. In the empiricist tradition there is a growing interest to combine qualitative and quantitative data.

Representing various partners in social interaction. Social learning research should give equal attention to all interacting partners. Students should be included when for example classroom research teachers are interviewed. This criterion may be related to the balance of power in social learning situations. Some researchers wish to give voice to the interest of the least powerful groups in the interaction as a means of empowerment. Political dimensions in research design can be difficult to accept for systematic observation researchers, although conceptions of power in social learning may be easily integrated in discourse analyses.

Generalizability and importance of sampling. All social learning research, including case study research should give attention to sampling problems. It may be for example that discourse patterns found in the data are restricted to a small subgroup of pupils, or to specific incidental circumstances (presence of the researcher, novelty effects for new learning-programs). It is the task of the researcher not only to demonstrate the rules that guide a discourse, but also to give some information concerning its stability. In case that random selection is not feasible, purposive sampling techniques may still guarantee sufficient variety in situations studied.

Moreover sampling should not just be directed at people studied, but also at setting, period, and type of actors.

For "single case" studies variety of situations may give a problem. In such cases as a minimum standard the researcher should discuss the representativeness of the case studied.

Conclusions should reflect theoretical frame and methods used. Conclusions need to be built on the theoretical frame and methods used. Researchers should look for alternative explanations when hypotheses are not confirmed. Moreover attention should be given to negative cases as well as to contra-evidence. It will be difficult to meet this criterion when a sound a priori theoretical basis for a study is lacking, or when studies consist of data that are predominantly used to *illustrate* conclusions instead of systematically *deriving* them from the data.

Little is discussed about merits and weaknesses of the multi method pluralism approach. The merits of other approaches can potentially be combined in this method, thus yielding the most valuable information. Two problems may arise however being the problem of underlying epistemology, and of cost. The first problem is concerned with scientific truth. Does an objective truth exist or are we investigating multiple perspectives of truth. The second issue is cost benefit. A multi method approach will be generally more time consuming, more expensive, and more disturbing for the field studied.

The studies that are included in the next twelve chapters on studies on the meaning of discourse for social interaction in learning and instruction all represent decisions in order to overcome problems that arise when social learning is investigated. We will discuss the strong points of these studies regarding the standards that we described in this chapter in the final chapter of the book.

3

Institutional Framings in Thinking, Learning and Teaching

Michèle Grossen

Introduction

Starting from the assumption that cognition is a situated activity rooted in social practices, this chapter aims at discussing the role of institutions in thinking, learning and teaching. After a brief theoretical overview which introduces some basic notions, the relationship between institutions and cognition will be observed in three respects: the framing of institutions upon the individuals' actions and competence in teaching–learning situations, as well as in test situations; the relationships between institutions and the representations which individuals have of a body of knowledge; the intertwining between institutions and social identities. It will be shown that institutions both determine and are constructed through interindividual interactions, a claim which will raise a delicate issue: that concerning the relationship between cultural innovation and reproduction, and between inter- and intrasubjectivity.

Theoretical Framework

Interactionist approaches to thinking and learning, such as the socio-cultural strand (see for example, Rogoff, 1990; Wertsch, 1991; Cole, 1996; Quelhas & Pereira, 1998) and the study of "situated cognition" (see for example Chaiklin & Lave, 1993; Engeström & Middleton, 1996; Resnick et al., 1997) have called into question three assumptions which underlie classical research into cognitive activity and development:

— the first assumption is that language is a *useful device* for studying internal activity. From this standpoint, language is considered as transparent, as if it were a window to the mind. Of course, it is implicitly admitted that this "window" is not completely transparent, nevertheless there is an ideal of reducing any "distorting" effect as much as possible;
— the second assumption is that *the situation in which a cognitive activity is carried out is an obstacle* — or a necessary evil — to accessing to the individuals' mental states. Here again, the ideal is to reduce any possible effect of the situation as much as possible in order to reach the subject's cognitive activity;

— the third assumption is that *cognition is an individual production* that can be studied independently of other individuals' actions. Of course, it is admitted, for example, that the researcher may "influence" the subject's actions, but the assumption still relies on various dualisms, such as "individual" vs. "social", "activity" vs. "thinking", "language" vs. "cognition", "context-bound" vs. "context-free", "ecologically valid" vs. "ecologically invalid", "reliable" vs. "unreliable", etc.

One consequence following from these three assumptions is that the context in which cognitive activities take place is neglected, or considered as a variable which can — at least to some extent — be neutralised. Taking an opposite stance, the socio-cultural approach claims that context and cognition cannot be disentangled and that institutions play an integral part in thinking and learning. The notion of "institution" (which, by the way, is rarely explicitly defined) has two inter-related meanings: according to the first, institutions are social organisations gathering a group of people whose aim is to achieve predetermined goals (for example teaching or healing) and to produce material or symbolic goods; according to the second, institutions are sets of laws, rules, norms, values, reciprocal expectations, tacit assumptions, common representations, routines, which are constituents of social organisations. According to the latter definition which is the one adopted here, school, family, marriage, research, testing, teaching, etc. are institutions or, to put it differently *social orders* which guide the actors' (inter)actions, but are also reconstructed or modified by them.

The role of institutions in thinking and learning has been studied in the field of developmental and educational psychology. Analyses of teaching-learning and test situations show that adult–child interactions are based upon "routines", common "ground rules" (Elbers, 1986; Edwards & Mercer, 1987; Hundeide, 1992; Mercer, 1995), "meta-communication contracts" (Rommetveit, 1978); didactic or experimental "contract" (Schubauer-Leoni & Grossen, 1993), a series of concepts which rely upon a common observation: teacher–student and experimenter–subject interactions are based upon implicit rules (or "hidden agendas") that children have to understand in order to learn or achieve the task in hand. These studies show that teacher–learner interactions, for example, are not mere interpersonal relationships, but are *mediated* by institutions which have the legitimacy of determining which bodies of knowledge should be taught, according to which curriculum, with which methods, for what purpose, etc. In this perspective, even a student working alone is in symbolic (or indirect) interactions with institutional representatives and therefore cannot be studied independently of the institutions which found the organisation in which he or she works.

However, as stimulating as these studies are, they run some risks which are common to functionalist approaches in general:

— a first risk is to consider social organisations as *homogeneous systems* and to forget that an activity may refer to various, and sometimes conflictual, institutions. For example, developmental studies carried out in school rely upon scientific institutions, but since the experimental subjects are also students within the broader experimental context, they are not only solicited as "experimental subjects" in relation to the experimenter who questions them, but also as "pupils" in relation to the school environment in which they are questioned, and as "children" in relation to an "adult" whose social status differs from that of a child in the broader social context;

— a second risk is to consider institutions as *static* systems of rules, routines, habits, etc., which directly determine the participants' (inter)actions. Such a view would underscore the fact that individuals are not passive but active participants who try to make sense of the situation in which they are involved, and interpret their environment. Their interpretation is of course partly based upon previous experience and cognitions, but cannot be reduced to them. In fact, an objectively "same" event may take on different meanings depending upon the situation and the moment in which it is experienced or the presence of other people. As a consequence, participants *negotiate* which institutions are at work in the situation in which they interact and this negotiation itself creates new institutions or modifying them in the course of their interactions. The term "negotiation" is indeed not to be understood as an explicit trade, but as a subtle and implicit way of constructing the meaning of a situation through communication. Since participants are part of the situation they seek to understand, this negotiation also relates to their social identities which are defined and redefined throughout their interaction. Constructing the context and constructing each other's identities, are thus two interdependent processes which develop diachronically and may be studied as an interactive event as a whole.

On the basis of this theoretical framework, I shall now examine how institutions and cognition are interrelated, considering the child's as well as the adult's activities. Illustrations will be taken from some studies my colleagues and I have carried out and which concern the role of peer interaction in cognitive development (Grossen, 1994; Grossen et al., 1996; Grossen, Perret-Clermont & Liengme Bessire, 1997), and adult–child interactions in test situations (Schubauer-Leoni et al., 1989; Grossen & Perret-Clermont, 1994). The reported examples will first show how institutions frame both the adult's and the child's activities, enable them to make sense of the situation and carry out a contextually relevant activity. The examples will then show that the adult's and the child's representations of the body of knowledge which has to be taught vs. learned are related to institutions and orientate the participants' activities. Finally, the examples will illustrate that institutions do not only relate to the construction of competence or to learning, but also to the negotiation and construction of social identities.

Institutions as Frames

Observations of teaching–learning and test situations show that the adult and the child carry out *complementary* tasks: the adult, whether an experimenter or a teacher, frames the situation in order to focus the child's attention upon the relevant features of the task, while the child seeks to determine which actions are expected from him or her, and which institutional rules (or "ground rules", "communication contracts", etc.) are relevant in this specific situation. These complementary tasks are mainly carried out by the use of two different tools: artifacts and language. Both are underlaid by institutional dimensions.

The Role of Artifacts on Institutional Framings

Teaching a body of knowledge and testing a child's competence are social practices which are based upon the use of *institutional artifacts* aimed at eliciting observable actions and verbalisations and at keeping track of them. In other words, in school and research institutions, children's productions are most of the time provoked by the adult's actions. By his or her actions, the adult collects traces that he or she may interpret as external signs of the child's internal activity. In this perspective, the mode in which the adult records the child's actions and verbalisations and the artifacts he or she uses to do it, may be considered to be an integral part of his or her understanding of the child's production. Example 1 offers an illustration of two different modes of collecting traces of the same event, namely the child's answers to the Piagetian conservation of liquid test.

Example 1: Two Different Modes of Recording a Child's Answers to the Conservation of Liquids Test

First mode	Second mode
Question	Adult: (conserving question)
=	Child: it's the same
why?	Adult: it's the same. How do you know that?
does not understand	Child: because I drink all the juice and you too
	Adult: OK, if we drink it all so/
	Child: there's no juice left
question	Adult: there's no juice left, yes, But what I'm asking is if you drink all that, do we drink the same amount of juice/
	Child: yes
=	Adult: or do you drink more, or do I drink more, what?
	Child: we both drink the same
identity argument	Adult: hmm. How do you know that?
⇒ Conserver	Child: because I poured the same amount of juice

The child's verbal productions are identical but, as shown in Example 1, the modes of transcribing his activity are quite different. The record in the left column might be that of a school psychologist who aims at assessing the child's stage of development, but not at analysing the child's answers, nor the adult–child interactions. The right column is taken from a previous study on the construction of intersubjectivity in experimenter-child interactions (Grossen, 1988). These modes of recording the child's activity refer to two different institutional practices. In both cases, the adult uses a set of procedures which have been institutionalised and legitimised within his or her community of practices (Lave & Wenger, 1991) and which is part of his or her identity of, let us say, school psychologist or researcher. The same may be said when school psychologists or researchers account for their practices in psychological reports or in scientific articles, since the writing of a report or an article is also based upon institutionalised practices. For example, the *Manual of the American Psychological Association* does not only provide typographic norms, it also institutionalises and legitimises certain ways of doing research and hence frames the researchers' practices within institutionally established boundaries (Budge & Katz, 1995). To sum up, the use of artifacts, such as questionnaire guidelines, modes of transcriptions,[1] academic writing handbooks, statistical instruments, refers to social practices which have been institutionalised in particular social organisations and are part of the observations and collected data.

However, these artifacts are not only symbolic, but also *concrete objects* which have their own affordances and constrain the observer's actions and interpretations (see for example Latour, 1994, 1996). Example 2 shows how the use of a tape recorder constrains the experimenter's and, indirectly, the children's actions.

Example 2

The following extract is taken from a study aimed at examining whether the social conditions in which an expert had acquired his or her expertise in the Kohs' Cubes task[2] would influence the interactional dynamics of novice–experts interactions (Grossen et al., 1995). The children are nine to 10 years old. The extract is situated at the very beginning of the peer interaction session when the experimenter introduces the task to Ibrahim, an expert who has been previously trained by the experimenter, and Stéphane, a novice. The study took place in an empty classroom of the school.

Exp.:   (explains to the children that they will have to carry out a task together) (...) and it's important, well I'm also interested in what you say to each other. This is why I put a microphone on the table, it's working now, so if you talk together, you don't need to go ps ps ps (she whispers), otherwise I won't hear anything in the microphone, and then I won't make any progress with my studies

---

[1] Let us think here of the widespread use of the transcription norms elaborated by Atkinson & Heritage (1984), even in studies which would not necessarily require such transcripts.

Stéphane: yes, no, but it's because when we work, we are not used to talking as we
            talk now, we just say well err we should do it like this, like this (she
            whispers)
Exp.:   yes if you talk like this, it's OK, but not ps ps (she whispers; the children
            laugh), well just normally
Stéphane: OK but we have always been very good at chatting (the children and the
            experimenter laugh).

Usually, interactions such as those reported in Example 2 are considered to be totally irrelevant for the understanding of the participants' activities and are never reported! However, the fact that they are judged as irrelevant can be interpreted as an effect of certain scientific research institutions which lead researchers to focus their attention upon certain events and to neglect the presentation (or staging) of an experiment. In this light, the controversy between Piagetian and post-Piagetian scholars concerning the effects of modified versions of Piagetian tests (Donaldson, 1978; see also Light, 1986; Grossen, 1988; Elbers, 1991; Säljö, 1991) represents far more than a scientific discussion concerning the "best" way of assessing the child's stage of development: it is a quarrel between institutional representatives who, by defending given research practices, also defend their own social identities and their membership of institutionalised communities of practices.

Using Language to Frame Each Others' Activity

From an interactionist stance, teaching-learning or test situations cannot be considered to be predetermined by rules, routines, norms, etc., which influence the participants' interactions (Goodwin & Duranti, 1992). Participants reinterpret the rules which are given in the situation, construct new routines, reconsider the values they previously attributed to certain events or attitudes, etc. On the basis of their former experience as social actors and of the intentions they attribute to the actors with whom they interact, participants engage in an activity aimed at determining which verbal and non-verbal activities are relevant at every moment of the interaction and which roles are expected from them. Language is one of the tools participants use to guide each others' actions, to construct a common definition of the situation and to negotiate common meanings of ongoing events. Analyses of adult–child interactions in test situations show for example that, despite the institutional claim that the tester is neutral, the adult uses guiding strategies which focus the child's attention upon the relevant features of the task and frame the child's actions within institutionally defined boundaries. Example 3, taken from the same study as Example 2, illustrates this point.

[2]This study has been supported by a grant from the Swiss National Research Foundation (FNRS) (credit n° 11-28561-90 attributed to Anne-Nelly Perret-Clermont, University of Neuchâtel, Switerland).

Example 3

This is the beginning of an interaction session between Amélie, an expert who has been trained by the experimenter, and Ludivine, a novice. Let us recall that the study took place in an empty classroom.

1 Exp.: (explains that she wants the children to speak loudly enough and not to whisper) (...) otherwise I won't hear anything and since I study these things it's a little bit annoying
2 Amélie: yes
3 Exp.: OK?
4 Amélie: yes but at school we are not allowed, it will be err ... (she laughs)
5 Exp.: yes but we aren't at school here, OK? (...)

In Example 3, the experimenter's request to speak loudly enough can be considered, as in Example 2, as an implicit reference to research institutions which require a scholar to provide attested data and to be accountable for them. It also anticipates that the children might behave according to different rules. By her request, the experimenter implicitly indicates that there is a change in one of the institutional rules that work in a classroom, namely that children should not speak too loudly. However, the institutional framing proposed by the experimenter is so strong that she apparently does not experience the slightest trouble in saying that «we're not at school here» (turn 5), when they obviously are! Of course, the "school" she speaks of is not the "school building", but the "school institution", so that her utterance may be interpreted as a clue indicating that her role is not that of a teacher and that other implicit rules are at work within the present situation. In brief, the experimenter does not simply request a behaviour (speaking loudly enough): she positions herself in relation to institutions which are relevant for her activity, and displays her role and social identity accordingly; by the same token, she invites the children to position themselves in complementary roles and to share a common perspective on the situation. The child's reaction («yes but at school we're not allowed ...» in turn 4) can be seen as an argument opposed to the experimenter's first attempts to change the definition of the situation (turn 1) and as a negotiation concerning the institutional rules which frame the situation.

However, institutions do not only frame the participants' interactions, they also affect the representations that the adult and the child have of a body of knowledge or a competence, and indirectly their (inter)actions.

Institutional Framings in the Representations of a Body of Knowledge

The term "representation" as it is used here refers to the meaning, values, relevance that an individual (or a group) attributes to a body of knowledge (mathematics for example) or, more generally, to social activities such as "learning", "teaching", or to concepts such as "knowing", "competence", "performance", etc. (Rochex, 1996). Representations are constitutive of teaching–learning situations or of any other situation requiring cognitive activity. As we shall see, they both guide the participants' (inter)actions and are constructed or redefined by them. Representations of a body of knowledge concern different fields of activity: in the *scientific field*, they refer to the various theories which may account for a phenomenon; in the *school field*, they refer to the bodies of knowledge which educationalists take as part of the school curriculum, and to the didactic methods for teaching them; in the *personal field*, they refer to the learners' appropriation (Rogoff, 1995) of a body of knowledge and to their personal interpretations. All these fields are underlaid by institutional dimensions, the role of which can be observed on the adult's as well as on the child's sides.

Example 4 is an illustration taken from a study analysing the adult–child interactions in the conservation of liquids test (Grossen, 1988; Schubauer-Leoni et al., 1989).

Example 4

It is the beginning of the test. The experimenter asks the child to pour the same quantity of juice into two equal glasses. The child pours the juice. There is more juice in one of the glasses.

1 Exp.: do we have the same amount of juice to drink or does somebody have more?
2 Child: I put a little too much in
3 Exp.: (gives the instruction again) what will you do?
4 Child: (silence)
5 Exp.: you can remove it if there is too much
6 Child: should we drink?
7 Exp.: no, do we have the same amount or (...)

On a cognitive level, drinking the juice in order to equalise the quantity, as suggested by the child in turn 6, may not be the best solution but it is not absurd. Though, the experimenter explicitly refuses it. Why? A plausible explanation is that she does not consider this solution as legitimate. As a matter of fact, this solution is not listed in scientific handbooks and would never be kept for a demo video on "how to be a good Piagetian psychologist"! In this example, the frame imposed by research institutions seems to be so strong that one could easily venture that the experimenter did not even imagine this as a solution. Drinking juice is an everyday activity which has no place in test situations, and the reference to this activity is only aimed at anchoring the task in a familiar activity. The child has then to understand that the reference to drinking is a hypothetical action and should not be treated as a real suggestion to drink. By preventing the child from drinking, the experimenter indicates which actions are authorised and institutionally frames the meanings of the situation and task. However, her action is double-sided: on the one hand, she orientates the child's actions, and contributes to the construction of a temporarily shared state of intersubjectivity (Rommetveit, 1992), but on the other hand she restricts the field in which a solution might be found. In other words, she both *promotes* and *limits* the child's activity, exactly in the same way as her own activity is both orientated and limited by certain research institutions.

Similar examples can be found in teaching–learning situations. Examples 5 and 6 are episodes reported by the teacher involved in these situations.

Example 5

In lower secondary school in Switzerland, English is taught as a second language and English lessons may sometimes include watching English-speaking movies. Speaking about this, an English teacher says to a colleague that she does not like to use movies in her lessons because students learn errors such as double negation ("this ain't no game"), that are, she says, very complicated to explain. Her colleague agrees but claims that certain students (namely those who will attend college) would nevertheless be able to understand. Then a third colleague enters the discussion, arguing that a language is alive and should be taught as it is actually talked by native speakers.

As Example 5 shows, a body of knowledge taught at school might be subjected to different definitions, depending upon:

(a) the teacher's representations of language and of teaching a second language;
(b) the teacher's representations of the students' abilities;
(c) the way the teacher takes up certain institutional categories, norms and values, in this example the hierarchy between categories of students who will attend college and those who will not.

The teaching of French as a first language also offers several examples illustrating how school institutions frame the representations of language and the types of answers which are considered to be "correct".

Example 6 illustrates that the teacher's and students' representations are liable to refer to different institutions and that these differences may give rise to debates which are not without consequences for both the learning–teaching process and the teacher's and student's identities.

Example 6

The students, who attend the last year of compulsory secondary school and are 14–15-years old, carry out an exercise consisting of indicating which sentences of a given list is an argumentation or not. One pupil answers that the sentence "this soup is good" is an argumentation, an answer considered as incorrect by the school handbook. Taking the perspective of the handbook, the teacher tries to explain why the answer is incorrect, but the pupil argues that "this soup is good" might be an argumentation, because, he said, «If I am invited somewhere and say that the soup is good, it might imply that the soup could have not been good, or that the soup I ate last time I was invited was not as good as this one». At this point, the teacher reports to have felt slightly uneasy! Confronted with his student's powerful arguments, he replied that if the context of the utterance was to be considered, the student would certainly be right, but that the exercise requests the students to consider only the linguistic form of the sentence. Unsatisfied by his own answer, he added that there is a gap between spoken language and language as it is taught at school and that pupils should stick to the context of the exercise.

The discussion between the teacher and his student cannot be fully understood if the school institutions which frame the body of knowledge to be taught are not taken into consideration. In fact, two differing representations of language may be identified: *the teacher's representations* which are the same as those of the school handbook and consider that language is a monosemic code system and that there is a one-to-one correspondence between a linguistic form and a function (for example argumentation); *the student's representations* which refer to a dialogical perspective on language and consider language as polysemic.

Even though their dialogue looks almost like a scientific debate between tenets of different schools of linguistic thought, the school context in which their discussion takes place and the institutional goals to be reached do not give way to such a debate. The teacher is led to defending handbook writers' arguments, rather than to discussing language itself. So he ends up the discussion with an authority argument: it is now more the teacher's status, social identity and role that count as legitimate than the characteristics of the body of knowledge. However, in the light of contemporary research into linguistics, one could ask who is the expert: is it the teacher or is it the student? The teacher actually seems to experience a conflict between research institutions in which opposing conceptions of language are available and school institutions which provide a unique definition of "argumentation". Here again, as in Example 4, the teacher both *orientates* the student's understanding according to the perspective of the handbook (and thus probably guides the student towards answers which are institutionally considered to be "correct") and *limits* the student's access to knowledge and to more complex and dynamic forms of knowledge.

This issue is also nicely illustrated by the Canadian writer Michel Tremblay who reports that he developed two completely different writing styles: «One for school because I wanted to get good marks, and another, more weird, infinitely more personal, for me alone, as a gift. It gave what it gave, but at least it resembled me» (1994, p. 214, my translation from French). The sentence "it resembled me" shows that certain representations of a body of knowledge, or more broadly of learning, maybe pose a threat to the student's face. Thinking, learning and teaching are thus closely linked to the issue of identity.

The Negotiation of the Participants' Identities

Learning and teaching are two complementary activities which involve social identity: the bodies of knowledge and competence we learn and are willing to learn, the way we learn, our motivation to learn, the value we attribute to learning and to certain bodies of knowledge, etc. are all dimensions which are part of our social identity, locate us in social groups and may function as identificatory landmarks between us and other individuals or groups. In this perspective, learning–teaching and test situations go hand in hand with the construction of the partners' identities. The notion of identity is to be intended here in a dynamic way which assumes that individuals, as members of several social groups (or communities of practices), display and develop different aspects of them depending upon the situation, its goal, and the individuals they interact with. According to this view, participants in an interaction do not only negotiate the meanings of their dialogue, but also aspects of their social identity.

Observations of peer interactions offer numerous examples illustrating that collaborative learning or joint problem-solving involve the management of partners' identities. Example 7 is taken from an experimental study aimed at understanding how children define a test situation, such as the conservation of liquid test (Grossen & Perret-Clermont, 1994). 6 to 7 year-old children were first individually subjected to this test and had then to take on the adult's role and give the test to one of their naïve classmates.

Example 7

Thomas, who gave conserver answers when he was questioned by the ex-perimenter, plays the experimenter's role with his classmate Vincent. Thomas proposes first to equalise the juice in two identical glasses and then pours the content of one of the glasses into a different glass:

1 Thomas: do we have the same?
2 Vincent: no
3 Thomas: yes we have the same because (he gives an argument), do you understand?

Thomas proposes a second similar sequence. Vincent answers that «it's the same».

4 Thomas: yes not bad you've understood

Thomas then proposes a third similar sequence. Vincent answers again that «it's the same».

5 Thomas: yes, and this (he shows some drops left in the glass)
6 Vincent: no, we don't have the same
7 Thomas: oh yes, if we could pour these (the drops) we would have the same
8 Vincent: (whispers something inaudible) well do we have the same here or not?
9 Thomas: (to the experimenter) well he doesn't understand then

Example 7 shows that the role-player Thomas is able to reproduce the conservation of liquid test rather accurately. As did the experimenter, he proposes an equalisation sequence followed by a transformation sequence; he is also able to formulate the conservation question rather precisely, even though his question does not contain any alternative formulation and tends to induce a conserver answer. There are however two major differences with respect to the experimenter's original presentation: the first is that after having received a negative answer (turn 2), Thomas gives some feedback to his classmate and explains to him why his answer was incorrect (turn 3); the second is that, after having received a positive answer after the second and third sequences, he introduces a new difficulty: the fact that some drops are left in the glass after the pouring. He thus changes the premises of the communication contract he previously established, with the consequence that his classmate gets confused and does not understand the question anymore. At this moment of the interaction, the state of intersubjectivity which seemed to be shared is broken.

This definition of the task and situation shows that the child interprets this new situation according to institutional rules that are at work in school. In this example, as in other interactions, the child behaves like a teacher who uses pseudo-questions as a strategy for guiding the learner. Moreover, his actions seem to show that for him, to be a teacher means to be — and to remain — the "one who knows more". The introduction of a new difficulty may thus be interpreted as a strategy for negotiating an identity which enables the "teacher" to keep an asymmetry between himself and his "student". In other words, the role-player's actions do also reflect the *social conditions* in which he was tested (Grossen et al., 1995; Nicolet, 1995) and contain a strong *evaluative dimension* which involves the participants' identities.

Evaluative judgements concerning a partner's performance or one's own performance also pervade novice–expert interactions, as illustrated in Example 8 which is taken from the "Kohs' cubes" study (see Example 2).

Example 8

Stéphane, the novice, has begun to construct a 9-cube model. After a while, the trained expert, Ibrahim, asks:

Ibrahim: are you constructing the top or what?
Stéphane: no, I'm doing this (shows the bottom of the model), it's very complex, you know, you need to be a genius, you need ... you need to have been at university to do this

Stéphane tries then to carry out the task alone, leaving Ibrahim out. The latter tries to impose his own point of view without much success. Competition dominates this interaction.

Later on, after Stéphane has made some mistakes and had some difficulties, Ibrahim suddenly declares in a serious tone:

Ibrahim: well Stéphane, you are not a genius
Stéphane: why?

Ibrahim: you don't know anything
Stéphane: (he laughs) thank you

The children continue to work. At a certain moment, Stéphane does not manage to place a cube. Ibrahim helps him and places the cube correctly:

Stéphane: yeah, well! you are intelligent (Ibrahim laughs)

Then the children construct a more complex model. Stéphane experiences more difficulties than before and does not know how to proceed. After some comments on the difficulties of the task, he says:

Stéphane: I think we'd better stay together because even with all my genius of course, I don't know if I can do it.

In Example 8, the children are obviously joking, but, as in other dyads, their evaluative judgements concern two themes which refer to values that are central for school institutions and contribute to the students' social identity: *intelligence* and *performance*. Categories such as "genius", "university", "intelligent", regularly pop out during their interactions, indicating that the children define the situation literally as a *testing* situation in which they are called upon to demonstrate their competence and to give proof of their legitimate membership of the school community.

This observation also raises another issue: does the way identity is managed during an interaction session influence the children's performance? As a first attempt to answer this question, we conducted an experimental study manipulating the reciprocal perceptions novices and experts had of their levels of competence (Grossen et al., 1996; Grossen, Perret-Clermont & Liengme Bessire, 1997; see also on the same topic but in school context Monteil, 1993). Results show that when the novices believed that their level of competence was equal to that of the expert, they got more out of an interaction session than when they believed that the expert had a higher level of expertise. Their belief that they had an equal level of expertise (even though it was actually not the case) led to more cooperation in the interactions and hence to more learning.

Discussion

In this chapter, I have tried to show that institutions play an integral part in thinking, learning and teaching, and that solving a problem or learning a new body of knowledge are only parts of a broader activity: constructing the interaction itself, and more specifically constructing the institutional frame in which some roles are enacted, others rejected, identities are negotiated, questions, bodies of knowledge or answers, are considered as legitimate or not.

The analysis of a series of examples illustrating how institutions and thinking are intertwined showed that learning vs. teaching a body of knowledge, or testing a competence vs. showing to have acquired it, are not mere interindividual processes, for at least four reasons:

(a) teachers, experimenters and students are *institutional representatives* and their relationships are symbolically mediated by other institutional representatives who do not participate in the situation and constitute an *invisible audience* which indirectly brings its own rules, norms and values into the situation;

(b) teacher–student or experimenter–child relationships are mediated by *artifacts* which belong to institutional practices and, as such, frame and orientate both the adult's and the child's actions and verbalisations;

(c) thinking, learning and teaching are activities linked to the *representations* adults and children have of certain bodies of knowledge, learning vs. teaching, the aims to be reached, and their roles and competence. Thus, teaching also consists of transmitting the institutional conditions in which bodies of knowledge are embedded and have been culturally transmitted;

(d) the way the adult frames the interaction on the one hand *guides* the child's activity, on the other hand *limits* it. This double-sided action is underpinned by institutional dimensions which do not only apply to the child, but also the adult who, as an institutional representative, is led to act within the very frame he or she has constructed.

Nevertheless, this double-sided action should not be considered as negative. On the contrary, one could formulate the hypothesis that under some conditions, which still have to be studied, the restrictive side of institutional framing might be a factor promoting innovation in thinking. As the French writer Marguerite Duras wrote it: «In order to create, it is necessary to put freedom into jail» (quoted by the painter Francis Bacon [1996], my translation from French). If we try not to reduce the notion of individual to the notion of group, or if we do not consider intrasubjectivity as a mere internalisation (not to say a reflection) of intersubjective phenomena (see Valsiner, 1997), Duras' claim raises a series of complex issues which, in my opinion, deserve more attention: What is the relationship between cultural transmission and personal appropriation? What are the conditions under which cultural transmission creates innovation?

4

"Shall we be Researchers Again?" Identity and Social Interaction in a Community of Inquiry

Ed Elbers and Leen Streefland†

Students of classroom learning typically view learning and interaction in the light of certain "external" educational goals and standards. However, for an understanding of how young people learn and cooperate we also need to know how they view themselves as learners. In this chapter we investigate students' and teachers' discussions about their roles and identities in an 8th grade classroom of a Dutch primary school (children between 11 and 13 years of age) and the importance of these discussions for learning and teaching. The introduction of an experimental mathematics curriculum in this classroom (in which pupils worked as a community of inquiry) compelled the participants to create new forms and expressions for their cooperation. The creation of these new discursive means can be understood by connecting them to participants' views on their new identities as members of a community of inquiry.

Introduction

In their study of cultures, anthropologists distinguish between "etic" and "emic" approaches. An "etic" description of a culture is based on concepts and categories "from the outside". Because these concepts and categories are derived from a general model, they are considered applicable to any culture. For instance, an anthropologist wants to describe family relationships in terms of a universal theory of kinship. In contrast, an "emic" approach attempts to see a culture "from the inside". It tries to understand the behaviour and ideas of the members of a society in terms of their own definitions. An emic analysis is culture-specific and reconstructs cultural meanings as the people themselves express them. In an emic account, kinship relationships are described in terms and understandings used by members of the culture themselves. There is no obvious criterion beforehand for deciding which approach has to be preferred. Both perspectives on culture have their merits. If we want to compare cultures, or if we want to measure cultures in terms of certain standards, e.g. of economic growth, we need to apply the same

†Leen Streefland died on April 29, 1998.

categories to all cultures involved in the study. But if we want to see what habits mean to the members of a culture or if we want to know what is reasonable behaviour in their own understanding, an emic approach is the appropriate one (Saville-Troike, 1989; Barnard, 1996).

It is a wide jump from the study of culture to the analysis of classroom behaviour. Nonetheless, the analogy is enlightening. If we apply the emic/etic distinction to educational psychology and to classroom interaction studies, we find that the etic approach is predominant: learning and classroom interaction are mostly studied "from the outside", by means of general categories. There is nothing wrong with this, since educational research reflects the importance attached to schools and learning by society at large. It is understandable that researchers try to clarify how children can reach certain educational goals, and borrow these goals from content areas such as biology or languages. Moreover, educational researchers develop general theories of learning and teaching, make observations in order to test these theories and derive suggestions for educational innovations. Many studies, implicitly or explicitly, compare schools or pupils and introduce overall standards for making these comparisons possible.

Very few researchers have applied an emic perspective and tried to understand learning and interaction at school "from within". Nonetheless, an emic perspective is necessary if we want to understand students' own views on school life and on their learning. We know little of what students feel is appropriate and reasonable in the classroom, of what they expect about the process of learning and about the interaction with their teachers. The introduction of a new curriculum or of a new didactic approach may fail, and indeed has sometimes failed, because schools and teachers do not take account of their students' understanding of learning and school life. Over the past two decades, such research as has been carried out on the perception and expectations of students gives an idea of the relevance of their own perspective for understanding learning and performance. Elbers and Kelderman (1995) showed that 5- and 6-year-old children's achievements on a simple task at school were influenced by these children's expectations about how the interaction with the adult, who gave them the task, would proceed. A recent study at Utrecht University about why so many students meet with delay in their first year at university, revealed that many students, especially from non-academic backgrounds, do not automatically understand what is expected of them. They have to learn "the rules of the game", before they can make progress (Taconis & Holleman, 1998). These examples show that an emic approach is more important than is generally realized in educational studies.

Changing Identities in the Classroom

The occasion for the above reflections was a study we carried out on learning and interaction in an 8th grade classroom in a Dutch primary school. In an experimental mathematics curriculum teachers and children worked, not in the traditional way, but as members of a community of inquiry. In this chapter, we will look at this classroom from an "emic" perspective. The introduction of the mathematics curriculum led to discussions and negotiations among the participants about their responsibilities and social identities. These discussions and negotiations are the subject of this chapter.

The motivation to set up the experimental curriculum originated from a view on mathematics learning. In Realistic Mathematics Education (Freudenthal, 1991; Goffree, 1993; Streefland, 1993) the students' activities do not aim primarily at learning mathematical subject matter, but rather at mathematizing: turning every-day issues into mathematical problems and using the mathematics evolving from these activities for solving realistic problems. Mathematics, taught and learnt in this way, should lose its character as only school knowledge. The lessons are directed at connecting everyday knowledge and mathematics, or rather, at enriching common sense with mathematical knowledge. The classroom activities help the students to build upon their current ways of knowing, which include both their informal knowledge of everyday-life situations and the mathematical means already available to them. The pupils contribute to the teaching and learning process by means of their own constructions and productions.

In order to increase the children's involvement in the learning process and to create opportunities for them to reflect on their mathematical ideas, the teacher asked pupils to collaborate as "researchers". The metaphor of a community of inquiry was used as a guideline for structuring the lessons. They were based on the understanding that children's learning is not so much an individual, but a communal activity. Children construct meanings and insights through interaction with others, through discussions and negotiations, by proposing, criticizing and rejecting hypotheses. Addressing pupils as members of a community of researchers means inviting them to actively state questions, to work at solving them in discussions, by making investigations and doing experiments (cf. Seixas, 1993). In a community of inquiry classroom life is not based on the authority of the teacher or on the instructions of a textbook. Learning occurs because children contribute to the construction of knowledge for which they themselves, to a certain extent, have been made responsible. The idea of a community of inquiry is in many respects similar to innovative curricula described by Rogoff (1994) and Brown and Campione (1994) as communities of learners.

For clarifying the differences between traditional school learning and working as members of a community of inquiry, we borrow from Rogoff's (1994) paper. In the traditional classroom, the teacher controls the students' activities by asking questions, giving directions and formulating the targets for group work. In a community of inquiry the students are involved in the organization of class work. They have been made co-responsible for their learning, which allows them to express their interests and to discuss the purpose of their activities. The interaction between teacher and students is two-directional rather than based on a traditional question and answer format. The teacher provides support and guidance without controlling all interactions during the lessons.

The success of a community of inquiry depends on the pupils' understanding of what is expected of them in the new situation. Children have to develop a view of their activities that is different from learning in a traditional classroom. They need to become aware of their new responsibilities and obligations, and of the different relationships between themselves and the teacher.

In the traditional classroom, in which interaction between teacher and pupils runs along familiar routines and rituals, there is generally little dispute about the participants' social roles. When a teacher tells a pupil to add 34 and 57, the pupil, knowing the conventions of traditional classroom interaction, is anything but unsure about his or her own and the teacher's roles. Rather, the pupil recognizes the teacher's question as the first part of the discourse structure of Initiation, Response and Feedback (cf. Edwards and Mercer, 1987), and gives an answer, knowing that the teacher will conclude the sequence with a feedback statement. This question and answer sequence is more than a matter of discourse conventions: there are social identities involved. The teacher is the authority and has every right to ask questions and to check whether the pupils can reproduce what he or she has taught them. Although recent studies show that negotiations about the participants' identities and responsibilities are a normal aspect of classroom life (Maybin, 1993; Orellana, 1996), these negotiations are seldom very explicit.

Identity is like an iceberg; most of it is invisible. The identities of teachers and pupils, in normal circumstances, are taken for granted. Only when difficulties arise, or when circumstances change, do the participants become conscious of the part of the iceberg which they, most of the time, are not aware of. These new circumstances may force the participants to reflect upon their social roles and to negotiate and redefine their responsibilities. Such difficulties are, for instance, found in young children, who go to school for the first time and have yet to become familiar with the speech and discourse conventions of school life (examples in Wells, 1983).

A situation in which we also may expect to see parts of the iceberg which are normally invisible, is the experimental mathematics curriculum. Here, a teacher announced that both teacher and children will work under new discursive rules. Because it broke with familiar conventions of classroom interaction, the introduction of the curriculum created a zone of uncertainty and forced the teachers and the children to redefine their roles and invent new patterns of interaction and cooperation. We will show in this chapter that the children did not only work at mathematics, they also worked at creating new social identities. The pupils' uncertainty about their new responsibilities and their attempts to clarify their identities as "researchers" led to discussions among themselves and with the teacher. The curriculum made questions about their roles and obligations topical, such as: what does it mean to be learners and teachers, what responsibilities do we have as members of a community of inquiry? Their discussions during the lessons reflected their uncertainty about: who am I as a member of this classroom, what are my rights and responsibilities, how are my relationships towards others? These discussions showed an awareness of these questions and attempts to answer them. These questions of identity were not only urgent and topical for the students, but also for the teachers. In raising and discussing these issues, the children and teachers worked at changing their identities.

Part of the students' identity work was in the construction of new forms of cooperation and of discursive means which belong to their new identities. The children had to invent new expressions for participating in the collective learning process, they learned how to use arguments and to criticize or support others' positions. By developing these new discursive means, by experimenting with them, the pupils reconstructed their relationships among themselves and also their own place in the classroom.

In conclusion, the introduction of the new curriculum confronted the children and the teachers with the challenge to develop a different view of themselves and to invent new forms of cooperation. In the next section we will present examples of the students' "identity talk" which reveal their awareness of their new identities. After that, we will discuss the problems facing the teachers because of their identities as "senior researchers" in the community of inquiry.

Identity Talk in the Classroom

Observations were made during mathematics lessons in an 8th grade classroom of a Dutch primary school (children between 11 and 13 years of age). The lessons of the experimental curriculum spanned a period of four months; there was a lesson of about one hour and a half once a week. Each lesson started with a repetition of the principle of a community of inquiry: we are researchers, let us do research. During the lessons the children were addressed as researchers. The teachers (there were two teachers, the regular teacher and the second author) introduced themselves not as teachers, but as senior researchers. The pupils were given a task or a problem as the subject for their research (often with reference to some example from everyday life, a newspaper clipping, a photo, etc.). Work in small groups of 4 or 5 children alternated with class discussions in which the results of the groups were made available for discussion in the whole class. There was no individual work. The teachers encouraged the children to make explicit which research questions were relevant and to work at answering these questions themselves. The children were expected to listen to one another, to take others' arguments seriously and to use arguments for convincing others. As the children in this classroom had already completed most of the regular mathematics program for their grade, during the experimental lessons the teachers had considerable opportunity for following the children's suggestions and solutions to problems.

We observed four lessons; we made video and audio recordings of both the class discussions and the discussions in small groups. These recordings were transcribed. The fragments discussed in this chapter have been chosen from these transcripts. In order to improve the readability of these fragments, we present them in a non-technical way, mostly leaving aside information on pauses, overlapping speech and pronunciation errors (following Mercer's, 1995, example). The teachers are indicated by the abbreviations T1 for Leen Streefland from the Freudenthal Institute and T2 for the class's regular teacher. It was often unfeasible to designate all pupils individually; in such cases we have used abbreviations P1, P2 etc. to indicate children in each fragment. Pupil P1 in one fragment may be the same but also a different child in the next fragment. Sometimes we had to use just P. The fragments shown in this paper have been translated by us into English.

The school had recently been accommodated in a new building and the teacher of this classroom had taken this opportunity to start a project in which children had to construct a map of their town with the new school on it, and had to make a scale model of the new school. The experimental mathematics lessons supported these activities by discussing the concept of scale. During one of these lessons, the children were presented with a photograph of a child standing next to a scale model of the Westertower (one of the most famous towers in Amsterdam). The scale model is about two times as high as the child. The photograph had been made in Madurodam, a miniature landscape in The Hague which presents models of major buildings of the Netherlands with a scale of 1:25. It is very common for Dutch children to be photographed in Madurodam, standing or sitting next to one of the model buildings. Using this picture, the children had to estimate the height of the real Westertower in Amsterdam and to estimate the scale of the model.

In the remainder of this section we give examples of how the children's awareness and uncertainty about their roles as "researchers" influenced the interaction in the classroom. We will focus on three aspects: the discussions about their new responsibilities as members of a research community, their talk about a collaborative style which is consistent with their new identities, and their invention of terms and expressions fit for their collaboration.

Responsibilities

Working as a community of inquiry entails a new division of responsibilities in the classroom. The children were more responsible for their learning than in the traditional lessons. Moreover, they had to rely more on their own creativity and powers of invention and less on support by the teacher. The metaphor of a community of researchers was very useful in this respect. The following fragment is from the start of one of the lessons. The teacher introduced the topic and then invited the pupils to work as researchers.

> *Fragment 1* (Class discussion)
> T1:   Now, shall we be researchers again?
> P1:   Oh, I thought that we already were researchers.
> Pupils: (laugh)
> T1:   I started with a couple of questions. Now it is your turn.

The small fragment shows that the pupils understand what is expected of them. Fragment 1 is from a whole class discussion. In the group discussions, too, we occasionally found spontaneous references to the idea of a community of researchers. For instance, in one of the groups, after the children had worked at formulating their own questions, one of them exclaimed: "These are real researchers' questions!". During the lessons, the teachers occasionally referred again to the idea of doing research, for instance by addressing one of the pupils as "researcher Tom".

Nonetheless, the new roles of the pupils and teachers were not always self-evident. The new curriculum led to many discussions in the classroom about who is responsible. Several times, the children reminded the teacher of the traditional division of tasks between teacher and pupils. They argued that the teacher already knows the answers to their questions. So, why can't he give the answer to these questions? The teacher, in these situations, repeated that it is a characteristic of researchers that they attempt to answer the questions themselves.

> *Fragment 2* (Class discussion)
>
> T1: I shall give Marieke a hand, because she can answer this question herself.
>
> P1 (= Marieke): Oh?
>
> P2: *You* should do that, Sir.
>
> (...)
>
> P2: Sir, I thought that the idea was that you give the answer and not that she herself answers her own question.
>
> P1: Yes.
>
> T1: eh, I think ..., I thought ...
>
> P3: Yes, they are researchers!
>
> P4: There is no need for you to do research. We ask the questions and you give the answers.
>
> P2: Yes.
>
> P1: Precisely. We put the questions.
>
> T1: Oh, I thought that the researchers put the questions and also give the answers. Did I make a mistake?
>
> Several pupils: No.
>
> T2: Both ways are possible.
>
> P1: Yes, but, Mr Streefland, there is no need for you to ask.
>
> T1: Pardon?
>
> P1: There is no need for you to ask, if you already know the answer.

Part of the problem in this fragment may be caused by the pupils' misunderstanding of what it means to do research. They think that their role is mainly to ask questions, they do not realize that this is only the first step and that after that they have to try to answer the questions. Sometimes, the teachers started the lesson with a whole class discussion in which they asked the children to come up with questions about the topic of the lessons. Therefore, the children may have thought that the main task of a researcher was to ask questions.

On the other hand, there are also examples of situations in which pupils clearly appealed to their own responsibility as researchers for declining the teachers' help. The following fragment shows this: children working in a group ignored the teacher's suggestions because they realized that they themselves are responsible for finding their own solutions to problems.

> *Fragment 3* (Group discussion. The students know by now that the height of the model in Madurodam is 3.60 meters and that the real height of the tower is 90 meters. Now they want to calculate the scale of the buildings in Madurodam)
>
> Anita: Now, you reduce the ninety until you have three meters sixty.
> Saskia: Let's do that. We make three point sixty. Now. (Silence, three seconds).
> Anita: What are you doing? (Pause, nine seconds, T1 from one end of the classroom loudly tells T2 the correct answer.)
> Saskia: Now, you divide it by ninety (Pause, eight seconds).
> Anita: We don't listen to that answer. We continue by ourselves. (Pause six seconds). Yes, that is twelve. No, it is not right. Look.
> Saskia: No, I see it (pause, three seconds).
> Anita: Ninety.

In fragment 3, the children were working in small groups at solving a problem. Unexpectedly, T1 communicated the solution to the problem to T2. The children did not only ignore this answer, but they also told each other explicitly that they wanted to find their own solution. This fragment exemplifies that children in this classroom realized that they are responsible for their own learning. What the teacher told them was less important for them than to follow their own course.

Forms of Collaboration

Children, as participants in a research community, have to become aware that cooperation is expected of them rather than individual performance. They have to work out forms of cooperation that tie in with learning as a collective or communal enterprise, rather than as an individual task. It is not surprising that discussions about collaboration were frequent. Children repeatedly fell into the old habit of individual problem solution. We observed many situations in which children became aware of this themselves and reminded each other that they should work as a group.

> *Fragment 4* (Group discussion. All groups have been asked to calculate the scale of the buildings in Madurodam)
>
> Arnaldo: One to twenty-five.
> Youssef: Look, Arnaldo, I know how to find it. You divide ninety

by three point six. That makes twenty-five. And now times three point six and then you can find it. One to twenty-five.

Kirsten: How many?

Richard: You divide. Look, do it this way. Divide ninety by three point six oh, is twenty-five.

Kirsten: Oh.

Youssef: And then twenty-five times three point six. I invented that. Ninety divided by three point six makes one to twenty-five and I and Arnaldo invented that.

Arnaldo: There is another way.

Youssef: We invented that for the first time, didn't we, Arnaldo?

Arnaldo: Three point sixty divided by ninety is oh point oh four, times twenty-five is one to twenty-five.

Richard: Yes, look, look, this way, one to twenty-five.

Kirsten: The answer is twenty-five.

Richard: One to twenty-five.

Youssef: That's what I and Arnaldo invented.

Richard: But I invented this, one to twenty-five.

(the teachers ask them to note their conclusion down. The children minus Arnaldo set themselves to write their conclusion down.)

Arnaldo: You do the same as I. I have the right (solution).

Youssef: We should do it together as a group.

Arnaldo: As a group. Youssef, you're not going to do it again, what I did, this way and that.

There is much to be observed in this fragment. First, we see how children offered to explain to others the way to the solution. Fragment 3 is one of many examples in which we found spontaneous peer teaching. Second, as a reaction to the proposal of an alternative solution, we find in this fragment the expression of rivalry and claims to authorship of a solution. Third, when the teachers encouraged the groups to write their solution down and all children start doing that, one of the pupils (Arnaldo) tells another (Youssef) that they should work as a group and that it is not necessary that they all individually repeat the same calculation.

We found several more discussions about authorship and about who found a solution first, but in many instances children made an end to this by stating: we work together, it doesn't matter who found a solution originally.

Expressions

The children do not have to answer questions by the teacher, as in a traditional classroom, but they have to formulate their own questions and make attempts to solve them. They have to engage in a collaborative process of thinking. This cooperation demands new ways of expression. Pupils have to develop terms and expressions for argumentation and discussion, expressions that bear witness to their new relationships as collaborating "researchers". We observed the use of metacognitive expressions, which the children used to communicate about the intellectual work they had to do together.

> *Fragment 5* (Group discussion. The students attempt to estimate
> the height of the child on the photograph)
> P: We have to estimate the child's height.
> P: Yes, just a moment, I have to finish this question.
> P: Then you don't know how many times it has been reduced.
> P: How tall is the girl, do you think?
> P: I want to finish this question.
> P: I guess one meter sixty, sixty-five.

> *Fragment 6* (Group discussion. The students use the model's door
> to estimate the height of the real door)
> Anita: That door, look the child, she has to go through that door, about here. Look, that child cannot go through, if it is that low, the child cannot go in, let alone her father and mother.
> Saskia: I don't understand it. Wait a moment, I am thinking.
> Anita: I think … I explain it like this.
> (Silence of three seconds)
> Saskia: If the tower in reality …, I think …, the door is two times …, how the door is in reality …
> Anita: It is logical that the door is higher than the child.
> Saskia: Of course.

In fragments 5 and 6 children use expressions that are suitable for collaborative work in a small group and that are used for talking about their own intellectual collaboration: "What do you think?" "Wait a moment, I am thinking". "I think that …", "I don't understand", "I will explain it to you", "Look, do it this way". Moreover, we also found expressions such as: (in a class discussion, addressing the teacher) "Sir, can I react to what she (another pupil) just said?". In another fragment from a group discussion, when children started joking and not acting seriously, their mates criticized them for not working and told them to "think along".

The Teacher's Role in a Community of Inquiry

In the previous section we looked at the way pupils brought up and negotiated their social identities as members of a community of inquiry. We saw that the children among themselves and with the teachers discussed their roles and responsibilities. The teachers, too, had to find their place in the new context of a "research community". We did not ask the teachers to systematically reflect on the transition from more or less traditional teaching to learning in a community of researchers. However, we gain access to the teachers' roles in this process by analyzing their contributions to interactions in the classroom.

The new role of being members of a community of inquiry brings with it a difficulty for the teachers: they cannot easily appeal to their authority as a teacher. They are senior researchers in interaction with juniors and their main tool for leading or influencing the discussion is to be convincing: they have to present solid arguments. If they do not, their contribution may be neglected or even rejected by the children.

The next observation is an example of one of the teachers inadvertently using a traditional teacher's expression, but realizing that he, in the new context, had no reason to prescribe what the pupils should do.

> *Fragment 7* (Group discussion)
> P1: Sir, sir, are we allowed to use a calculator?
> P2: I think so.
> T2: Now, you can do without a calculator.
> P:　Where is mine?
> (Later, T2 tells T1)
> T2: He asked if he could use a calculator. I thought that the calculation was simple enough, but then they said: we are researchers, we are not going to make calculations.
> T1: I think they are right.

In this fragment, the children asked T2 if they could use a calculator to circumvent the work of mental arithmetic. The teacher discouraged this because he thought that the children could easily handle the problem without a calculator. But the children, while discussing the issue with the teacher, had already brought out their calculators. A couple of minutes later, the teachers, talking about this, realized that they agreed with the children's argument that doing research is beyond making tedious calculations.

Their role as fellow researchers allowed the teachers to make contributions to the discussion themselves. The two teachers sometimes did so in a provocative way by bringing forward and defending different and incompatible hypotheses. More often, one of the teachers took on the role of manager of the discussion while the other contributed by bringing forward suggestions, more or less on an equal footing with the children.

All this does not alter the difference between teachers and pupils, which remains despite their common roles as participants in a community of inquiry. Although the pupils get more responsibility for their learning, in the end the teachers are responsible for the learning process and the procedures in the classroom. For all the new responsibilities of the children, the role of the teachers is, of course, considerable. The teachers introduce a problem, they influence the formulation of the tasks for the group discussions and they lead the class discussions.

However, the teachers have to solve the problem of how to correct their students who give a wrong answer or make an inadequate contribution, without falling back in a teacher's role and instigating a traditional exchange. Our observations show that the teachers did not, as in the traditional teacher–pupil exchange structure, evaluate the statements made by the children in a direct way: if they were to have done so, they would have destroyed the "contract" of interaction within a community of researchers. In order to solve this difficulty, the teachers used the discursive tool of reconstructive recapitulations (Edwards & Mercer, 1987). They repeated part of what children had said, not in a literal way, but by paraphrasing it and recasting it in a more acceptable form, eliminating errors or less preferable terminology. The teachers guided and influenced the class discussions by rephrasing a statement, adding information to it, or reminding the pupils of earlier conclusions. They also introduced examples to help all children understand the discussion and to give them the opportunity to grasp the argument on a less abstract level. In their recapitulations, the teachers used their positions as senior researchers for contributing to the discussions and at the same time had the possibility of directing the discussion.

The teachers' use of reconstructive recapitulations is different from the function of this discursive tool in the traditional classroom. In the study by Edwards and Mercer, the teacher's recaps are mostly used as feedback in the Initiation Response Feedback structure, that is, as a means for reacting to children's elicited contributions. We suggest, that the teachers in the classroom we observed used these recaps as means for participating in and contributing to the discussions. A recap allowed them to influence the discussion.

Nonetheless, as we showed in a different paper (Elbers, Derks & Streefland, 1995), the teachers' means for directing the discussions among the pupils were limited. This is mainly so because the teachers could not easily reject statements made by the children ("junior researchers"), but had to accept them as suitable for further consideration. Therefore, the teachers did not always succeed in preventing misunderstandings and confusion. In sum, working as a community of inquiry also brought about difficulties for the teachers, which they did not always know how to solve.

Moreover, sometimes, children stopped making progress and the discussion appeared to repeat itself. In these cases, we occasionally observed the teachers resorting to more traditional forms of teacher–pupil exchange. Traditional exchanges were also used as a means to repeat the conclusion of (part of) a discussion. Especially if a conclusion had been reached in a discussion with some children and the teachers wanted to make sure that all other children had grasped the argument, teachers used traditional interaction patterns. We also found several examples of children asking a question which was solved before. Here, the teachers did not allow a repetition of the entire discussion, but used a traditional IRF-pattern to briefly repeat the main results of the discussion.

Discussion

Antaki and Widdicombe (1998) point to the dual aspect of identity as both a tool and an achievement. Pupils' identities provide the resources through which their actions are moulded and their experiences are shaped (Widdicombe, 1998). Without a sense of their identities as learners, children would neither know their responsibilities in the classroom nor what is expected and demanded of them by the teacher. This is the tool side to identity. However, identities may appear to be stable, in fact they are never ready or self-evident. Part of what happens in a classroom is identity work. In their dialogues and statements in the classroom, the participants, at the same time, express how they view their position in relation to others. In doing so, they challenge, renegotiate, maintain or change their own and their interlocutors' identities (Maybin, 1993; Muller & Perret-Clermont, in press).

The achievement aspect of identity is clearly visible in the classroom observed by us. When discourse conventions change, social relationships and identities are questioned and have to be redefined (Orellana, 1996). In an otherwise traditional school setting, the teachers asked the children to work as members of a community of inquiry. The mathematics lessons were therefore particularly suitable for making observations of identity work. Familiar and automatic patterns of interaction were no longer adequate, they no longer worked and had to be replaced. The announcement by the teacher: from now on we work as a community of inquiry, created uncertainty about how to conduct and interpret what happened in the classroom and made it necessary for the participants to renegotiate their roles and responsibilities (Gumperz & Cook-Gumperz, 1982). Eventually, we may expect, these discussions and negotiations will give rise to new conventions and routines of learning and interaction.

There was much identity talk in this classroom. We saw how children talked about their new responsibilities as members of a community of inquiry, how they criticized each other when somebody fell back into the habits of the traditional lessons. They also discussed the role of the teachers and their relationship towards them. The examples show that the students did not only talk about the question: "who am I? what are my responsibilities?". In order to find the answers to these questions, they also worked out new forms of cooperation. The children relativized competition and claims of authorship. Against these, they emphasized that they work as a group and that the solution matters, not who found it originally. They attempted to find new expressions that would fit their collaboration and their interaction with the senior researchers, their teachers. In brief, the children created an awareness of their new identities as co-researchers and invented collaborative and discursive tools for doing their work as members of a research community.

The identity talk was, of course, not restricted to the students. We showed that the teachers themselves clarified the differences between their traditional role and their role as senior researchers. More importantly, the teachers, because they dominated the talk during the class discussions, made a vital contribution to the students' understanding of their new responsibilities. The introduction of a problem, the formulation of a task for a group discussion, the way a class discussion was led — all these could be used by the teachers as occasions for clarifying what it meant to be researchers and to collaborate. The class discussions were particularly helpful because they provided the students with a model of argumentation and cooperative talk, which they could use themselves in their work in the small groups.

It is a common finding of research on collaborative learning that children need help in order to interact successfully according to the conventions of working together (Bennett & Dunne, 1991; Cowie et al., 1994; Rogoff, 1994; Brown & Campione, 1994; Mercer, 1995; Rojas-Drummond et al., 1998). Mercer (1995) writes that teachers often take it for granted that pupils already have a good understanding of the ground rules of collaborative learning. Teachers may even think that it is wrong to guide the activities of the learners too directly. But, as Mercer points out, students are often unsure of what is expected of them. The teachers in the project described by Mercer encouraged the pupils to work together by introducing awareness-raising activities for rehearsing the ground rules of collaborative work. Cowie et al. (1994) started cooperative group work sessions with trust-building exercises and used debriefing sessions in which the teacher discussed with group members their experiences of working together. Rojas-Drummond et al. (1998) prepared the pupils by exposing them to cooperative learning training sessions, in which the teacher gradually transferred responsibility for handling the tasks to them.

The teachers of this classroom did not use such exercises, although they occasionally encouraged the students to listen to each other or to do their best to cooperate. For making clear what they had in mind, the teachers referred to the metaphor of a community of researchers. This metaphor proved to be very useful for the teachers to structure the pupils' activities. By referring to a research community the teachers could help the pupils articulate their roles. This is not to say that the children easily grasped the meaning of the metaphor and their new social roles as researchers. The example above in fragment 2 shows a confusion originating from some children's suppositions that their part is mainly in asking questions, instead of, as the teachers try to make clear, also finding the answers. Fragment 2 also shows that the teachers used the incident to clarify the responsibilities of researchers.

However, the use of the metaphor of a community of inquiry also put restrictions on the teachers' means for influencing the discussions in the classroom. The teachers were reluctant to openly make corrections because of the students' status as "junior researchers". This status made it necessary for the teachers to accept the students' contributions as meriting a discussion. This sometimes led to confusion. In such situations we observed that the teachers, as a way out of confusion and repeated argument, sometimes resorted to IRF exchange patterns (Elbers, Derks & Streefland, 1995).

Other innovative curricula show comparable problems for teachers. A dramatic example of this is to be found in Brown and Campione (1994). Here, students (the same age as the children in this classroom) talked about the results of their collaborative work in a public presentation. During this meeting, one of the students informed the auditorium that, like malaria, AIDS can be disseminated by mosquitos. No other student questioned this statement. Ann Brown who was present as an observer of this meeting, because she wanted to prevent the circulation of this error, stood up and told the student that he was wrong and that AIDS is not spread by mosquito bites. The student then asked her to give evidence for her claim, which Ann Brown could not. She only managed to say, that she was sure about this. The student did not accept Brown's comment and came up with good arguments to back his claim, making recourse to biological and epidemiological data which Ann Brown could, for the moment, not refute. Brown and Campione write that Brown's claim to her authority was justifiably impermissible in this community of learners. The incident had a favourable follow up: it was a starting point for a semester of inquiry into the analogies and differences between malaria and AIDS (Brown and Campione, 1994, pp. 240–244).

Working as a community of inquiry changes the character of what counts as knowledge and learning. Learning under these circumstances consists of children's participation in class discussions and group discussions. Here, learning to reproduce knowledge is less important than learning to listen to others, contribute to solutions to problems, convince others, argue and ask for arguments. We do not know if all pupils participated sufficiently in the discussions to make sure that they all learnt during these lessons. On the other hand, we have examples of ideas, invented first in one of the groups, and then appropriated quickly by other children during class and group discussions (see Elbers & Streefland, 1997, 1998).

In the traditional classroom children seldom refer to their thinking process (except for having to tell the teacher that they forgot the right answer or that they did not understand): talking about the process of learning is traditionally the teacher's privilege (Edwards & Mercer, 1987; Wood, 1988). In the classroom observed by us, however, children not only communicate about the task which they are trying to solve, they also have to organize the process of collaborative thinking. For the organization of their work, they need terms and expressions fit for reacting to each others' contributions and for explicating their own thinking process. Collaborative learning, which means listening to others and bringing forward and criticizing hypotheses, cannot be successful unless the children have a command of terms for referring to the process of collective thinking. By inventing and using metacognitive expressions, the pupils fulfil an important condition of peer teaching and learning together.

Rogoff (1994) views learning as a process of learners' transforming participation in social activities. This view can help us understand how children learn in a community of inquiry. Learning, here, is essentially collaborative, children have to learn to coordinate their activities with their fellow students and to support each other. They feel responsible for their own and others' learning and are able to express their own interests in the subject. This process of learning is different from the traditional classroom with its value put on individual performance and the reproduction of knowledge. Instead, the students' interaction with the teacher is based on their motivation to learn. However, as Rogoff points out, being skilled in a community of learners does not mean that children are unable to work in a different educational context. Different models of learning prepare children differently for participation in the life of a community. Rogoff writes that "individuals can become 'fluent' in more than one philosophy of learning and its practices" (1994, p. 225). We learn from the present study that this flexibility can only exist if children become aware of the social identities and responsibilities which the various philosophies of learning demand of them.

This is not to say that children's learning in the Dutch classroom is just a temporary adaptation to the rules of a community of researchers. The teachers, in this classroom, appealed to the pupils' own interests; in doing so, they strengthened the students' motives for learning. The students learnt to be creative and convincing, to trust their own interests and abilities and to share these with their classmates. They have learnt to take responsibility for their own learning and for their collaboration with others. It is reasonable to expect that working as members of a community of inquiry influenced the students' long term motives for learning and had a formative impact on their identities as learners which they also wanted to express in other learning circumstances. Although the experimental curriculum spanned only a short period of time and was a separate event in a fairly traditional school, the regular teacher of the class told us that the students proposed to work as a community of inquiry in other lessons, particularly in the history lessons.

Although we occasionally used the term "social role" in this chapter, we do not find role theory adequate for interpreting our results. Role theory defines roles as sets of activities or behaviours that belong to social positions (cf. Potter & Wetherell, 1987). People conform to roles because of socialization processes. The disadvantage of this way of thinking is that it defines roles positionally: they belong to the situation, in a way they already exist before the people involved have to learn how to adopt them. They are more or less determinate categories, which the students only have to take on, and on which they can have little influence. However, the invitation by the teacher to work as a community of researchers does not result in the children playing a new role which they can just as easily lay aside again. These new identities have to be constructed by the participants in their talk, by inventing discursive means and by creating new forms of cooperation. The students and the teachers have to build their different identities and the new relationships in the classroom themselves. They have to find out what works and what does not, and to discover the implications of their new identity as researchers. They need to explore what it means to be a researcher. For understanding the pupils' roles, it is not sufficient to look at the structural properties of these roles. We also have to study the microprocesses of conversation and interaction in which the new identities take shape (cf. Elbers, 1996).

The difference between role theory and a study of the discursive construction of identities corresponds with the difference between an etic and an emic perspective. In this chapter we approached identity from the perspective of the participants, the students and the teacher. We reconstructed their negotiations about the responsibilities of a community of inquiry and we studied how they created discursive tools fitting their new relationships. This reconstruction of pupils' sense of who they are gives us an access to grasping how they learn. A telling example that we want to repeat is that children's identity as researchers provides them with a critical attitude. They no longer accept so easily what the teacher tells them. Even the teacher has to give good arguments and justify statements. In the new situation, argumentation and intellectual collaboration are more important than the solution to a problem. The conventions of the traditional mathematics classroom make room for the new rules of collaborative work in a community of inquiry. By studying the talk in the classroom, we got hold of what these new conventions and rules amount to and how the participants understand them. An emic perspective on classroom life shows how much identity work is involved in making a community of inquiry successful.

5

Collective Argumentation: A Sociocultural Approach to Reframing Classroom Teaching and Learning

Raymond A.J. Brown and Peter D. Renshaw

For a number of years we (Brown, 1994, 1997; Brown & Renshaw, 1995, 1996; Renshaw & Brown, 1998a, 1998b) have been exploring how to reconstitute classroom practices in the upper primary school using a sociocultural perspective as a tool to generate new practices and to critically reflect on change as it has occurred (Renshaw, 1998). One pedagogical strategy that we have used is "Collective Argumentation". Brown (1994) initially employed this term following the work of Miller (1987), who had defined three principles of interaction that were required to coordinate different views held by students. First, the "generalisability" principle requires that students attempt to communicate their ideas, so that the other students can participate in sifting the relevant from the irrelevant ideas. Second, relevant ideas can be rejected only if they can be denied through reference to past experiences or logical reasoning. If ideas cannot be denied then they must remain part of the discussion regardless whether they support or reject the point of view of some of the participants — the "objectivity" principle. Third, ideas which are contradictory to each other or that belong to mutually exclusive points of view must be resolved through group argument — the "consistency" principle.

Brown (1994) extended Miller's principles to include a principle of "consensus" and a principle of "recontextualisation". Consensus requires that all members of the group understand the agreed approach to solving the problem. Interactively it requires that all members of the group contribute to the co-construction of arguments in support of the solution process, and can articulate the arguments in their own words. If a member of the group does not understand, there is an obligation on that student to seek clarification, and a reciprocal obligation on the other group members to assist. Finally, the "recontextualisation" principle involves children re-presenting the co-constructed argument to the other members of the class for validation. Communicating to class members outside the group, challenges students to rephrase their ideas in terms familiar to the class, to defend their thinking from criticism, and perhaps to reassess the validity of their thinking.

Our research on Collective Argumentation has been informed, in addition, by Vygotsky's emphasis on the centrality of communicative and cultural tools in learning (Vygotsky, 1987). In Vygotsky's analysis, the changing functional relationship between speaking and thinking exemplifies the general developmental process where social tools, such as speech, are transformed into internal tools of thinking. The movement from the social plane of functioning to the internal plane of functioning, however, requires active engagement by children in social interaction with peers and adults. During social exchanges, children and their partners employ speech and gesture to regulate joint attention, to conceptualise objects, to integrate experiences, to recall and recast events, to devise plans, and offer explanations. It is the socially situated and functional use of speech during activities that enables children to transform their thinking. Vygotsky suggested that speech becomes a powerful tool for thinking only when it is employed in a socially situated and instrumental capacity. The opportunity to use speech, therefore, in collaborative activities with others is central to learning from the sociocultural viewpoint.

Collective Argumentation Format

In developing Collective Argumentation, we sought to create more diverse communicative spaces in the classroom — that is, spaces for speaking and engagement that differed from the typical IRE formats in classrooms where teachers do the majority of the talking and thinking (Wertsch, 1998). To achieve greater diversity we introduced students to the key word format of Collective Argumentation, namely, "represent", "compare", "explain", "justify", "agree" and "validate". The key word format provided a guide to students in coordinating the phases of their interaction in small groups (2 to 5 members) and facilitated opportunities for students' to co-construct understanding. The students are guided by the teacher to organise their group discussions so that they initially represent the task or problem alone, compare representations with the other members of their small group, explain and justify the various representations to each other in the small group, reach agreement within the group, and then present the group's ideas and representations to the class for discussion (validate) so as to test their acceptance by the wider class community of peers and the teacher.

The Teacher's Role

The teacher has an active role throughout each phase of Collective Argumentation (see Renshaw & Brown, 1997). The tasks of the teacher include: (a) allocating management of the problem-solving process to the group; (b) facilitating co-operation between students by reminding them of the norms of participation; (c) participating in the development of conjectures and refutations; (d) modelling particular ways of constructing arguments; (e) facilitating class participation in the discussion of the strengths and weaknesses of a group's co-constructed argument, (f) introducing and modelling appropriate language for different curriculum areas, and (g) providing strategies for dealing with the interpersonal issues that arise when working with others.

Teacher participation in the activities of the small groups involves an on-line assessment of progress. The teacher needs to learn how to listen and observe the small group processes before challenging the children to engage in and demonstrate different types of representations, explanations, and justifications. The teacher may do this by asking questions about the representations, adding to the representations, noting similarities and differences in representations, redirecting children to problem information, providing a personal representation to challenge children's ideas, seeking explanations or justifications, and challenging children to provide more abstract or general justifications for their ideas.

The final phase of Collective Argumentation — recontextualisation — is important for the progressive building of understanding over time. In managing the reporting process, the teacher can rephrase, paraphrase, and re-represent the contributions of particular groups, draw connections between contributions, refer to previous problems and recall the way similar situations were approached. In this way, the teacher can create for the class a sense of continuity in their work, and ensure that the consensus that is emerging in the local classroom is an effective bridge for the children to eventually participate in the conversation of a broader community of inquiry.

Initial Research on Collective Argumentation

In previous papers (Brown & Renshaw, 1995, 1996; Brown, 1997) we reported research findings relating to the quality of talk within episodes of Collective Argumentation. We found that students in Collective Argumentation classes do work consistently with the ideas of their peers. Brown (1994) recorded the number of *transacts* (see Kruger & Tomasello, 1986) during episodes of peer interaction in two classes — one class employed the key word structure of Collective Argumentation, and the other simply encouraged students to discuss ideas in small groups but without the key word structure. Kruger and Tomasello (1986) refer to "transacts" as spontaneously produced verbal behaviours that clarify, critique, refine, extend, justify or paraphrase a student's point of view. In an analysis of matched groups of students from the two classrooms (see Brown & Renshaw, 1995), the students in the Collective Argumentation groups were found to employ a significantly higher proportion of transacts than students in the other discussion groups [33.3% as compared to 23.1%, $t(5) = 3.8011$, $p < 0.006$], with requests for clarification, justification and elaboration of ideas showing the largest differences.

Subsequent analysis of the types of student talk focussed on the *validation* phase of Collective Argumentation. There is evidence (Brown & Renshaw, 1996, Brown, 1997) that students who participated in Collective Argumentation share a symmetry of authority with the teacher during classroom discourse. Two 15-minute segments of video-taped mathematics lessons in two Collective Argumentation classrooms (one Year 6 and one Year 7) were transcribed for analysis. These segments occurred in the phase of each lesson where groups of students present their agreed methods and solutions to the whole class for validation and assessment.

The talk in each class was divided into conversational turns (that is, student-turn or teacher-turn) with each turn often containing multiple utterances. One-hundred conversational turns in each class were coded according to the following categories: (a) "Request-for-answer": a turn in which the speaker asks another speaker to provide specific information without elaboration; (b) "Request-for-explanation": a turn in which the speaker asks another speaker to elaborate on a statement previously given; (c) "State-answer": a turn in which the speaker provides a specific answer; (d) "Explanation": a turn in which justifications or rationales for a point of view are given; (e) "Restatement": a turn where a speaker repeats what another has said; (f) "Expansion": a turn where a speaker adds to or completes another's statement; (g) "Rephrasing": a turn where a previous statement is modified but the meaning remains the same; and (h) "Evaluation": a turn where a speaker makes a statement about the accuracy, conceptual correctness, completeness or relevance of a previous utterance (see Forman et al., 1995).

When we examined the ratio of teacher to student talk, we found that students in both these Collective Argumentation classrooms generated a high percentage of conversational turns — 65% in class A and 44% in class B. Although the students provided all the answers, which is consistent with the Initiation–Response–Evaluation pattern characteristic of traditional classroom talk, they also provided almost all of the explanations which is inconsistent with traditional classroom talk. The percentage and type of student contributions indicated that the control of topics and the direction of classroom discourse and action was shared between teachers and students. The occurrence of restatements, rephrasings, evaluations, and explanations by students indicated also that they were beginning to work with each others' ideas rather than the teacher's ideas only, and that they were expressing ideas in diverse and multiple ways rather than seeking a single correct solution.

Individual Problem-Solving

The content of Collective Argumentation talk, therefore, resembles what Mercer (1995) refers to as "exploratory talk", that is, talk which foregrounds and facilitates the development of reasoning. In examining the reasoning of students working individually, we found that Collective Argumentation enabled them to solve new and challenging problems. In a study of students' thinking about a novel balance-scale problem (see Siegler, 1976, 1978) we found that two-thirds of the students from the Collective Argumentation class displayed a mature quality of thinking in terms of an adaptation of Siegler's taxonomy, whereas only one-third of the students who had experienced unstructured collaborative talk displayed such thinking (see Brown & Renshaw, 1995). Further examination of the problem-solving protocols of the students suggested that hypothesising, setting sub-goals and monitoring subgoal achievement, and empirically validating outcomes were the features that most distinguished the thinking of the Collective Argumentation students from that of the other students. This evidence suggests that engagement in Collective Argumentation provides a set of resources that students are able to transfer to novel problems when working individually.

Establishing a Sub-community of Collaborative Learners

The research reported above was field-based, that is, conducted in a real-life school setting. The changes brought about in the ways that students talked and interacted with each other were not limited to episodes of Collective Argumentation. The introduction of Collective Argumentation scaffolded different speaking positions for students and invited them to adopt a more egalitarian view of schooling. In short, the introduction of Collective Argumentation in one classroom created new challenges within the school as a whole.

As children became aware of the expectations and tacit norms of Collective Argumentation, more dominant outgoing students needed to adjust their actions to take account of more reserved students who, in turn, needed to find the courage to express themselves more forthrightly. We found that some students did not like Collective Argumentation and refused initially to participate in discussions. Others found it difficult to maintain membership in specific small groups due to clashes with group members. These tensions had to be faced and to be worked through.

Tensions also arose between the teacher in the Collective Argumentation classroom and his colleagues, for example, specialist teachers entering the classroom would insist that the children adopt a more traditional seating pattern and approach to the teaching–learning process during their lessons. During their time with the children, these teachers sometimes contrasted their experiences in the Collective Argumentation classroom with their experiences in more traditional classrooms where the children were thought to be "better mannered" and "more focused" on the teacher.

Reflecting back on these events, it became clear that Collective Argumentation could not remain a discrete pedagogical device, since it involved a systematic change in the relationships of the students to each other and to their teachers. It became clear also that is was going to take time for Collective Argumentation to be accepted by the whole school community and that the children needed to be scaffolded in their growing awareness of what it meant to be a collaborative community of learners within a traditional school setting. To facilitate the promotion of student involvement, thoughtfulness, tolerance and responsibility inside and outside the classroom, we set about negotiating a class "Charter of Values" with the students.

A Class Charter of Values

For students whose most frequent experiences of schooling involve listening to teachers and following directions, negotiation might be misinterpreted as simply agreeing with the teacher after an apparent open-ended discussion. To facilitate a new classroom culture where negotiation and discussion with the teacher could be seen as genuine, the children in the Collective Argumentation classroom were offered the opportunity to organise everyday aspects of classroom life that are normally decided by teachers. Everyday routines are powerful ways of maintaining the teacher's dominance in the classroom, so offering students the opportunity to participate in remaking classroom routines helped to convey a more active view of the role of "student". For example, the students were offered a choice in their seating arrangements as to where and with whom they sat. They were able to eat "breakfast" or "lunch" type foods in the classroom during lessons and they were allowed to leave the classroom to go to the toilet when they decided. The students tested the limitations of these routines and the teacher had to justify to his colleagues, to administrative authorities, and to parents why children were allowed to leave the classroom during lessons, eating during class time, sitting next to students deemed to be "distracting", and sitting with their backs to the black-board. However, the fact that these new routines remained in place when significant others complained, brought authenticity to the negotiation process.

As these changes were introduced, the teacher also guided the students to consider the charter of norms and values that would guide collective activity in the classroom. Small groups constructed their ideas using the keyword format of Collective Argumentation and presented their charters to the class for discussion and validation. Over a period of weeks, a negotiated class "Charter of Values" took shape and was given pride of place on the black-board in the form of a student designed poster. The class "Charter of Values" was finally presented to the whole school community at a general meeting attended by the school administration, teachers, students and many parents. The presentation involved all members of the Collective Argumentation class who named each value that had been negotiated and the class's accepted definition of it. In the words of the students (quoted from the teacher's journal records), their agreed values included commitments to: sharing — "telling people about your ideas"; industriousness — "to work hard"; persistence — "to keep at the job or problem even when it looks hard"; patience — "to wait your turn and to listen to each others' ideas"; courage — "to give things a go that we don't want to do"; openness — "to be open to everyone's ideas"; respect — "to be kind to each other and not hurt others or put them down"; friendliness — "to support or give assistance to those who need help, even if they are not your friend"; awareness — "to be aware of others' ideas and to listen to others around you"; trust — "to have some form of confidence in our class members and to not cover the truth"; humility — "to not think of yourself at the expense of others"; honesty — "to do what you can, and admit to what you can't do" and; willingness — "no matter how hard the task, you are happy and ready to do what is necessary".

Each class that has been introduced to Collective Argumentation has negotiated and presented its own charter of values with some being more extensive than the list outlined above, some less. All, however, contained reference to "openness", "honesty", "courage" and "humility" deemed necessary to establishing a collaborative community of learners (see Lampert, 1990; Bereiter, 1994).

Over time, aspects of Collective Argumentation have been adopted by the school community. For example, references to Collective Argumentation as being a worthwhile pedagogical practice have being made in curriculum documents at the school for both language (English) and mathematics. Aspects of collaborative learning seen operating in the Collective Argumentation classroom, such as letting children work in groups and having them present their ideas to the class, have been appropriated by other teachers. Parents have also requested that their children be placed in the Collective Argumentation classroom with one parent writing to the Principal: "The reason that I am making this request, is that I feel that (my other child) profited enormously from (the) classroom work ethic, (the) philosophy generally about learning, and in particular (the) approach to Maths teaching".

In summary, the history of the implementation of Collective Argumentation in this primary school reflected four crucial elements — *agency, reflection, collaboration*, and *culture* — that Bruner (1996) has recently employed to frame the relationship between teaching and learning. Through the "key-word" format of Collective Argumentation children were enabled to take more control of their social and intellectual activity — *agency*. Small group and whole class discourses assisted children to explore their own and others' ideas and to make sense of their learning — *reflection*. Sharing ideas and resources with each other brought about new ways of speaking, acting, and valuing both within the classroom and the broader school community — *collaboration*. The way of life co-constructed and negotiated in the Collective Argumentation classroom came to be recognised by others (administrators, teachers, children and parents) as an important aspect of the life of this school — *culture*. As such, the Collective Argumentation classroom may be said to be contributing to the sense of renewal and possibility in the school, a key element in what Bruner (1996, p. 43) refers to as "a complex [educational] pursuit of fitting a culture to the needs of its members and of fitting its members and their ways of knowing to the needs of the culture".

Voice

In our most recent investigations, we have begun to employ the notion of voice, derived from Bakhtin's theory of language (Bakhtin, 1981; Vice, 1997), to analyse small group talk, and to explore how students appropriate different speaking positions during Collective Argumentation. Each step in the key word format of Collective Argumentation challenges the students to adopt different speaking positions or voices. The initial step of representing a problem alone, provides space for the personal voice to be heard — "my representation is". The representations produced by the students even at this initial step are not monologic expressions of a personal voice, since each student will draw on diverse experiences at home, at school, and from the media in constructing their representations of problems and issues.

The small group processes that follow this individual work are designed to move students to an agreed representation (or set of representations) of the task. Here the speaking positions alternate between explaining or defending personal representations and moving towards a common view. There is a movement from "my ideas" and "your ideas" to "our ideas". That is, each member of the group must have a sense of their shared authorship of the group's ideas. Finally at the last step of Collective Argumentation, where the small groups present their ideas to the rest of the class, the students have the opportunity to explain their ideas to a broader audience. "Our ideas" (ideas of the small group) are brought in contact with a range of other possibilities, producing an opportunity for inter-animation and re-articulation.

Shifting Voices in Collective Argumentation

To illustrate how Collective Argumentation can create a space for different voices in the classroom, a short extract from one episode is presented. One student, Angela, is reporting her group's ideas to the whole class. The task had been to represent the idea of infinity. Prior to Angela's presentation, a number of other groups had already presented their ideas to the whole class — these consisted of drawings of lines, spirals, circles, and other closed geometric shapes which were meant to convey the idea of infinity as endless space and distance — with neither beginning nor end. Angela's presentation of her group's ideas begins by focusing on a different dimension-time, and she uses the image of a clock with a very large array of hands to convey the idea of infinite time.

Angela: We drew a clock and we had, um, about, an infinite number of handles, because time goes on for an infinity. That's how we represented that, because time goes on.

Teacher: I didn't understand that phrase, could you say it again please.

Angela: Well, we drew a clock and we had an infinite amount of handles, the little things that go around, because time never stops. It just keeps going around.

[Teacher clarified with Simon and Angela the term for the hands of the clock, and then Angela continued]

Angela: Time has no beginning and no end like numbers. And we had the dictionary meaning which says this — infinity has the state of being infinite, infinity of the universe, infinity of space, time, quantity — so infinite space, so, it's so that you can't describe it. Um, (infinite) mass is the concept of increasing (mass) without volume. So we thought that we would make a meaning of our own. So we thought that infinity means everlasting number, object and the universe. So infinity is an everlasting thing.

[Teacher recalled the key ideas from Angela's presentation.]

Angela: Infinity can(not) be determined or explained over a vast amount or period of time, because it is an everlasting idea. And I made this up. I think the word infinity is similar to life. No one can fully explain it and just like infinity it has many definitions. We can't really explain life and we can't really explain the word infinity.

Angela's presentation to the class shows an explicit awareness that particular ideas are related to the stance or position of the speaker — notice how Angela uses "we", "I", "you", and "no-one" to signal her adoption of a series of different speaking positions, as shown below:

(a) the authoritative voice of the dictionary, (*"And we had the dictionary meaning which says this"*);
(b) the voice of her group (*"so we thought that we would make a meaning of our own"*);
(c) a personal voice (*"... And I made this up. I think the word infinity is similar to life."*); and
(d) the generalised voice of an expert (*"No one can fully explain it and just like infinity it has many definitions. We can't really explain life and we can't really explain the word infinity"*).

"No one" and "We" convey Angela's intention to speak authoritatively not on behalf of her small group, or personally, but generally on behalf of humankind.

Angela's presentation reflects the social practices and dispositions that we had envisaged in initially designing "Collective Argumentation", namely, that students be made aware through the social practices of the classroom that knowledge is always constructed from a particular viewpoint and that the same idea can be expressed in many different ways depending on the context, the audience and the speaker's own goals.

Revoicing — A Social Practice in Collective Argumentation

Our observations and analysis of students' talk in this classroom has shown that the effort of students to translate ideas into their own words, to make sense of the concept of infinity, did not happen by chance. It was scaffolded over many months by the teacher as he introduced them to the practices of Collective Argumentation. There was specific evidence of this scaffolding process in Angela's talk where she used the word "so" which appeared to be a ventriloquation of the teacher. The teacher often prefaced his transformations of student contributions (summarising and rephrasing) with the word "so".

Summarising and rephrasing have been referred to by O'Connor & Michaels (1996, p. 76) as "revoicing", and like us, they have noted the use of "so" as a salient marker of revoicing as it occurs in the classroom. Teachers within collaborative classrooms are likely to employ revoicing quite often as they attempt to incorporate students' contributions into whole group discussions. A student whose contribution has been revoiced by the teacher or another student, is positioned to make a judgement regarding the relevance and acceptability of the revoiced utterance. By revoicing and naming a particular student as the author of an idea, the teacher also positions the student in relationship to other participants in the discussion. In this way students acquire shifting identities within the discourse as they are required to either assent to or challenge ideas or stances accredited to themselves or other speakers in the class.

Revoicing also raises dilemmas about the individual and collective authorship of ideas. To revoice another's contribution without reference can be seen as copying, as illegitimate appropriation. In a previous paper Brown (1998) noted the sensitivity of students to reconstituting ideas that had previously been accredited to others. In the particular episode analysed by Brown (1998), a small group of students were presenting their solution to a task when one of their classmates asked them if they had "copied" the idea from someone else. They replied that they had not copied it, but had remembered the idea from a previous session and had employed the idea as a solution to the current problem. Why did the classmates challenge the authorship of the idea being presented? The challenge demonstrates that these students were sensitive to the authorship of ideas and that they interacted within a specific set of "ground rules" that required ideas to be referenced to their original source where possible. This indicates that revoicing is not an isolated phenomena within a set of pedagogical practices, but is embedded within a set of implicit norms which govern the authorship and sharing of ideas within a knowledge building community — a set of norms which relate students ideas to each other and to the content of the lesson in a manner constitutive of authority and student identity.

Authority in Collective Argumentation

Collective Argumentation is based around a set of social practices and shared norms that challenges the traditional authority framework of the classroom where the teacher is assumed to be in control and where students are expected to listen and comply with teacher directions. One of the students included in our analyses of Collective Argumentation moved to a school where more traditional teaching methods were employed. Her teacher complained that she was too argumentative during lessons. The voice she had appropriated in Collective Argumentation — a voice accorded authority and status in that context — appeared disrespectful to the new teacher. However, the student did not abandon the stance promoted in the Collective Argumentation classroom, rather she negotiated with the teacher a time outside of formal lessons in which to engage the teacher in argumentative discourse about lesson content. In this manner, the student was able to create a space, even within the traditional classroom, where she could engage the teacher in a form of Collective Argumentation.

The practices and shared norms of Collective Argumentation take time to establish and requires the teacher to constantly embody a different stance to issues of authority. There are times, however, when both the teacher and students may revert to more traditional voices or stances. Below we explore one such instance when the teacher's attempt to influence the direction of a group's thinking is strongly resisted by one of the students. This episode is particularly interesting because it is the student who remains within the norms of Collective Argumentation and who resists the teacher's momentary adoption of the traditional authority space.

We enter the dialogue where the students are attempting to find the area of an eight-pointed star enclosed within a square, and the teacher has joined the group to review their progress. Annie has employed a conventional representation to successfully move towards a solution to the problem. However, her partner, Allan, has adopted an imaginative, but inadequate representation which requires viewing the figure as two equivalent rectangles. Annie is exploring Allan's idea to see if it can be successfully adapted to solve the problem. Annie's attempt to work with Allan's idea demonstrates that revoicing can have an explicit instructional purpose. O'Connor and Michaels (1996) make the point that the "revoicer" of a speaker's contribution often sees more significance in the ideas than the speaker was aware of. This clearly occurs in the following episode where Annie sees potential in Allan's idea where neither the teacher nor Allan had seen any. In fact, the teacher demands that Annie cease her attempts to co-construct a response to the problem, and comply with his directions.

Teacher: You've turned the eight-pointed star into two rectangles, but you're no longer measuring the eight-pointed star.

Annie: So what we did. I found the area of these little triangles and it was twenty-four centimetres squared. So I got that idea off mine and took it away from Allan's answer.

Teacher: No, that's not going to work. You just can't make things fit together. Okay? You can't get two different ideas and make them fit together.

Annie: No, I just knew that …

Teacher: Stop arguing and listen to me for a moment. You can't take his ideas and take your answer away from his answer. He's coming at the problem from a completely different perspective to what you are. You have to work with your ideas and convince him that your ideas are accurate.

Annie: I didn't take my answer away from his.

The teacher and Annie re-visit the calculations evoked by her representation of the problem space, confirming Annie's response that the area of the star is 40 square centimetres. The teacher then re-visits the calculations evoked by Allan's representation and compares the two results.

Teacher: (To Allan) See you haven't got the eight-pointed star there. You got this section here which is not part of the eight-pointed star (points), you've taken this which is not part of the eight-pointed star (a triangle) and put it here. So those two sections don't belong to the eight-pointed star. Your idea is brilliant, it's a beautiful idea, but to find the area of the eight-pointed star it doesn't work. So can you work the next one out (the next problem on the sheet) on this (Annie's) idea.

In the above sequence the teacher engages a voice uncharacteristic of previous student–teacher interactions. Statements like "stop arguing and listen to me" and "can you work the next (problem) out" using Annie's idea, imply that the teacher has adopted a new position within the discourse of the group — that of the traditional teacher.

In response to the teacher's statement that "You can't get two different ideas and make them fit together", Annie maintains the argument that she is not simply subtracting her answer to the problem from Allan's answer ("I didn't take my answer away from his"), but combining his ideas with her ideas to solve the problem in a novel way ("So I got that idea off mine and took it away from Allan's answer"). This contradiction of the teacher's voice is not an act of defiance by Annie, but an example of "wise restraint" — where a mathematical point of view is not changed wantonly, without serious examination (see Lampert, 1990). In this way, Annie's mathematical voice resonates with the confidence of the knower, struggling to represent what she knows and to connect that to the knowledge of others — an emotionally risky resonance, but necessary to developing authority of voice (Kutz, 1990). Annie wants all participants in her group (Allan and the teacher) to integrate the group's existing ideas to co-construct a solution. She persists with this goal in the following sequence:

Annie: Okay, let's go with your idea.
Allan: No.
Annie: Yes.
Allan: We don't have time.
Annie: No, we're going to fix up your idea. We're going to find out where you went wrong.
Allan: But it (the work-sheet) is wrecked.
Annie: Allan, we'll do your idea. Can you draw that shape (the figure) please on the back (of the sheet)? On the back of this and we'll fix up your idea.

(Allan commences to draw the problem figure on the back of the work-sheet. Teacher approaches the group.)

Teacher: How are we going?
Annie: I know where he went wrong.
Teacher: It doesn't work!
Annie: I know, but I think it can.
Teacher: I'll get you another sheet.

(Teacher gives the children a new problem sheet and leaves the group.)

In the above sequence, Annie first recruits Allan's participation in the co-construction of a solution by expressing confidence that his idea can be "fixed" and by organising their work-space so that time can be used efficiently (working on the back of the work-sheet). Annie then recruits the teacher's tacit participation by her confidence ("I know where he went wrong"), affirming the teacher's argument that the idea does not initially work ("I know ..."), and expressing faith in the status of the idea as being an important element of a co-constructed response ("I think it can"). Annie's confidence and her authority derive from the norms of the Collective Argumentation classroom.

Annie's stance continues to give direction to the discourse as the other participants (Allan and the teacher) take up reciprocal positions relevant to the norms of Collective Argumentation. The teacher's attempt to enforce his authority by adopting the traditional teacher voice has been successfully resisted by Annie's maintenance of the voices of Collective Argumentation. In the sequence below it is the teacher who now tries to follow Annie's definition of the task and grants her the status of the "knower", beginning to work with her as a co-participant.

Annie: Okay. Talk to me. Talk me through what you did.

Allan: I went Oh! and got this here (a triangle) and put it here (points). Then I went Oh! and saw there was another one there and another one (both children reconstitute Allan's original representation).

Teacher: But if you keep putting the parts which are not part of the star onto your rectangles, are you finding the area of the (indicates the area of the whole figure)? You've got a big problem with the middle anyway, because it overlaps (shades in the middle square that overlaps both big rectangles).

Annie: Ah ha!

Allan: What are you doing?

Teacher: But that can be solved by finding out the area of that square and taking it away once. That problem can be solved.

Annie: So you've got to find the area of the square …

Teacher: Yeah, we're not interested in that at the moment. But the question you have to ask yourselves is by putting these bits (the triangles) of the square which are not part of the star onto the end of this rectangle, are you finding the area of the star?

Allan: No.

Teacher: Or are you finding the area of the whole square (the figure)?

Allan: We're kinda finding the area of the whole square.

Annie: I'm not particularly worried …

Teacher: You are, you're finding the area of the whole square. Aren't you?

Allan: Because we've got all these parts (the triangles) which were the square, on the end.

Teacher: In other words you've turned the square into two rectangles. You've got the other problem here … that these two rectangles overlap here.

Annie: So we've got to take this square here (the overlapping square) away from our answer.

Teacher: So if you take that square there away from your answer you should get the area of the square which is sixty-four square centimetres. See if it works.

In the above sequence, it is the teacher who is learning to master the children's definition of the situation. For example, as we pointed out earlier, the teacher has often prefaced his scaffolding of student ideas (paraphrases and summaries) in this classroom with the word "so" and students have signalled their appropriation of this scaffolding by using "so" to preface a transformation in their mode of thinking. As can be seen in the above sequence, it is Annie who prefaces her scaffolding of the teacher's contributions with the word "so" — "So you've got to find the area of the square ..." and "So we've got to take this square here (the overlapping square) away from our answer" — and it is the teacher who signals his appropriation of Annie's mode of thinking by prefacing his contribution with the word "so" — "So if you take that square there away from your answer you should get the area of the square which is sixty-four square centimetres. See if it works". Clearly, Annie and the teacher share a symmetry of authority rarely seen in primary classrooms (Edwards & Mercer, 1987).

Conclusions

In our recent research we have explored issues of authorship and authority in the classroom using analytical concepts derived from Bakhtin's theory of voice. We have attempted to show how authorship and authority are shifting and dynamic aspects of classroom practice. In the *infinity* episode, Angela explicitly adopted different speaking positions that simultaneously involved changing authorships and changing bases of authority. Her speaking position varied from a spokesperson for her group ("so we thought ...") to a spokesperson for human kind ("no one can ...") and at the same time her utterances drew on different authority bases that invited her classmates to vary the criteria they employed in evaluating her ideas.

A second issue of interest in our recent research has been the occurrence of *revoicing* as an integral aspect of collaborative talk. The teacher's use of revoicing in this classroom places students on a more equal footing by allowing them the opportunity to evaluate other interpretations or extensions of their utterances. By revoicing a student's utterance the teacher assigns authorship and authority to the student in a manner which encourages the co-construction of ideas and the formation of identities congruent with the culture of Collective Argumentation. Students' revoicing was shown to occur in relation to their classmates' contributions as well as in relation to the teacher's utterances. In the interaction between Annie and Allan, Annie's revoicing of Allan's ideas went beyond his initial understanding and revealed a hidden potential in his ideas — a clear case of instructional dialogue within the ZPD. We also demonstrated that unacknowledged revoicing appears to break the norms of a Collective Argumentation classroom, as shown when classmates asked one group whether they had copied an idea. While copying is unacceptable, acknowledged use of others' ideas is valued.

The analyses presented in this chapter are part of our on-going research program and commitment to create new spaces in the classroom where a diversity of speaking positions is made available to students on a regular basis, and where authority and authorship are spread among the members of the classroom rather than held by the teacher alone. Research on the social construction of knowledge needs to demonstrate that exploratory classroom discourse can be facilitated on a regular basis in ordinary classrooms and that in such circumstances children's learning is enhanced. Collective Argumentation is only one of many possible ways — one of many different types of social scaffolds — that promote the occurrence of such discourse. Our purpose in writing this chapter is not to promote Collective Argumentation as the solution to all pedagogical challenges. Rather it is offered as a possible pedagogical approach — one that might be adapted and explored by other local communities of teachers and learners.

6

The Development of Children's Social Representations of the Primary School Curriculum

Gabrielle Ivinson

Introduction

The curriculum is an organising device that determines the way knowledge is framed and classified within the school context. The wider study, from which this work is drawn, investigated how children re-construct the curriculum through their experience of everyday classroom practice. The study was both *social* in that it was concerned with differences between classrooms and *developmental*, concerned with the way children develop cognitive structures between the second and sixth years of primary schooling. Cognitive structures are investigated in this study within the theoretical framework of social representations (Moscovici, 1976, 1981, 1984) and specifically the work within this field which has called for a greater convergence between social and developmental approaches (Duveen & Lloyd, 1990; Moscovici, 1990; Duveen, 1994, 1997).

A Social and a Developmental Approach

Within psychology there has been a growing awareness that cognition cannot be adequately studied without taking account of social context. Social context may refer to the practices found in specific classrooms, to school practice, to social and political contexts and to cultural contexts. The specific classrooms occupied by the children who were involved in the study are the social contexts that are relevant here because it is through everyday classroom practice that children experience the curriculum. However, classrooms are not fully insulated from other social contexts. Local classroom practice may resist or reinforce social and cultural forces. The curricula instantiated in classrooms are mediated by the values and beliefs of specific teachers, yet teachers have to operate within the constraints of prevailing political and social conditions, and the pragmatic demands of classroom life.

Curricula as Social Representations

The curriculum both as a whole and in its parts can be understood as a social representation, fulfilling symbolic functions for different groups according to their position within society and the economic and political pressures impinging on their everyday life. Each sub-group adopts a representation of the curriculum which is functionally useful and which in turn locates and defines the group within a wider social context. The concept of a social representation elaborated in the work of Moscovici derives from both sociological and psychological traditions and claims Durkheim, Piaget and Freud for its ancestors (cf. Jovchelovitch, 1995). Social representations provide collectives with the resources to interpret and make sense of social situations and to communicate with one another. According to this perspective, social realities are constantly under construction, the continuous production of specific groups functioning in their local contexts. Moscovici has defined them as:

> *system(s) of values and practices with a twofold function; first, to establish an order which will enable individuals to orient themselves in their material and social world and to master it; and second to enable communication to take place among the members of a community by providing them with a code for social exchange and a code for naming and classifying unambiguously the various aspects of their world and their individual and group history* (Moscovici, 1976, p. xiii).

The term "social representation" refers to both the *structures* that allow communication to take place through inter-subjective shared meanings and the *process* whereby shared meanings are created. The theory takes a particular epistemological stance, which treats the subject and object of knowledge as correlative and co-constitutive. The content of a representation is therefore afforded the same significance as the process. Further, a social representation is always the representation for some thing. The object, which this study focuses on, is the curriculum. The consequences of taking this epistemological position are that empirical investigations had to identify the group for whom the curriculum was a *significant structure* (cf. Duveen & Lloyd, 1990). This necessarily limits the findings to specific contexts and to the time when the research was conducted.

Curricula have deep historical roots that can be traced to the organisational structures in different societies. The degree of differentiation within the organisational structure of the curriculum at any time and in any society can be viewed as the outcome of competing interests within different factions of society. As an organising device, the curriculum determines the boundary between what should be imposed on the child and what should not be imposed. For example, the unstructured curriculum advocated by the radical reformers in the 1920s was underpinned by a notion that knowledge would spring from the child as a natural unfolding so long as the social context was sufficiently liberating. Underlying the curriculum in any era are contradictory views about man as good/evil, as rational/irrational and therefore requiring more or less constraint.

The curriculum instantiated in classrooms in mid to late 1990s is generated through a nexus of influences some of which have deep historical roots and others which reflect local political contexts. When this study was conducted official directives were beginning to drive the organisation of the primary school curriculum away from topic and thematic structures towards a more classified curriculum. Since the study was completed the government has prescribed one hour of literacy and one hour of numeracy each day, confirming the trend towards a classified curriculum.

Classrooms as Social Contexts

Moscovici (1998) reminds us that the important difference between traditional and modern societies is not that one practised barter and the other practises exchange, but the degree of differentiation among domains. "Through the course of history, the economic setting has become detached from the surrounding setting and affirmed a separate domain" (ibid. p. 193). Elements of the curriculum such as literacy and numeracy have their own symbolic fields and although these may appear to be neutral, they are highly contested social categories. Once afforded curriculum time and space a subject or activity acquires a distinct domain and the classroom practice becomes *visible*. For example, children may be given specific colour coded exercise books and allocated a place at a table with children perceived to be of a similar *level* or *ability*. These kinds of classroom practices provide symbolic markings, which indicate the "value", attached to an element of the curriculum.

When the child enters a classroom she enters a highly structured space. The curriculum instantiated in teachers' everyday classroom practice and discourse maintains different contexts that provide messages which children will come to interpret. Elements of the curriculum have different social status and thus the everyday practices and routines associated with them are not value free. Teachers communicate these values, often implicitly, through their everyday classroom discourse. For example, chairs placed in a circle are intended to provide a different message from chairs placed in rows behind desks. The codes underlying classroom practice become particularly visible when children transgress boundaries and are reprimanded. Classrooms constitute what Moscovici (1990) has referred to as "thinking environments" and what Shweder (1990) calls "intentional worlds".

Through their everyday practice and discourse teachers mark spaces, objects and other aspects of the material culture of the classroom with significant meaning. Social marking "connects relations of a cognitive order with those of a social order" (Mugny, De Paolis & Carugati, 1984, p. 137). Therefore a classroom may be viewed as a semiotic field with a range of linguistic and non-linguistic signifiers. The specificities of each classroom environment can be viewed as a projection of the teacher's representation of the curriculum. The material culture, for example, wall displays, positioning of tables and chairs, the use or not of specific text books and even the size, quantity and possibly colour of exercise books have significance. However, it can not be assumed that children have the cognitive resources to interpret the material culture of the classroom according to adult conventions; for them this is a developmental process. The important point here is that teachers intend objects, routines and activities to have significance. Therefore, to achieve a successful performance children have to approximate towards adult conventional understandings. It is through trying to make sense of everyday classroom practice that children develop social representations of the curriculum.

Children as Social Actors in the Classroom

Schooling introduces children to a specific set of institutional practices which necessitate new ways of being, acting and speaking. Children elaborate social representations of the curriculum as they become social actors within the classroom context. They internalise the curriculum, not as passive agents, but through an active process of re-construction according to the development of their own cognitive resources (Duveen, 1997). This approach views cognition not as decontextualised structures but as internalised forms of practice. Between the cultural code and the child's idiom there is a level of mediation that relates to social identity (cf. Duveen & Lloyd, 1986). As children re-constructing the curriculum they situate themselves in classroom life and in doing so they develop social identities.

> *"As a social psychological process, the construction of an identity is a way of organising meanings which enable a person to position him or herself as a social actor. An identity provides a means of organising experience which contributes towards a definition of self, but it does so by locating the self within the collective world"* (Duveen, 1997, p. 71).

Work on the development of gender identities (Duveen & Lloyd, 1986, 1990, 1993; Lloyd & Duveen, 1989, 1990, 1992) has shown that while children shared representations of femininity and masculinity they adopted different positions with respect to these symbolic systems. Taking up a position involves defending a social identity. So, although individuals may have the same knowledge of a semiotic code such as gender or mathematics, they position themselves differently with respect to that knowledge. Taking up a position is also an expression of a value and the values associated with social identities are, like all symbolic processes, arenas of conflict and negotiation.

Piaget defined "representation" as the "simultaneous differentiation and co-ordination between signifiers and signified". Lloyd and Duveen (1990, p. 32) suggest, the emergence of differentiated signification is a gradual process which corresponds to the internalisation of social representations. Different relations between the signifier and signified characterise the genetic development of social representations (Piaget, 1951; Wallon, 1970). The distinction between signification and representation is important for both developmental (or genetic) and semiotic perspectives since it cannot be assumed that young children have the cognitive resources required for developing social representations. In order to understand how children develop social representations, Lloyd and Duveen (1990, p. 28) have emphasised the importance of distinguishing between different types of significa-tion (signals, symbols and signs). Initially, differentiated signification remains embedded in the immediate context of activity.

The gradual process by which children differentiate functions and context relates to what Vygotsky referred to as "the decontextualisation of semiotic means" (cf. Wertsch, 1985). Lloyd and Duveen point out that it will be in the context where children are offered the greatest amount of scaffolding that they will develop signs. Their work elaborates the semiotic character of social representations and thus indicates how the material culture of the classroom acts as scaffolding (Wood, Bruner & Ross, 1976) for the child's entry into specialist subject discourse.

The Research Stance

Within the broader study, classrooms were viewed from a particular perspective, determined by the object of investigation; the curriculum. In this chapter my focus is less on the ontological subject and more on the collective phenomena, or social representations, produced by social practices within classrooms. The question here is whether the specificities of everyday classroom practice provide children with resources to re-construct the curriculum in different ways. I chose therefore to work in schools with different types of curricula. The developmental angle was concerned with whether the form and content of representations of the curriculum change between two moments, the second and the sixth year of schooling. Lloyd and Duveen (1990) have compared a social representation to an iceberg. The visible part is accessible via verbal formulations and the submerged part, which consists of a network of ideas and inferences, is not. There is no unequivocal way to tap these hidden aspects and in this study a range of quantitative and qualitative methods was used within an ethnographic approach.

Methodology

Primary schools were selected to reflect three types of curriculum according to Bernstein's typology of curriculum types (1971, 1974, 1981, and 1990). One tended towards a collection type curriculum, one tended towards an integration type curriculum and one combined aspects of each, hereinafter referred to as a mixed type curriculum. The study focused on two moments in the development of curricular structures; Year 1 (children in their second year of schooling, aged 5/6 years) and Year 5 (children in their sixth year of schooling, aged 9/10 years). In each school, two parallel classrooms (note 4) in each year group were studied. In all, five schools and twelve classrooms took part as described in Table 1 below. The term "classroom" will be used throughout in order to prevent ambiguities over classes of children and social class background.

Comparable case studies were carried out in each school. The fieldwork

Table 1: Schools and classrooms in the study by curriculum type

School	Copse School	St Helen's Infant & St Anne's Junior	Dart Infant & Dart Junior School
Type of curriculum	Integration	Mixed	Collection
Date opened	1990	Infant: 1960s Junior 1991	1927
Architecture	Open plan	Infant: enclosed Junior: semi-open	Enclosed
Sites & buildings	Same site Same building	Different sites Different buildings	Same site Different buildings
Headship	One headteacher	Different headteachers	Different headteachers
Number on roll	221	Infant: 275 Junior: 322	Infant: 186 Junior: 277
Infant classrooms	Classroom 1 Classroom 2	Classroom 3 Classroom 4	Classroom 5 Classroom 6
Junior classrooms	Classroom 7 Classroom 8	Classroom 9 Classroom 10	Classroom 11 Classroom 12

consisted of two cycles; first the Year 5 classrooms were the objects of investigation and the second focused on the Year 1 classrooms. Each cycle lasted one academic year and consisted of two phases. In phase one the aim was twofold; firstly, to compile a typology of semiotic messages within classrooms and secondly, to design instruments to investigate children's representations of the curriculum. Ethnographic tools included fieldnotes based on classroom observations and event sampling gained through video recording a series of lessons in each classroom. The typology was constructed from fieldnotes and video recordings. There is now a sizeable literature on recognition and realisation rules (cf. Bernstein, 1981, 1990, 1996; Diaz, 1984; Daniels, 1989; Morias, Fontinhas & Neve, 1993; Singh, 1993; Whitty, Rowe & Aggleton, 1994a, 1994b). The typology is illustrated in Table 2.

The typology was used to show how many and which types of classroom activity had distinct and recognisable domains. The crude summary of a selection of recognition and realisation rules, provided in Table 3, points to differences among classrooms.

In the second phase children's representations of the curriculum were investigated through individual interviews with a sample of children (controlled for age and sex group — ten boys and ten girls) from each classroom. This chapter reports findings from one of the psychological instruments, a modified version of Kelly's

Table 2: Typology of recognition and realisation rules

Tending towards Closure/restricted Visible pedagogy	Tending towards Openness/less restricted Invisible or less visible pedagogy

1 PLACE

specialist space (e.g. art room, hall)-------------------------------------in the classroom
furniture positioned in lines, rectangles -------------------------------------in groups
rectangular and square tables---round tables
tables face the teacher's table or board--------------------------tables face each other
children have their own place-------------------------------------places are communal
storage room at individual places --------individual drawers in a communal trolley

2 EQUIPMENT

children own personal everyday equipment -----everyday equipment is communal
(e.g. pencil, pen)
children keep subject specific items----------------------------kept in communal places
(e.g. exercise books, text books)
children can access specialist equipment ----teacher controls specialist equipment
(e.g. apparatus, paint brush)

3 CURRICULUM STRUCTURATION

activity has an identifiable beginning----------------------------arises in an ad hoc way
activity has a set procedure-------------------------------------the procedure is novel
activity has an identifiable end-----------------------------------the end is contingent

4 TIME INTERVALS

regular and often (predictable) ----------------------------------irregular and infrequent
(e.g. happens each day or week)   (e.g. one-off activities)
short time cycle---long time cycle
(e.g. a few minutes   (e.g. across a term)

5 SETTING AND GROUPING

ability groups--no ability groups
assigned to groups for activities--work individually
equipment for specific (ability) groups--------------------------all use same equipment
seated in specific groups---individual places
groups have a different teacher--same teacher

6 SPACE AND MOVEMENT

restricted --less restricted
(e.g. children sit in a fixed place)   (children occupy a variety of seats)
homogeneous---diverse
(e.g. the same place for each activity)   (e.g. different places for different
                                                             activities)
teacher strongly controls movement----------------------------children have autonomy

(continued)

Table 2: *Continued*

Tending towards Closure/restricted Visible pedagogy	Tending towards Openness/less restricted Invisible or less visible pedagogy
7 WALL DISPLAYS	
curriculum subject oriented--child-centred	
(e.g. gives information, functional)	(e.g. illustrates "creativity")
child's name appears---no names used	
label indicates subject--label indicates topic	
teacher's individual style--school aesthetic code	
hierarchical--equal	
(e.g. sample of the "best work")	(e.g. every child is represented)
8 TEACHERS' CLASSROOM DISCOURSE	
subject focused--child focused	
(e.g. instructional)	(e.g. regulative, moral)
subject criteria made explicit------------------------------------individuality emphasised	
sameness emphasised--difference encouraged	

(1955) repertory grid. During the ethnographic work 11 regularly occurring curricular activities were identified. These were then used as the elements of the repertory grid. Variations in practice meant that different instruments had to be designed for each classroom. Year 5 children were presented with elements of the curriculum as names written on strips of paper. Since children in Year 1 classrooms were unlikely to be able to read subject names and may not have been aware that activities had specific names, photographs were used instead (cf. Ravenette, 1975). Items usually used for one activity were positioned in their familiar setting and photographed. For example, the mathematics cubes, the worksheet scheme, pencils and some of the children's exercise books were placed on a table. Six sets of photographs were created to reflect the material culture specific to each infant classroom.

Procedure

The task was administered to children on an individual basis. Each child was taken to a quiet place outside the classroom and presented with the set of photographs/names: at each turn the child was shown three of the 11. He or she was asked, "Can you point to the two that are like each other, or a bit like each other?" and then "Why are these two like each other?" Their responses were both written down and audio taped. The remaining eight photographs/names were then placed on the table and the child was asked, "Are any of these also like those two?" If they

Table 3: Summary of selected recognition and realisation rules

Classroom	Place Children have a set place to sit	Equipment 1 Where personal property is kept	Equipment 2 Number of exercise books	Curriculum Structur'n Activities with a beginning, middle & end, per week	Time cycles Number per day	Setting & grouping Number of clues (e.g. differentiated worksheet)	Movement Restricted, variable & not restricted	Wall displays Curriculum oriented, variable & child-oriented	Discourse Subject criteria or individual difference made explicit (other)
Copse Infant 1	variable	communal tray	4	7	3	3	variable	child	individual
Copse Infant 2	variable	communal tray	4	8	3	2	variable	child	individual
St Helen's Infant 3	variable	communal tray	6	10	4	6	variable	variable	language of emotion
St Helen's Infant 4	variable	communal tray	6	9	6	6	variable	variable	language of emotion
Dart Infant 5	set place	At own table	6	12	4	5	restricted	variable	subject
Dart Infant 6	set place	At own table	6	10	4	1	restricted not	variable	subject
Copse Junior 7	no set place	communal tray	4	8	5	1	restricted not	child	individual
Copse Junior 8	no set place	communal tray	4	8	5	1	restricted not	child	individual
St Anne's Junior 9	no set place	communal tray	7	10	5	3	restricted	variable	individual
St Anne's Junior 10	set place	communal tray	7	10	5	2	variable	variable	individual
Dart Junior 11	set place	at own table	9	12	5	1	variable	curriculum	subject
Dart Junior 12	set place	at own table	9	12	4	1	restricted	curriculum	subject

did not understand they were prompted with, "Can any of these also be described like that?" Finally, they were asked, "Why is the other one different?" These responses were recorded in the same way. A record was kept of the activities, which were described as "similar" and "different" for each turn. The procedure was followed for each of 11 permutations of three subjects, resulting in 22 justifications of similarity and difference for each child. Justifications of similarity and difference were later transcribed in full and coded according to a specially designed coding scheme described below.

Repertory Grid Analysis

Both task performance and children's talk about the task were analysed which yielded both quantitative and qualitative data. Task performance was analysed using a specially designed program, IGRID (Smith, 1986)[1]. The three curriculum categories with the highest positive/negative loadings were used to illustrate the poles of a bipolar construct for that child. This gave approximately 20 bipolar groupings of curricula categories for each of the classrooms in each of the schools. Since the aim was to investigate social representations of the curriculum by classroom, rather than individual constructs, a classroom component was sought. This was achieved by selecting the three curricular elements with the highest positive and the three elements with highest negative loadings that occurred most frequently in each classroom. These were used to identify each pole of what will now be referred to as the principal curriculum component.

Principal "Curriculum" Components

The principal "curriculum" component for each classroom provides insight into hidden aspects of representations, that is, aspects which children were unlikely to verbalise. Tables 4 and 5 show the subjects that emerged at each pole by classroom.

---

[1]The program supplies tables for identifying or naming principal components by detecting underlying trends in the relationship between elements. A component is a construct expressing a contrast between elements. It also provides loadings for each element (curriculum category) by calculating distances between elements. The elements with high positive loadings when contrasted with those elements with high negative loadings epitomise the contrast, the nature of which is indicated by those grid elements with high loadings on the component. In a further step the number of significant constructs is calculated. In the majority of cases the first principal component accounted for 30–75 percent of the variance. More than one significant principal component was found only in a very few cases (about 1 in 20). On the basis of this finding it was decided to investigate the content of only the first principal component for each child. Usually no more than three trends are considered because these tend to make up 75 percent of the total variance. The Bartlett test was applied to determine if there was any significant difference between trends. In nearly all cases there was a negative result from the Bartlett test for the 230 children in this study.

Table 4: The principal "curriculum" component in the infant classrooms

Pole 1			Pole 2	
Copse Infant School				
Integration curriculum				
Classroom 1	physical education	12/15*	handwriting	11/15
	story time	11/15	English	9/15
	play	9/15	mathematics	8/15
Classroom 2	play	15/18	science topic	12/18
	physical education	14/18	English	12.18
	story time	8/18	science topic	10.18
St Helen's Infant School				
Mixed curriculum				
Classroom 3	PSE	15/20	topic, science	14/20
	physical education	12/20	mathematics	11/20
	play	10/20	handwriting	9/20
	reading	10/20		
Classroom 4	physical education	12/20	numbers	17/20
	reading	12/20	mathematics	16/20
	PSE	11/20	English	13/20
	play	11/20		
Dart Infant School				
Collection curriculum				
Classroom 5	art	13/20	science topic	10/20
	music	11/20	English	10/20
	design	12/20	mathematics	9/20
Classroom 6	physical education	20/20	science topic	16/20
	music	18/20	mathematics	12/20
	art	13/20	handwriting	10/20

*The proportions given in the table indicate the number of children out of the total number in one classroom for which the element occurred as one of the three elements with the highest negative or positive loadings.

Work and Play

A bipolar opposition between fixity and movement holds across types of curriculum and across age groups. The subjects represented at pole 1 in both infant and junior classrooms usually took place either outside the classroom or in places not normally used for "work" such as the carpet area. These activities require the

Table 5: The principal "curriculum" component in the junior classrooms

Pole 1			Pole 2	
Copse Infant School				
Integration curriculum				
Classroom 7	music	18/20	handwriting	16/20
	singing	17/20	English	16/20
	art	9/20	spelling test	13/20
Classroom 8	music	15/20	handwriting	18/20
	singing	14/20	English	15/20
	art	9/20	spelling test	13/20
St Anne's Junior School				
Mixed curriculum				
Classroom 9	physical education	15/20	English	15/20
	story time	10/20	topic	14/20
	singing	9/20	handwriting	12/20
Classroom 10	art	13/19	English	14/19
	physical education	12/19	spelling test	11/19
	reading	8/19	handwriting	12/19
Dart Junior School				
Collection curriculum				
Classroom 11	technology	14/19	history	13/19
	art	13/19	science	10/19
	physical education	9/19	geography	9/19
Classroom 12	art	18/20	history	11/20
	technology	11/20	science	10/20
	physical education	11/20	English	10/20

*The proportions given in the table indicate the number of children out of the total number in one classroom for which the element occurred as one of the three elements with the highest negative or positive loadings.

use of parts of the body that have to be kept relatively immobile when writing. In physical education children ran, crawled and skipped, all of which required gross motor activities. In art, children usually stood up and used their arms and hands. In music, the hands, arms and the mouth were used to play instruments. In reading and singing children used their voices. Without exception children were required to sit at a table for all the activities which appeared at pole 2, most of which involved writing either in exercise books or on sheets of paper. English was represented at this pole in all but two classrooms and mathematics in five out of six infant classrooms but none of the junior classrooms. Elsewhere, (Ivinson, 1998b) findings from a sorting task, reported that mathematics emerged as a basic level curriculum category in the junior classrooms. The sorting task demonstrated that mathematics had become a distinct curriculum category for children after six years of schooling and for children in some classrooms after only 18 months of schooling. It is likely that mathematics did not emerge at either pole in the principal "curriculum" component in the junior classrooms because it had already become a category with strong boundaries and a distinct identity and was not considered similar to any of the other curriculum elements.

In essence, poles express an opposition between desk-bound and non desk-bound activities. Desk-bound activities involve physical constraint because children have to sit at a table and hold a pencil to write. Activities, such as art, play and physical education involve relative freedom of movement. These activities also take place in a variety of classroom and non-classroom spaces. The activities associated with pole 1 can be described as aesthetic, physical and recreational. The activities associated with the pole 2 can be described as literacy and numeracy. In the infant classrooms this can be viewed to a bipolar opposition between work and play.

These findings suggest that firstly, all children differentiate the curriculum according to space and restriction of movement. The homogeneity at pole 1 across the infant classrooms in the same school is particularly striking because it demonstrates that young children did not recognise the specific differences between classrooms in the same school. This suggests that the kinds of body movements involved in activities such as physical education, art and play were salient for young children. They were also attending to large-scale differences in place. For example, reading, story time and music usually took place in spaces other than the places used for the desk-bound activities associated with the opposite pole. In infant classrooms, reading was different to other literacy activities because it did not involve working independently at a table and often took place outside the classroom.

The recognition and realisation rules in the Year 5 classrooms had a greater influence on the constitution of each pole than in the infant classrooms. The two Year 5 classrooms in Copse School shared a common space and material culture and these similarities can be seen reflected in the principal "curriculum" components. The greatest difference between poles was found in St Anne's Junior School with the mixed type curriculum. In Dart School the structuration provided by a collection type curriculum is reflected in the homogeneity of the two poles. In this school, and not in the others, science and history emerged at pole 2.

Analysis of Talk by Classroom

Social representations provide the code, which connects the signifier (e.g. a photograph or a name), to the signified. Forming social representations of the curriculum requires interpretative effort and for children this involves coming to recognise semiotic messages. Although talk provides access to the *tip* of the social representation *iceberg*, the way talk is analysed can also throw light on hidden aspects. A coding scheme was devised which comprised four discrete categories: feature talk, function talk, structure talk and other talk. Each type of talk indicates a different process of signification. Feature and function talk point to connections between the signifier and the signified which rely on personally motivated meanings or *symbols* and structure talk indicates adult conventional categories or *sign* use. The point about sign use is not that children's representations have become identically matched with those of their teachers, but that the meanings they attach to words have become aligned with the meanings that are fixed by public convention and used by adult members of the speech community. The purpose of analysing children's talk according to different forms of signification was to find out if classroom practice had influenced the development of sign use.

Feature talk was context dependent and usually based on visual perception. This type of talk indicated that children had few resources for interpreting classroom life: their understanding remained tied to surface features such as shape, colour and position.

Function talk pointed to a qualitatively different relation between signifier and signified which was characterised by the use of action verbs. Signification was based on functions of everyday classroom practice. Children spoke about fetching and replacing equipment, about sitting, running, writing and about where to do things. In this category social representations of the curriculum were anchored in practice, in physical movements and in local contexts such as "at tables", "in the hall" and "outside".

Structure talk indicated by signs. Social representations of the curriculum had become decontextualised, no longer tied to specific practices and functions. Children who used structure talk had developed cognitive resources that allowed them to manipulate ideas and to transcend immediate contexts. They had started to develop reflexive understandings of themselves as learners which is also part of constructing social identities. The coding scheme is illustrated in Table 6.

Analysis of Talk by Year Group

Each of the 22 justifications produced by one child was coded. A justification which may have been as short as one word or comprise a lengthy paragraph was treated as one utterance. Each utterance was assigned a code according to the highest level judged to be present. For example, the utterance, "I put these together because they are used for doing maths and they are all red" would be assigned the code structure talk for "doing maths" even though it includes feature talk, "they are all red". This section relies on aggregated data from the 22 * 20 utterances produced in each classroom. Separate analyses were carried out for each type of talk — feature, function, structure and other. The mean numbers of utterances for each year group are illustrated in Figure 1.

Table 6: Coding scheme for children's talk

FEATURE TALK
Context dependent, based on visual perception.

That's got a green box and they have.	year 5
That ones near the cupboard and that's the teacher, reading book.	year 1
That isn't work.	year 1
Got flowers, one pair of scissors and paint box and piece of paper.	year 1
Because that one is outside and that one is inside.	year 1

FUNCTION TALK
Self referred to as the subject in a general classroom activity or performing a function with objects visible in the photographs. Concrete action verbs used.

In English you are never wrong what you write. You can not make it up in maths, it has to be correct all the time.	year 5
Just sit down and listen to a story. PE you're up on your feet, jump. You can do anything, jump, skip.	year 5
Those two are play. PE is sort of play really.	year 1
You've got to play in the sand and you've got to make numbers with the buttons.	year 1
Maths and art, don't have to listen to anything or write any notes down.	year 5

STRUCTURE TALK
About a subject, subjects named. Abstract action verbs.

Because you're expressing your feelings in music and art, rather than reading. Reading you're reading someone else's feelings.	year 5
Them two, that one maths in books, you work, reading is work you have to work in reading, you understand more in books, they explain better. Maths learn to juggle with numbers.	year 5
Science learn things about the world.	year 5
PE, play games, in technology concentrate on your work.	year 5
RE is about learning about faith, people who live in different places. Mostly olden days, faiths, too RE, could be about Muslims and history could be Muslims, long time ago, them and their faith.	year 5

OTHER TALK
Any justification which could not be coded according to the above categories.

On its own	year 1
Forget now	year 1
I ain't got nothing for them two.	year 5
I couldn't find any other reason	year 5

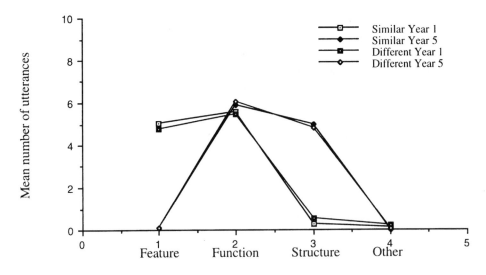

Figure 1 Types of talk by year groups

As could have been predicted, year 1 children produced more feature talk and less structure talk than year 5 children did. Younger children tended to rely on physical features and classroom functions to differentiate activities.

Analysis of Talk by Curriculum

Repeated measures analysis of variance was used to analyse the quantity of each type of talk produced by children from each school. The within-subject variables were the amounts of each type of talk produced in judgements of similarity and difference and the between-subjects variables were curriculum, sex group and year group. There was no significant difference in the quantities of feature, function and structure talk produced in justifications of similarity and difference. Three significant interactions were found. With feature talk there was a between subjects interaction, year group with sex group (df 2,217: $F = 2.05$: $p < 0.05$). Post hoc analysis using Tukey's b found that Year 5 children produced significantly less feature talk (mean 0.09) than the Year 1 children (mean 4.92, $p < 0.05$) and the Year 1 girls produced more feature talk (mean 5.45) than the Year 1 boys (mean 3.20, $p < 0.05$).

A two way interaction between curriculum type and year group for function talk was significant (df 2,217: $F = 3.73$: $p < 0.05$). More function talk was produced by the Year 5 children than by the Year 1 children. However, in the classrooms with a collection type curriculum, the Year 1 children produced more function talk than children in Year 5. Across both year groups more function talk was produced in the integration and mixed type curricula (mean 6.25) than in the collection type (mean

4.77, $p < 0.05$). The difference between the Year 5 children from the collection type classrooms (mean 4.20) and the Year 5 children in the mixed and integration type classrooms (mean 6.84) regarding function talk, was not significant.

More structure talk was produced in the classrooms with a collection type curriculum than in the others. There was a two way interaction, curriculum by year group (df 2,217: F = 3.73: $p < 0.05$). The difference between the amount of structure talk produced by the Year 1 and the Year 5 children was significant, and as had been expected the younger children produced significantly less (mean 0.41) than the older children (mean 4.90, $p < 0.05$). The older children in the collection type (classrooms 11 and 12) produced significantly more structure talk (mean 6.75) than the older children in the mixed and integration type classrooms (mean 4.00, $p < 0.05$).

These findings suggest that the production of talk was influenced by curriculum type. Less function and more structure talk was produced by children from classrooms with a collection curriculum and the effect increased for the older children.

Analysis of Talk by Classroom

In the introduction it was suggested that teachers mediate the curriculum according to their beliefs and values. Therefore differences in the production of talk between classrooms in the same school could have been predicted. The production of each type of talk in the infant classrooms is illustrated in Figure 2.

The greatest quantities of function talk were produced in classroom 4 which had a mixed curriculum and in classroom 5 with a collection curriculum suggesting that

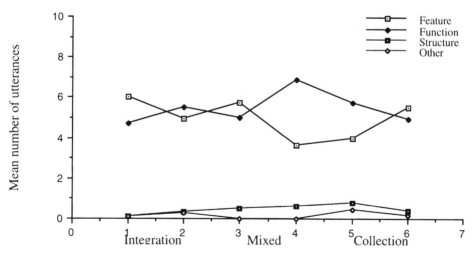

Figure 2 Types of talk produced in the infant classrooms

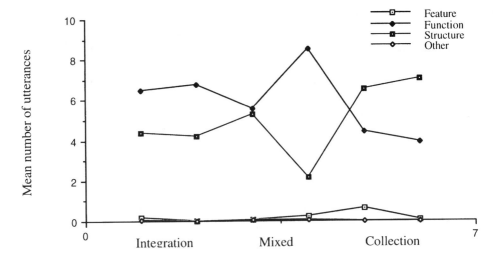

Figure 3 Types of talk in the junior classrooms

effects due to individual teaching style had at least as much influence as curriculum type. In order to investigate this further, the quantities of each type of talk were compared using *t*-tests for pairs of classrooms in the same school. Talk for both similar and different groupings was aggregated.

Significant differences were found between classrooms 3 and 4 in St Helen's Infant School with a mixed curriculum and *not* for the other two schools. More feature talk was produced in classroom 3 (mean 5.76) and in classroom 4 (mean 3.65, $p < 0.05$). Conversely, less function talk was found in classroom 3 (mean 5.02) than in classroom 4 (mean 6.90, $p < 0.05$). More function talk was produced in classroom 4 than in any of the others. It may well be that the flexible structure of a mixed type curriculum allowed for greater variation in teachers' practice. However, the result may also have been due to differences between the two groups of children.

It was only when children had a greater experience of school life that curriculum type began to noticeably influence the way children spoke about the curriculum. The pattern of talk produced in the junior classrooms is illustrated in Figure 3 below.

Children from Dart Junior School, which had the greatest curriculum structuration, produced the greatest quantity of structure talk. Girls in classroom 12 produced the greatest quantity of structure talk, although the difference did not reach significance. Children from junior classrooms in Copse School with the least curriculum structuration produced less structure talk and more function talk than their peers in the collection type classrooms.

As with the infant data, *t*-test were used to compare the talk produced in parallel junior classrooms in the same school. Significant differences were found between the two classrooms in St Anne's School which had a mixed curriculum. More structure talk was generated in classroom 9 (mean 5.28) than in classroom 10 (mean 2.03, $p < 0.00$). As would be expected, this was matched by less function talk in classroom 9 (mean 5.58) than in classroom 10 (mean 8.68, $p < 0.00$).

Findings suggest, once again, that variations in teaching style had a greater impact in schools with a mixed type curriculum. The teacher in classroom 10 was more formal than the teacher in classroom 9. In classroom 10 children had set places which they were expected to occupy during most of the day and the teacher had developed strategies for keeping children in their places. For example, there was a pot for sharpening pencils on each table to prevent children walking to the wastebasket during lessons. Teacher 10 had abandoned the mathematics textbook used in classroom 9 because she said the children did not have good enough literacy skills to understand the exercises. Either the teacher's low expectations or some other aspect of classroom practice may have contributed to the relatively small quantity of structure talk produced by the children in classroom 10.

As children gain experience of schooling their representations of the curriculum become more differentiated and more elaborate. The following sections rely on an extensive qualitative analysis of talk, which is reported in more detail elsewhere (Ivinson, 1998a, 1998b), to illustrate the kinds of developmental changes associated with feature, function and structure talk.

Work and Play in the Infant Classrooms

Younger children consistently produced the same kind of bipolar opposition (work/play) irrespective of curriculum context. Work was an over extended category that included classroom activities that involved sitting at a table, with paper and a pencil. Play, was a less extended category and referred to activities which involved relative freedom of movement and choice. The infant children used predominantly feature and function talk to describe this opposition and in doing so they referred to objects and their position within the classroom, to spaces and to their bodies. Children described functions such as when and where they sat, stood, moved and which parts of the body they used to listen, to do art and particularly to do physical education. The phrases used most frequently to describe the basic work–play opposition are listed in Table 7 below.

"Writing" was mentioned more than any other verb when children described "work", whereas "toys" and "Lego" were mentioned most frequently with "play" and "choosing". There were a few references to place, such as, "these are in the classroom and these are not", "they are both done on the table", "done on the carpet", "that is done on the board". There were also references to time such as, "all on the same day" and to pace, such as "dash through your work". Other verbs frequently mentioned were "sticking", "colouring", "drawing" and "skipping'. Mathematics and reading were named as separate categories by many of the Year 1 children and a few also mentioned handwriting.

The science experiment represented in one classroom by a plastic bowl with soil in it attracted various distinctive comments. Science experiments often involve

Table 7: Bipolar constructs in the infant classrooms

Feature
  1   On the table — not on the table (on the floor)
  2   In the classroom — not in the classroom (in the hall, outside)
  3   Pencils and book — apparatus (for physical education), toys
  4   Books — no books
  5   Has words — has not got words

Function
  6   Writing — something you do
  7   Using your hands — running around
  8   Sitting down — standing up
  9   Moving around — isn't moving around
 10   Listen to the teacher — not listening to the teacher
 11   Don't make a noise — make a noise
 12   Tidy — messy
 13   Harder — fun
 14   Things we don't like — things we like

Structure
 15   Have to concentrate — sing, move

---

unusual and interesting equipment and the photograph of the soil in which worms were kept elicited comments which reflected children's excitement such as, "a big fat worm" and "because it's got worms in the soil".

Fixity and Movement in the Junior Classrooms

The opposition between "fixity" and "movement" was articulated as a mind/body distinction in the junior classrooms. In general, activities relating to the body, physical movement and posture were differentiated from those relating to the mind. A transitional moment was recognisable in some children's talk when they used parts of the body to indicate mental activity. Jamie described, "listening with your ears" and "using your brain for your own things that you're doing".

> Cos in story time you're listening again, you're and in English and spelling you're writing down and you're using your brain for your own things that you're doing. Is listening and you're not doing anything the only thing that you're doing is with your ears. You're just listening with your ears. English and spelling, not listening to somebody, you're listening to your brain really and writing down. (Year 5 Jamie, classroom 1, Copse School)

This kind of description was qualitatively different to those given by the younger children. "The brain" was clearly meant to indicate mental activity and was used for this purpose by children in all the junior classrooms except those in Dart Junior School where mental activity was referred to using conventional terms such as "learn", "concentrate" and "practice". Although many Year 5 children continued to use action verbs such as "do", "read", "write", "draw", "make up", "paint" and "colour", the use of abstract verbs and phrases increased.

Year 5 children often used the terms "reading" and "writing" to indicate many different functions within the classroom. The specificity with which they used the terms indicated different meanings underlying linguistic terms. The following extract illustrates the range of meanings Sarah attached to the term "writing", capturing the fluidity that Walkerdine (1988) referred to in the relationship between the signified and the signifier:

> Because when in English we do stories and write in handwriting, we write as well. Maths is different because English and handwriting is all writing. In maths the teacher says something, like do your seven times table, you don't write anything. When you have a book you look at the writing and then you write your answer. It's usually learning, not a story, not making things up. (Year 5 Sarah, classroom 2, Copse School)

Clearly, Sarah had a number of context-specific understandings of writing. She referred to "handwriting", writing "stories", writing in "text books" and the writing involved in "an answer". The signifier "writing" was bound up with specific classroom contexts and it would have been helpful if Sarah had had access to a number of linguistic expressions to signify these. By differentiating the category "writing" she has demonstrated the importance of keeping two curriculum categories, English and mathematics, separate. Writing stories involved "making things up" and mathematics was often described by children as "getting the right answer" rather than as "writing".

A further example of this kind of fluidity was found in the way Sarah described different kinds of learning. In the extract below she explains why "art" and "reading" are different to physical education (PE):

> In art you read and you can learn a lot at reading. In art you can learn a lot, sometimes you make a mistake and say you can do this and that and then you learn it. You can learn a lot in PE but you don't. You can fall over in PE but you can do it again. In story time and art if you make a mistake, you can do it again, but you learn it. In PE you just fall over it nearly all through your life you can fall over, you can't really learn not to fall over. (Year 5 Sarah, classroom 2, Copse School)

Falling over did not count as "learning" because the act was confined to an immediate concrete context — the here and now of the acting. Subject knowledge was often represented in ways which suggested a greater distance between a function and its completion, opening up a space for practice, reformulation of the task and therefore for the possibility of re-doing. This became clearer in one of her later comments when she related "making mistakes" to "learning". Further on, she differentiated "learning" and "making things up", and by doing so implicitly linked "learning" to mathematics rather than to English, although, "learning" proved to be an unstable category. Her talk about the curriculum is characterised by references to functions. This indicates the use of symbols rather than signs.

By examining the full corpus of Sarah's utterances three underlying dimensions were recognisable in the structure of her social representation. The first identified knowledge that was new or old, the second identified knowledge that was malleable or fixed and the third identified knowledge that allowed for a wide or narrow range of possible (i.e. correct) responses. This level of analysis focuses on the specificities of individual representations and begins to demonstrate the relation between ontogenetic development and social representations. Individuals elaborate particular social identities by reconstructing social representations at a psychological level. Social identities embody knowledge of the social representations of a particular group yet by investigating the difference between individuals in the same classroom it becomes possible to show how each child takes up a position with respect to collective meanings.

The contrast between the physical, the immediate and the embodied on the one hand and the malleable or flexible properties associated with the mental on the other was reworked and articulated in a variety of ways by children in each of the junior classrooms. We turn now to the justifications given by Alan from Dart Junior School to illustrate a social representation that relied on a high level of sign use. Abstract action verbs were taken as one of the indicators of structure talk. Alan used the term "learning" six times during the interview and, unlike the previous example, the term was used consistently throughout. Other abstract terms such as "working things out" and "create" were also used.

Alan described mathematics as "the most mental" because information (possibly mathematical symbols) could be "expanded" beyond what was already there. This was expressed as a creative process:

> Take a bit of information and create something from it. Take, expand it into something that is really. Maths, expand it, create something. (Alan, Year 5, classroom 1, Dart Junior School)

In contrast, actions such as running and play were represented as if they remained embedded in the immediate context:

> Action, run, play. Not like taking information and making it into something much bigger than you started from. (Alan, Year 5, classroom 1, Dart Junior School)

However, this was not the way other children represented mathematics. Ben, in the same classroom, described mathematics as "an exact science". His talk indicated that mathematics was strongly differentiated from other activities. He contrasted mathematics with music that he said, "can be given to you in many forms".

> Sometimes music can picture in your mind, but it's mostly learning, not so much pictures in your mind. Maths, is an exact science. Music can be to given to you in many different forms. (Ben, Year 5, classroom 1, Dart Junior School)

Some of the Year 5 children, particularly in Dart Junior School, demonstrated that they had social representations of the curriculum which showed an awareness of the inner logic of a subject category, that is, the way ideas can be aligned. Some also demonstrated an understanding of the nature of the ideas associated with different areas of the curriculum. Alan was able to talk about subjects in this way. He distinguished "learning things, fictional characters" from "reading in real life". He suggested that physical education was concrete — that it was action-bound — while mathematics and technology were, in a sense, constructive because the basic or raw information "becomes something bigger than you started from". Later, he suggested that technology was not "learning something" because the (raw material) was already given. Mathematics was about "working things out" and technology was about "making things". Another boy in classroom 12, who said, "technology is making models, that's building" made the connection between building and technology very explicit.

Alan associated religious education and English with something, which arose initially from books rather than from "real life". He also considered art to be fictional but this time he associated the subject with "landscapes and people". He talked about the subject matter of art as — "not real" — and to do with the "imagination". Through his talk it was possible to recognise domains. For example, he described geography as being about "real people" and "real places". He also linked music to people and places and in doing so he identified a humanities domain. He linked physical education to science by describing them both as diagnosing problems to do with the body — "fitness" — and the environment — "pollution". Patrick, also from Dart Junior School, stated that science was "all about drawing pictures, how the human body, what we have learned from the past". He also said, "physical education is about sport, activities and that, making stuff, the human body."

Qualitative analysis of Alan's talk showed that his representation of the curriculum was structured according to four domains: constructing and working out (mathematics, technology); fictional, imaginative and the "not real" (English, art and religious education); "real" people and places (geography and music) and an accumulated body of knowledge which provided "information" (science and physical education).

Discussion

In this study, classrooms were viewed as micro-social contexts that make the curriculum available to children in different ways. Different types of curriculum entail different forms of control, which facilitate modalities of social interaction and practice. One of the important differences among classrooms was the extent to which curricular elements had distinct domains. It was hypothesised that classrooms, which offered the greatest quantity of curricular scaffolding, would facilitate the use of signs.

It may not be particularly surprising to find that it was in classrooms, which differentiated curriculum elements more clearly, that children had developed the greatest use of signs. Children have to go beyond the specific content of classroom discourse and the surface features of practice to recover the hidden aspects of curriculum categories. Although different modalities of control play a structuring role, how children internalise these varies between different moments in the formation of curriculum categories. It was found that the young children did not possess the cognitive resources to recognise the specificities that, from an adult perceptive, clearly distinguished infant classroom practice.

Initially, children differentiated curriculum elements according to context dependent features such as whether or not they could move parts of their bodies. The generative nucleus at the heart of infant children's representation of the curriculum comprised an over-extended category "work" and an under-extended category "play". Reading was the first activity to split-off from the nucleus and acquire a distinctive category. In each infant classroom, reading involved working with an adult on a one-to-one basis. Children had reading book bags, reading record books, identifiable reading schemes and were usually given written feedback about how well they had read. Reading was also the only regular homework children were expected to undertake. In short, reading had many semiotic markers so that the practices associated with reading were highly visible. Analysis revealed that salient features of classroom life for the younger children were the physical and spatial structuring of classrooms.

Qualitative analysis of children's social representations revealed transformations in both form and content. In feature and function talk, curricular categories were relatively undifferentiated and had fuzzy boundaries as with the over-extended category "work". At the moment when a category starts to acquire a distinct domain, children are less likely to associate it with other categories. For example, mathematics did not emerge as part of the principle "curriculum" component in the junior classrooms even although it had been identified as a basic level curriculum category in a sorting task (cf. Ivinson, 1998a, 1998b).

When they had developed sign use the links children made between subjects were based less on general classroom functions. For example, in the Dart Junior classrooms "writing" was mentioned far less with respect to mathematics than in Copse School where children had fewer structures. The objectification of a subject category, characterised by sign use, was coupled with an increase in the range and quantity of technical, subject-specific vocabulary. As children's social representations of the curriculum become more elaborate and more differentiated we can say that they participate more fully in the specialist speech communities which constitute subjects, albeit the subjects made available to them by specific teachers in local classroom contexts.

Concluding Remarks

The psychological instruments devised for the study investigated children's social representations of the curriculum. However, curriculum was defined from a specific, adult perspective. For example, the coding scheme for children's talk relied on a developmental scale based on a teleological projection away from the kinds of categories used by young children towards the use of conventional, adult categories.

The approach differs from that taken by Piaget because the teleological projection did not assume that an adult perspective involves a relatively stable, universal form of logic. Instead, the notion of an adult perspective is rooted in an understanding that adult conventional organisations are both temporarily and culturally specific. Since a national curriculum had been imposed in England in 1988 it seemed reasonable to accept only those curriculum categories as the criteria for structure talk. Therefore if children used the name "reading" and elaborated what they meant by reading, the utterance was not coded as structure talk because strictly speaking reading is a sub-category of the national curriculum element, "English". Devising the coding scheme therefore involved strategic decisions. Although this particular example is likely to have influenced the quantity of structure talk produced in each classroom only marginally it points to a more important issue.

Social representations are not cognitive structures in the strict Piagetian sense. Duveen and Lloyd (1990) have compared them to Lucien Goldmann's notion of a "significant structure", which implies an organisational whole which is functionally useful for a group. The theory of social representations focuses on phenomena which underlie practice and therefore foregrounds the active, constructive and dynamic features of social structures.

The notion of learning used in the study involved the process whereby children develop more elaborate categories for defining the curriculum that allow them to attain a greater involvement in everyday classroom life. In the infant classrooms in Copse School children were learning a great deal about social relations that was not indexed by the coding scheme for analysing talk. While it has been stressed that it is through the social relations experienced in specific local settings that children develop social representations, the psychological instruments privileged children's understanding of curriculum *content* rather than their understanding social relations and social participation.

Different forms of relationship have different consequences for learning. Piaget (1932) distinguished co-operation and constraint as two forms of social interaction which play different functions in cognitive development. The former refers to symmetrical relations, for example those found among peers, which he linked to autonomy, and the latter to asymmetric relations, for example between children and adults, which he linked to heteronomy. The two requirements for genuine cognitive advance are that a child is confronted with socio-cognitive conflict and has the prerequisite competence to recognise the difference between the two positions. Some adult–child relations result in imitation or compliance rather than genuine cognitive advance.

According to Piaget, learning takes place when children have opportunities to elaborate ideas in non-hierarchical social interactions. The typology of recognition and realisation rules devised for this study demonstrated that children in Copse School enjoyed relatively more liberty than those in Dart School.

Findings from this study suggest that opportunities for peer interaction without strong curriculum structuration is an insufficient basis for the development of sign use and therefore for learning. Further investigation is required to determine how peer group interaction affects learning. The strong curriculum structuration in, for example, the Dart classrooms may have influenced the nature of children's classroom talk, possibly keeping it "on task" while the peer interactions in the less structured environments may have been interfering with learning. Children are the most conservative actors in classrooms (cf. Lloyd & Duveen, 1992). Strong classroom structures can interrupt the spread of crude or less differentiated social representation and force children to confront challenges which, in turn lay the foundations for learning.

7

Learning the Communication Skills and Social Processes of Peer Support: A Case Study of Good Practice

Paul Naylor and Helen Cowie

Introduction

"Children, unlike adults, do not have many places where they can operate as a collective group. Adults have factories, workplaces, and the community in which they live. For children, a primary place for interacting as a group is at school" (Dalrymple & Hough, 1995, p. 47).

Peers have a crucial role to play in the scaffolding of one another's learning. Group learning environments, if properly structured, encourage questioning, evaluating and constructive criticism, leading to a restructuring of knowledge and understanding. The case study presented in this chapter illustrates the collaborative learning that takes place when young people in partnership with an adult team are trained in the skills of peer support. Most children and young people state that they dislike bullying (MacLeod & Morris, 1996) but only a minority, estimated to be around 10 per cent will spontaneously take action to prevent it (Craig & Pepler, 1996; Rigby & Slee, 1991). The most common roles are "assistants to the bully", "reinforcers of the bullying behaviour", "outsiders" who remained detached from the bullying and with only a minority taking the pro-social role of "defenders" who offer emotional or physical support to the victims (Salmivalli et al., 1996). Why is this? One compelling explanation is that bullying is a social event and that the social context has a powerful influence on whether bystanders act responsibly or remain "neutral" (Hazler, 1996).

The Elton Report (Department for Education and Science, 1989) stressed the important part schools should play in creating an atmosphere in which staff consistently encouraged pro-social values and where there were clear sanctions against bullying behaviour. How do teachers learn to facilitate in their students a helpful, pro-social stance when there may be pressures from other pupils to remain neutral or even hostile to a peer's distress?

Peer support offers one effective method for training young people to challenge anti-social behaviour and to support the victims of peer-led aggression. As a form of co-operative group work, training in peer support has two major strands. On the one hand, the students learn a range of skills including active listening, empathic response, learning to use a vocabulary of the emotions, facilitating a problem-solving stance. On the other, the method provides the opportunity through individual and group supervision for the students to develop a reflective stance on their learning. In this two-way process, the young person's development as a learner reflects his or her social experience in the group; in turn, significant group experiences become internalised into the structure of the young person's intellect. Vygotsky's (1978) theory stresses the role of interpersonal processes and the role of the social group in providing a framework within which the child's construction of meaning develops.

Researchers (e.g. Carr, 1994; Cowie, 2000; Cowie & Sharp, 1996) have found that over time peer support systems improve the social climate of a school (Cowie, 2000), reduce aggressive behaviour in the playground (Cunningham et al., 1998) and are appreciated by actual and potential users (Naylor & Cowie, 1999).

But there is also evidence that this learning can be impeded by other social factors in the environment. This is especially the case where the school has not provided supervision and where role models for the implementation of the skills are not in evidence (Cowie & Olafsson, 2000). Male peer supporters also report ridicule and sabotage of their role from other pupils, especially boys. Studies in the UK (Cowie, 1998; Naylor & Cowie, 1999) have found that teachers in charge of peer support systems tend to be women and that they report hostility from some of their colleagues, particularly men. In general, boys are under-represented in the establishment of peer support systems in schools (Cowie and Olafsson, 2000) and men teachers are under-represented in the running of these systems (Naylor & Cowie, 1999). ABC (Anti-Bullying Campaign) peer support system has been chosen because it has avoided or overcome, in one way or another, some of the difficulties found in similar systems in schools in the UK.

The Case Study

Elliott Durham School is a mixed comprehensive school of 460 11–16-year-old pupils taught by 30 teachers in an inner city, socially and economically disadvantaged district. Pupils' attainment is well below national average standards (OFSTED — the UK government Office for Standards in Education, 1998). In 1998, only 10 per cent of the school's Year 11 (15–16-year-old) pupils gained five or more GCSE grades A* to C whilst the national average was 46.3 per cent (Department for Education and Employment, 1999). Despite the socially and economically disadvantaged backgrounds of many of its pupils, the school enjoys an "ethos of care" (Gilligan, 1982) as acknowledged in the recent OFSTED Report:

> "… The respectful attitude and sensitive management (of pupils)
> by all staff sets an ethos in which pupils learn to value everyone's
> contribution and to respect different lifestyles and circumstances
> …" (OFSTED, 1998, paragraph 49).

Elliott Durham was one of 54 UK schools selected to take part in a research project evaluating peer support systems. (The findings are reported in Naylor & Cowie, 1999). Data were elicited from the school's questionnaire responses, documentary evidence obtained from the school, the school's most recent OFSTED (1998) report, and interview data from pupils and adults.

Individual interviews were conducted with seven adults: the deputy head teacher with overall responsibility for peer support; the teacher with day-to-day responsibility for the system; two other teachers; a classroom assistant; the school educational psychologist, and the school counsellor. Group interviews were conducted with six peer supporters, and ten other pupils, actual and potential users of the system.

Setting up the ABC Peer Support System

The staff had worked hard to facilitate and model positive interpersonal relationships in the school:

> "… the teachers are excellent models. Senior management make it quite clear that all handling of pupils should be done in a calm manner, and shouting is out in this school. Pupils are treated with the utmost respect …" (Naomi Posner, head of languages).
> "We've got a very understanding staff. I've never seen teachers bullying pupils, and I've been in virtually every classroom" (Adrian Dyer, classroom assistant).
> "The style of management here isn't a male bullying system. If you're trying to put a scheme like this into a hierarchical school system, I think you'd work yourself into the ground" (Terry Whysall, deputy head teacher).

So the peer support system grew out of a school environment in which relationships are valued and where adults try to model the pro-social behaviour that they are hoping to promote.

However, as in all schools, bullying behaviour did occur amongst the pupils and there was understandable concern to reduce its incidence. A key reason for setting up the system was to increase the avenues through which bullied pupils could talk to someone about their distress. Discussions with pupils in class had revealed that there were problems for some pupils who were reluctant to talk about being bullied for fear of reprisal or ridicule on the part of peers. A visit to another school with a well-established peer-support system encouraged Derek Wilson, the educational psychologist, and Robin Tinker, the head of personal and social education (PSE), to propose the idea to the staff at an in-service education and training day. During this session, they and the deputy head teacher presented the case for establishing the scheme, stressing that without the support of most members of the school community the scheme would be unlikely to succeed. The staff agreed to support the establishment of a peer support system despite initial anxieties:

> "I think all of us were very aware of the risks involved and we were all scared when we took it on board: 'Is it going to be positive?' 'Is something going to go wrong?'" (Meryl Salt, school counsellor).

Derek and Meryl, trained in counselling, were to be responsible for selecting, training and supervising the peer supporters while Robin was to have day-to-day responsibility for managing, administering and monitoring the system under the oversight of Terry, the deputy head teacher. As Terry suggests, this sharing of the responsibilities works well:

> "We're aware of one another's strengths, what is actually best to ask one another to do. I think that's good, ... that's positive".

Thus, each of these people has a clearly defined role in the system with the active support of a large majority of the school staff.

The selection of trainee peer supporters was rigorous. Derek and Meryl interviewed the first cohort of applicants. Subsequently, as a result of discussions within supervision groups, peer supporters were also involved in the process. The empowerment of the peer supporters by involving them in selecting the trainee supporters has not been without its problems, but these hurdles have been turned into an opportunity for professional development:

> "We've had to spend time helping them draw the boundary between being somebody's friend and liking them and being a colleague in a team and trying to make it clear that you don't have to like somebody to work well together" (Derek Wilson, educational psychologist).

Adults and peer supporters, in the course of discussions and supervision, agreed that if peer supporters were to work effectively in the school they had to be viewed positively by the peer group:

> "I'm very clear in my own mind that you're aiming to recruit the kids that are the top of the tree in the peer group, who've got big cred (credibility with the peer group), are shiny, attractive and people will think that if they're doing it then it must be a good thing. ... Often they'll be a bit naughty but you need the cred that they bring with them. You can't always get them to apply but when you can, I very much want to get them on to training and see what we can do" (Derek Wilson, educational psychologist).

In many schools, there is a reluctance to give the responsible task of peer support to younger pupils. However, in Elliott Durham, adults and peer supporters have made the decision to offer training to younger age groups. The policy has been successful, particularly as some younger pupils found it easier to go to a same-age peer.

Unusually, for most mixed-sex schools that have a peer support system (Naylor and Cowie, 1999), there is a gender balance amongst the supporters in Elliott Durham School.

> "The ethnic balance I would bear in mind more. The gender balance hasn't really come up as an issue. We've always had enough boys to make it reasonable. I wasn't aware until quite recently that ... this tends to be a feminine activity. Maybe it was down to the first year when we did have enough boys and it's always been part of the mind set in the school that this is something that boys do. ... It's fallen in our lap and somehow it's part of the culture of the school" (Derek Wilson, educational psychologist).

After selection, pupils are trained as active listeners, with the emphasis on facilitation of problem-solving on the part of their peers rather than advice-giving. The two processes by which this training is achieved are through shared activities, such as role-playing, working with personal issues, trust-building and problem-solving.

In the process of learning skills and reflecting on that learning, the peer supporters discover the value of giving in turn to the users of the service a safe space in which to reflect on the relationship problems they bring, for example, being socially excluded or being intimidated by an aggressive fellow student:

> "You don't actually solve their problem. You try and get them to think of ways they can sort ... it out. ... We help them solve it" (Jason, peer supporter).

The peer supporters learn to be non-judgmental:

> Interviewer: "Do you ever think to yourself: 'I'm listening to what this person is telling me and ... I really don't think this is bullying'?"
> Amraz (peer supporter): "Everyone has their own different ways of classing things as bullying and not bullying".

However, as Derek Wilson (educational psychologist) suggests, it is not only the supporters who learn from the adults but also that the adults do too from the supporters:

> "In the last couple of years we've thought that it's … important to give them (the supporters) more words that identify feelings, but often we underestimate kids. It's a constant lesson you learn from them, how sharp socially they are. It is only a question of asking the right questions; it isn't a case that they don't know it. … It's humbling really. … You think come on, these kids know their stuff, they know why he's off the rails or misbehaving".

Derek continues this theme of learning from the young people with an anecdote about one girl peer supporter:

> "She's got a sort of social intelligence about her that's humbling. There was a lovely little anecdote she was relating; … she said she sat down with the client at the first meeting and said 'Do you want to talk about what's happening'. The client said 'No'. Unfazed by this, she said 'Do you want to talk about anything else then?' They got talking about something unrelated and I think this intuitively put them at ease, … and she said 'If you don't want to talk about it would you like to do a drawing about what's happened to you?' The kid said 'Yeah' and did a drawing and they were able to talk about it … We didn't do anything in training about reflecting feelings through drawing but it just came to her. She couldn't abstract what she'd done, … but here's a context for her where her … social intelligence can be recognised in a way that's very hard to within the academic curriculum".

In light of his supervision experiences with the supporters Derek also acknowledges that adults have much to learn about childhood and adolescence:

> "One of the things they (peer supporters) seem to have success with, is … the best (of them) seem able to get the bullies to come to an interview and talk to them. I don't know what it is that they're using to do that or what's in it for the bullies. … I'll always quiz them about why do you think they came and what was in it for them. I'm still working on it. I don't know (the answer). This is an interesting area … about peer relationships, the differences and equalities and the power exchanges that go on that as adults we're not party to. We think we know it all but we only know it in outline really".

As Derek explains, his experience of working with a group of peer supporters has influenced the way he thinks educational psychology might improve its practice. He says that many educational psychologists are:

> "locked into an individual casework model so that many (educational psychology) services are overwhelmed with statutory work based on formal assessment ... (rather than) ... more preventative things like this (peer support work) and more systemic things that involve groups and are about the health of the school. ... Some educational psychologists have been talking about it (peer support) for years without there being much uptake ... but if there was a message that could come out of this it would recommend services to look more at what work they do with pupil groupings rather than with individuals".

The peer supporters also learn clear guidelines about ethical practice, including the balance between confidentiality and the boundaries of their own expertise. Peer supporters are trained to pass on to an adult in the school all serious non-bullying matters, and to clarify to users the meaning of confidentiality within the service:

> " ... they are taught that anything they can't handle must come to myself or Derek and if it's child abuse it will go to someone straight away" (Meryl, school counsellor).

One of the peer supporters explained it in this way:

> "We can't tell a teacher without asking the person's permission first, unless its life threatening or sexual harassment or something like that ..." (Amraz).

Another drew on this knowledge when a girl came to her with a difficult issue to disclose:

> "At the meeting I said this is confidential unless it's serious, like life threatening and then we do have to report it and she goes 'Alright then'. When she told me, I thought I need to tell someone, as this is serious. So I asked her and she goes 'Yeah' but I don't want you to tell the names ..." (Debbie).

Of the way in which the supporter handled this case in subsequently passing it on to an adult, Meryl (school counsellor) says:

> " ... the team acknowledged that it was a real positive, even though it was a difficult situation because it demonstrated that what we had taught the kids had gone through".

However, the fact that the users unanimously confirmed that they were unaware of a supporter ever having betrayed a confidence highlights the professionalism of the supporters regarding this issue.

Adults and Young People Negotiate Change

Group supervision meetings are facilitated by at least two members of the system management team and are held every week during lunchtime. These meetings usually last for 30 minutes. Unnamed individual cases are discussed and so too is other ABC business.

Through the interplay between the practice of skills and reflection on their experiences in supervision, the pupils have collaborated with the adult team to make changes and adaptations over time. An example of this is demonstrated by the sensitivity with which the peer supporters dealt with the issue of arranging meetings with users of the service. In discussion with the adult team, peer supporters had pointed out that some users might feel self-conscious about going in the company of a peer supporter to the ABC room to keep an appointment, so they had collectively worked out a strategy for safeguarding the confidentiality of the meeting:

> "… we send them up first while we get the key. And we hide the key … this room is used for many other things. It's used for teachers' meetings and open days and the inspectors used it, … and when pupils have a problem" (Debbie, peer supporter).

Initially, the first cohort of peer supporters and the adult team made the decision to adopt an appointment system as opposed to a "drop-in" service. One of the peer supporters explained that pupils contact the system by posting a note in a box near reception which is then cleared by a peer supporter:

> "… if it's got a slip in it for them (the peer supporters), they put an appointment slip in that pupil's register. Then the ABC room is booked and you bring them in here (the room) and help them get through it" (John, peer supporter).

A key factor in this decision — and one highlighted by the peer supporters — was the need to preserve confidentiality. However, over time, the peer supporters have found that nearly 45 per cent of users come directly to them and choose not to use the appointments system. In addition, around 10 per cent of users are referred to the system directly by teachers. The issue is discussed in detail during supervision and the system has adapted to the needs of the users and the teachers' increasing referral to the service.

> "The two systems of adult support and peer support are getting enmeshed. I don't think we've got a pre-determined idea of how it will grow. … It's more this is how it's developing for us and the needs of our children" (Terry Whysall, deputy head teacher).

A problem perceived by supporters and teachers who run systems in many schools is that the service is underused (Naylor & Cowie, 1999). Typically, the supporters and teachers report that there are not enough users to maintain the supporters' interest and enthusiasm:

> "When we started, we had 16 ... and there just wasn't enough for them to do. They were really enthusiastic and they did a load of publicity. ... but they weren't getting the cases. ... By May, the eight Year 11 (15–16-year-olds) ones had gone, we were left with eight Year 10 (14–15-year-olds) and we found that much easier to work with so we said: 'Right, we don't need those big numbers'" (Robin Tinker, teacher in charge of the service).

Robin raises an important issue in this comment. Through careful monitoring of the use of the service, the managers and peer supporters have taken the pragmatic decision to reduce the number of supporters through "natural wastage" and thereby create a better balance between "need" and "provision". Such "needs analysis" is based on the outcomes of the regular supervision that the supporters receive, which has been discussed earlier, and from the records of the use of the system.

Evaluating and Disseminating the Peer Support System

One of Robin's key tasks in the management of the support system is that of monitoring and evaluating its effectiveness. He does this by maintaining a list of unnamed users of the service, though, as he acknowledges, the list is probably incomplete because of the confidential nature of the service. However, at the end of the 1997 autumn term, in a written report to the school staff, Robin was able to say:

> "This term, ABC has handled 18 cases involving 20 pupils as victims. This is the greatest number of referrals in any one term; all were Year 7 and 8 pupils. This makes a total of 47 cases and 62 pupils since the service began ... It seems that pupils are much more ready to 'tell' about bullying, and this may be due to the 'culture' of ABC".

Robin also conducts an annual questionnaire survey of all of the pupils and teachers in the school. The pupil questionnaires ask for responses to a number of questions which test pupils' knowledge of the system and their attitudes towards it. The questionnaire and interview responses of many of the Year 7 and Year 9 users of the system revealed that they have a very good knowledge of the school's system. These pupils said that they had learned about the system in PSE lessons, in assemblies, from posters around the school and from letters to their parents.

The ABC system has been promoted beyond the school in a number of ways.

All of the peer supporters spoke to parents and children from the school's feeder primary schools (for 5–11-year-olds) at an open evening, and some visited classes in the feeder primary schools with Terry where they spoke to pupils about the school's ABC scheme. In addition, three of the supporters helped to facilitate an in-service event for teachers and other professionals. Robin and the peer supporters have also collaborated on an article about the service (Tinker, 1998).

Since August 1997, the school's ABC scheme has had its own Internet website linked to the Canadian site "Peer Resources" (http://www.peer.ca./peer.html), the "Peer Support Networker" site (http://www.mhf.org.uk/peer/psn and, most recently, to the Nottingham City Educational Psychology Service site (http://www.inotts.co.uk/~colinn/epsweb.htm).

Discussion

As Vygotsky (1978) argued, it is the process of turning round and reflecting on one's own thoughts, using language that enables one to see things in a new way. Learning is first achieved through co-operation with others in a whole variety of social contexts and second through the symbolic representations of the child's culture — through its art and language, through play, through metaphors and models. A central concept is the zone of proximal development (ZPD) which provides an explanation of how the child learns with the help of others — under the guidance of more expert adults or in collaboration with more competent peers. So the young learner is initiated into the intellectual life of the community and learns by jointly constructing his or her understanding of events and issues in the world. Some contexts are particularly conducive to learning for example, where the expert adult asks open-ended questions or where the learner is in the company of supportive, trusted peers.

From this perspective, the young person's understanding grows out of the process of making the shift from *actions*, through *symbolisation* to *formulation*. Action in the present case study involved direct exploration of the subject through training and practice in the field, as the peer supporters experienced a range of carefully structured, collaborative training activities. These training exercises included learning to paraphrase what another young person has said, checking back for accuracy, learning to be aware of another's emotional state, finding appropriate words to capture that emotional state, and learning to listen in an active, person-centred way. Symbolisation was achieved once the young people were able to find ways of representing relationships among things that they have observed, for example by being flexible in applying the skills of peer support, adapting to needs as they arose, and developing new strategies. Formulation of broader principles came when the peer supporters could clearly state principles that go beyond the specific subjects of their supportive work, for example, when they demonstrated their understanding of the complexities of the meaning of confidentiality, or showed a deeper sensitivity to the concepts of bullying or abuse.

At each stage, the concept of the ZPD provides an essential framework for evaluating young people's development as thinkers.

Peers have a crucial role to play in the scaffolding of one another's learning. Group learning environments, if properly structured, encourage questioning, evaluating and constructive criticism, leading to a restructuring of knowledge and understanding. It is not just the encounter that brings about change, but the internalisation of this joint intellectual activity.

As we have seen, Vygotsky (1978) and his followers (for example, Tharp & Gallimore, 1988; Wood, 1988) suggest that it is "expert adults" largely, who construct children's social and cognitive learning experiences; this is true of Elliott Durham's support system. However, as we have seen in comments made by adults involved in the system, it is also the case that there are ways in which the supporters have scaffolded the learning of adults. The implication is that Vygotskian ideas about social learning and scaffolding need to be reinterpreted. Such a reinterpretation is that these ideas can be generalised to all learners, adults and children alike, and it includes the likelihood that "expert children" often can and do scaffold adults' learning.

The willingness of the adults to learn from the supporters is one of the strengths of Elliott Durham School's ABC system. Other good practice features of the system are:

- It has the strong support of the school's governors and senior managers, the great majority of the teachers, parents and pupils who are well informed about the system.
- The system was established only after careful planning and consultation with all of the interested groups of people.
- It is well managed by a co-operative team of adults each of whom has a clearly defined and understood role in the running of the system.
- The selection, training and supervision of the peer supporters is carefully thought out, thorough and meets standards of good professional counselling practice.
- It has a clearly defined and limited function which is understood by all, particularly by the supporters and users of the system.
- It is positively promoted both within and outside the school and its successes are justifiably celebrated.
- The views and ideas about and attitudes towards the system of the peer supporters, teachers and potential and actual users are regularly sought and acted on so that the system is sensitive to changes which are perceived to be necessary.
- All aspects of the confidentiality issue have been carefully considered so that "mistakes" are unlikely to happen.

Acknowledgements

We wish to thank the participants for the time which they have freely given to us. The research was funded by The Prince's Trust.

8

Co-Construction in Kindergartners' Free Play: Effects of Social, Individual and Didactic Factors

Paul P.M. Leseman, Linda Rollenberg and Eveline Gebhardt

Introduction

Free play is a common part of many early childhood curricula, whatever further differences there may exist. Play is a natural, developmentally appropriate didactic arrangement for young preschool children, but its value for education, more in particular for stimulating cognitive development is not undisputed. Free play typically involves child-initiated choices of centers ("corners"), play topics, toys and materials. It usually involves peer-interactions and it is marked by low participation of teachers. Doubts about the cognitive value of free play are related to these typical characteristics, and culminate in the question whether more or less symmetrical social interactions of young developing children in largely self-determined situations of free play can be seen as actualizing cognitive potential. The current study addresses this question from the theoretical point of view of cognitive co-construction and reports the results of an observational study into co-construction and peer-interaction in four-year-olds' free play in Dutch kindergarten classrooms.

A neglected topic in cognitive play research with young children concerns the effects of social background, especially socioeconomic status as referring to particular socialisation practices, and children's personality and cognitive ability. It will be argued in this chapter that the educational potential of free play depends upon the quality of social processes and the knowledge and skills of individual children that are put together in creative processes of co-construction. Taking this as a starting point, one may expect that individual differences in social background, personality and cognitive ability influence this potential. Therefore, this study is also about the role of individual differences in free play and will report on the relationships between play behavior and child-characteristics.

Play, Development and Learning

Traditional empiricist and cognitivist theories of learning and development emphasize the transmission of cognitive content (knowledge, skills) as the basic mechamism of learning and development, which seems to require a teacher — an expert relative to the children — who possesses the knowledge to be transmitted and instructs the children (cf. Case, 1998). Theories based on Vygotsky's work, though different in many respects from traditional learning theory, also stress the role of a more experienced other — teacher, parent, older child — in inter-psychological processes with clearly unequal roles for the expert and the novice (cf. Rogoff, 1990, 1997; Wood & Wood, 1996; Case, 1998). In contrast, children's play typically involves more symmetrical relationships between the participants, who, as a rule, are peers of roughly the same age and same abilities, and who are no experts in the conventional sense of the word. Seen from the angle of asymmetrical, expertise-involved models of learning and development, curricula that rely heavily on the free play arrangement easily seem to boil down to a laissez faire approach (cf. Dickinson & Smith, 1991).

Theories based on Piaget have traditionally foregrounded the intrinsic cognitive aspects of play, yet not without ambiguities. According to Piagetian theories, children's play follows a developmental sequence from functional play, constructive play, symbolic play, fantasy play to games with rules (cf. Smilansky, 1968; Pellegrini, 1991). This sequence *parallels* children's cognitive and social development, every step manifesting the further decentration and abstraction of cognitive structures. However, the potential surplus value of joint play for cognitive development has not always been fully recognized in the Piagetian tradition. Play development has often been studied from the assumption that cognitive development precedes it (Aureli & Colecchia, 1996). Further, the focus has been on conflict and dispute, instead of collaboration (Verba, 1994). Finally, as certain socio-cognitive competences were assumed to be prerequisite for higher forms of interactive play (such as social perspective-taking), children under a certain age were not thought to be capable of interactive play.

Therefore, the question is: Can children even as young as four years stimulate each other's cognitive development in largely self-initiated and self-determined situations? What role do teachers as experts play, if any, in these situations?

The Concept of Co-Construction

In recent work on the sociocognitive aspects of children's play Piagetian and Vygotskian insights have been combined (cf. Rogoff, 1990, 1998). A balance is sought between the disputational and collaborative aspects of children's play. There is awareness of the fact that even within a disputational–conflict approach, there should be basic cooperation and mutuality in order to get the play started, to reconcile differences of views and motives, and to continue and extend joint play (Garvey, 1993; Musatti, 1993; Verba, 1993, 1994; Mercer, 1996; Rogoff, 1998).

Central to these new developments is the concept of co-construction that seems to unite as no other concept does, the converging (neo)Piagetian and (neo)Vygotskian lines of thinking. The term is taken here as entailing three basic notions: First, that knowledge acquisition and development involve *active construction processes* on part of the subjects involved; second, that the construction processes of an individual subject are *coherently linked with* the construction processes of other subjects; and, third, that there is *reciprocity* between the participants.

Construction means that new knowledge is acquired on the basis of old knowledge structures. Already available knowledge provides the categories, schemata, strategies and skills needed to understand new information and to integrate it into the existing knowledge structures.

Coherent links of individual construction processes with other minds is a necessary assumption to understand social-cultural influences on learning and development, and to avoid solipsistic accounts (cf. Fodor, 1975). The notion of coherence is well-studied in the philosophy of language, text-linguistics and psycholinguistics (cf. de Beaugrande & Dressler, 1981; van Dijk, 1987; Kintsch, 1998). A recent view is that in everyday conversations (and also in reading and writing) coherence is established in reference to a *situation model*, a kind of cognitive representation with concrete-analogue properties that represent relations of time, space, cause–effect, intention–action, possibility and permissibility between the basic constituents of the model (cf. Johnson-Laird, 1983, p. 413). This model may be a model of the actual situation ("here and now") and being close to the mental models yielded in perception processes. It may also be a model of a non-immediate, but real situation (for instance, about an event that took place yesterday), or of a fictitious, but possible situation (like in fairy tales).

It is beyond the scope of this article to discuss the theory and its implications in greater detail. Important for the present purpose, however, is the definition of intersubjective coherence of co-construction processes that can be derived from this briefly sketched theory: Intersubjective coherence is defined here as the meaningful "connection" between each participant's verbal utterances and non-verbal actions that roots in and is represented by a shared situation-model, the *possible world* to which utterances and actions refer and make sense. This situation-model is constructed in the process of play or problem-solving, specifying what the play is about or what kind of problem is at stake.

Co-construction, so defined, further presupposes a social-relational basis, a shared motivation to understand and make understood, a preparedness to co-operate and to abide by basic maxims, much like the ones formulated by the language philosopher Grice (1975). Without this, the processess of (social and situated) learning and development are incomprehensible, in the same way as a pragmatically successful conversation is logically impossible without assumptions about conversational maxims and constituting rules (Searle, 1965).

Peer-Interaction and Cognitive Stimulation

A basic dimension to evaluate cognitive significance common to different authors is the *level of abstraction* or *distancing* of play, which requires children to construct mental representations of their and others' activities and ideas (cf. Cocking & Renninger, 1993; Sigel, Stinson, & Kim, 1993; Wertsch & Bivens, 1993). In the traditional (Piagetian) accounts of play, the level of distancing is identified from the type of play. Practice play or functional play is regarded as lowest in representational demands, whereas games with rules are seen as highest (cf. Smilansky, 1968; see also Pellegrini, 1991).

There are two problems with the classical view. First, classifying the type of play says little about the quality of the social processes involved, nor about the individuals' participation in the social processes. Second, it can be assumed that within the same type of play, there may be differences in creativity, informativity, and cognitive complexity, dependent upon what the children make out of it.

To evaluate cognitive demandingness from the co-construction point of view that was outlined earlier, reference should be made to the underlying shared mental model of the situation. It is common in psychology to take perception (not withstanding the extreme complexities involved, both neurologically, psychologically and philosophically) as the most *direct*, thus *least distanced* form of cognition; on the other hand, reasoning about abstract mathematical theory of an entirely symbolic problem seems a good candidate to represent the other extreme of distancing dimension (Johnson-Laird, 1983; Cocking & Renninger, 1993). So the question becomes: What is the underlying model's "psychological distance" to the actual, here-and-now perceptual world?

In recent play research, the traditional Piagetian approach that focussed on type of play has been extended so as to include the social-relational quality of collaboration and new cognitive aspects. According to Verba (1994), mere cooperation requires children to observe each other's activity, to coordinate perspectives and eventually resolve conflicting ideas, which means that they have to distance themselves to a lesser or greater degree from the actual situation and to reflect upon their own ideas and activities, opening a kind metacognitive discourse.

However, taking each other's perspective, though cognitively demanding itself and probably contributing to the development of social perspective taking, does not imply that the collaboratively created play is cognitively demanding and "distanced", and therefore promotes cognitive development. For instance, collaboration may concern sociodramatic play in which children enact stereotypical roles of familiar, "everyday characters", such as their parents or teachers, and imitate script-like events. To get the play going, children need to coordinate their ideas and motives, they have to define, adjust and readjust constantly the topic and objective of their play. But the resulting play itself, from a cognitive point of view, can still be relatively simple, at least as compared with true fantasy-play in which children sometimes invent completely new stories referring to fictitious worlds.

Similar ambiguities can be expected to arise with regard to constructive play. Playing with Lego® or similar construction materials may sometimes involve highly sophisticated "plans" which are called in to attain difficult "goals" (e.g. a very complex, fantastic construction). However, play with construction materials may also be limited to merely assembling a few parts without an interesting, comprehensive underlying plan.

Musatti (1993) associates collaborative play with Vygotsky's notion of the *zone of proximal development* (ZPD). In collaborative play, she argues, a ZPD is created, surpassing each participants' actual level of development (note that this places the ZPD outside the individual child and makes it a property of the child's social interaction with others). In Musatti's research, however, the emphasis is again on the social aspect — the establishment of intersubjectivity — but not on the cognitive (distancing) aspects and the informativity of what children subsequently do within the shared frame of reference, that is, within their jointly constructed model-world. Typically, however, what seems crucial for learning and development is where this intersubjectively created zone is about and what happens within this zone (which we identify with the notion of shared situation model).

Based on the preceding considerations, we expect the cognitive potential of children's free play to depend upon children's active participation in the play activities, their mutual informational coherence with is defined with respect to an underlying shared situation model, and this underlying model's psychological distancing level.

The Role of Individual Differences

Differences in social skills, cognitive skills, experience with peer-interaction and in social-personality characteristics may profoundly influence the social and cognitive quality of play, and thereby its developmental potential.

The structuralist approach of the predominant (neo)Piagetian play research has traditionally paid little attention to the role of individual differences in cognitive competence and socially relevant personality characteristics. Part of this lacuna is complemented by research into cooperative learning arrangements, carried out mostly with somewhat older children in more formal learning situations. This research has revealed that strong differences in cognitive ability, low average level of cognitive ability, strong differences in social status, and unwillingness of some of the participants to acknowledge other participants' perspectives and interests, influence the educational potential of these arrangements negatively (Webb, 1991; Cohen & Lotan, 1995). Whether these findings apply to early education and free play settings, is not clear. However, it underscores the importance of taking individual differences into account.

Another program of research is devoted to the role of children's personality or "temperament" in social interactions in educational settings (for overviews, see Keogh, 1986, 1989; Martin, 1989; Bullock, 1993). A number of studies have focused on the consequences of particular temperaments on peer-interactions. Greenwood et al. (1982) found that children who were rated by their parents as "withdrawn" (or shy, with low activity and emotionally overcontrolled) initiated and received fewer social initiations with peers and responded less frequently to peer initiations. Rubin (1982) reported that withdrawn, anxious and socially less-agreeable children engage in less mature forms of play and receive fewer social overtures of their peers. Lewis (1977) found that high distractability of children, as rated by parents, was associated with erratic social interactions in preschool, whereas high persistence, high task orientation and long attention span were correlated with higher levels of constructive activity and verbal communication in peer play interactions. High activity level and strong approach tendencies (or impulsivity) were found to relate to high social proximity (more initiating of social interaction and more prompt responses to social initiations by others). A study by Fabes, Eisenberg and Eisenbud (1993) revealed yet another temperamental dimension with relevance for social interaction and peer collaboration. The ability to control (negative) emotions (or "inhibitory control", including low levels of anger and aggression) correlated with prosocial behavior and promoted better social relationships between preschoolers.

The Role of Family Background

In the Piagetian view, peer collaboration in play requires certain sociocognitive competencies which are thought to be dependent upon the physical and neurological maturation of the child with growing age (Case, 1998). In addition to the maturational stance, it can be presupposed that also some kind of social-pragmatic content knowledge is involved, such as knowledge of play-genre-conventions, specific situational conventions (classroom rules), conversational maxims and also background world knowledge. This pragmatic and world knowledge is acquired in social interactions, in the family (Bruner, 1983; Ninio & Snow, 1996) as well as in group settings preceding kindergarten, such as the crèche or preschool (Howes, 1988; Aureli & Colecchia, 1996). As it is assumed that at least part of children's competence to interact and collaborate is socialized, peer-interaction in free play provides an interesting arena of cultural and socioeconomical differences.

There are numerous studies that relate young children's knowledge and skill to family socialization patterns. Well-documented is, for instance, the meaning of preschool oral language and literacy interactions at home on children's vocabulary, literacy and world knowledge (Bus, van IJzendoorn & Pellegrini, 1995; Leseman & de Jong, 1998; Leseman & van den Boom, 1999). Home language and literacy use is known to be strongly related to the family's socioeconomic status, especially to parents' educational level and cultural capital (Bourdieu & Passeron, 1977; Leseman & de Jong, 1998; Leseman & van den Boom, 1999).

Children may also have learned different codes about how to cooperate, depending on the family's socio-economic status. For instance, Leseman and Sijsling (1996) found that low-SES mother–child pairs were more product-focused in joint problem-solving than high-SES pairs who were more process-focused (see for related findings Renshaw & Gardner, 1990). Low-SES mothers more often took full responsibility for the joint task in order to solve it in an efficient and "correct" way, whereas high-SES mothers apparently found it more important that their children were in charge, although this often took more time and did not always lead to a correct solution.

The Current Study

In the current study, freeplay sessions in normal kindergarten classrooms were videotaped and analyzed with respect to children's participation and interaction, the intersubjective coherence of their interaction, and the cognitive demandingness or distancing level of their activities. A coding system, to be described in the next section, was developed to evaluate observed play behavior regarding participation, cooperation, coherence and distancing. The research set out to provide answers to the following questions:

- to what extent do four-year-old kindergarten children collaborate in free play instead of playing solitarily or parallel to each other?
- does interaction and collaboration lead to higher distancing levels of free play activity of individual children, that is to say, does playing with a peer or interacting with a teacher make a difference?
- do individual characteristics, i.e. socioeconomic background, cognitive ability and temperamental style influence peer-collaboration and the distancing level of play activities?
- and finally, what is the role of other children and teachers, taking children's individual characteristics into account?

Method

Sample

The present study involved 39 children from 7 kindergarten classrooms in a middle-sized town in the western part of the Netherlands. Kindergartens in the Netherlands are part of primary schools. Although attendance to kindergarten is compulsive only from age five, 95% of the Dutch four year olds attend kindergarten, starting usually directly after their fourth birthday. When children are between six and seven years of age, they enter grade three (grade one in US and British schools) where formal instruction starts. The children in this study, 60% girls and 40% boys, had varied socioeconomic backgrounds and all spoke Dutch as their first language. The mean age of the children was 53 months (SD = 2.8; range 48–58 months).

Procedures

The focus of the present study was on children's behavior and social interactions in a free play situation. In free play, children could freely choose a play center in the classroom, and the toys and objects to play with. They could choose to play alone or select a play mate. The observations of free play took place a few months after the target children started in kindergarten. In every classroom five to six target children, all other children playing parallel to or in interaction with the target children, and the teachers if involved in the situation were observed, using a videocamera and small wireless microphones that were attached to the target children.

Videorecordings were made in periods of exactly two minutes in order to obtain a representative sample of observations covering begin, middle and end-stage of the free play sessions (lasting approximately 35 minutes) for all target children. In each observation period, one target child was in focus. After the first cycle of five two-minute obervations was completed, the next cycle started. In all classrooms three cycles were completed, yielding a total amount of six minutes observation for each target child, evenly divided over beginning, middle and end of the play session.

The recorded two-minute fragments of the free play session were transcribed both to the verbal and nonverbal behaviors of the target children and of other children in the same situation close to or playing with the target child. The teacher's behavior was also included in the transcripts when it related to the target child or to another child in the situation.

Regarding the non-verbal behavior, a level of analysis was chosen that may be described as the level of meaningful but elementary actions. The nonverbal behavioral units were labelled by simple action verbs and action predicates and were easily observable; if an action consisting of two distinct but functionally related elements appeared as one fluent movement, it was considered as one single action.

With respect to language use, units were defined in accordance with common practice in developmental linguistics and pragmatics. A speech unit — an utterance — was either identified by interruptions and naturally occurring breaks, marked by characteristic intonation patterns or conversational turns. In the case of an extended turn consisting of a series of interconnected utterances, an utterance was defined as a string of discourse that contains one complete meaning proposition.

In addition to observational measures, the target children's cognitive ability was assessed. A test was administered individually in a separate room at school. A few target children were not tested. The major reason was absence due to illness.

Finally, the parents were requested to fill out a written questionnaire on the child's temperament and the family's socioeconomic background. The questionnaire was handed out to the parents by the teachers; 95% of the questionnaires were returned.

Measurements

Play behavior: A multi-dimensional coding scheme was developed for coding the transcribed verbal and nonverbal behavioral units recorded in the play situations (Rollenberg & Leseman, 1997). All verbal and nonverbal units were coded in the following categories of the coding scheme:

(1) *Participant*:
  (a) target child;

     (b) other child(ren); and
     (c) teacher.
 (2) *Behavioral Mode*:
     (a) verbal utterances;
     (b) paraverbal utterances (such as exclamations, onomatopeia); and
     (c) nonverbal actions.
 (3) *Function for Cooperation*:
     (a) solitary play or work actions (apparently not in response to or as a coherent extension of a previous initiative);
     (b) initiatives towards another child or the teacher, to start a new episode;
     (c) immediate coherent responses to questions or requests;
     (d) coherent extensions within the initiated play-episode;
     (e) interruptions or disruptions of ongoing activities, or rejections of initiatives by others.
(4a) *Cognitive Distancing Level Verbal Behavior*:
     (a) relational, thematically not to the play related utterances referring to the immediate situation or to the social relationships between the participants, often containing negative affect;
     (b) procedural utterances preceding actual play (for instance, negotiations on what to do) or following it (for instance, instructions to clear up);
     (c) low distancing level verbalisations such as labelling and giving concrete directives;
     (d) intermediate level utterances concerning representation, planning and evaluation of play-theme related activities; and
     (e) higher distancing level of analytical-explanatory reasoning about the play, reasoning about rules in a game-with-rules and extensions of a non-immediate discourse related to a pretend situation.
(4b) *Cognitive Distancing Level Nonverbal Behavior*:
     (a) distracted nonverbal behavior (fiddling, staring, thumbsucking);
     (b) nonverbal actions (e.g. gestures) referring to the immediate situation or to the relationships between the participants, often containing negative affect;
     (c) procedural actions preceding actual play (for instance, fetching play materials) or following it (for instance, clearing up);
     (d) low distancing level nonverbal pointing, functional-manipulative actions and simple, isolated performative actions apparently not part of a planned sequence of actions;
     (e) intermediate distancing level nonverbal actions apparently part of extended, planned chains of performative actions relating to the play; and
     (f) extended chains of performative behavior if part of pretend or fantasy play or games with rules.

Two coders independently coded 385 behavioral units (5% of all observed utterances and nonverbal actions) collected in three classrooms. Cohen's κ's were computed for each main category and ranged from 0.71 (function for cooperation) to 1.00 (behavioral mode, participant).

Because all behavioral units were coded in all categories, cross-combinations of these categories could be computed, yielding, for instance, the number of verbal utterances by the target child or the number of non-verbal, thematically unrelated actions by the teacher.

Children's Temperament. Six subscales of the Child Behavior Questionnaire were used to determine parents' perceptions of their children's temperament. This instrument consisted of 15 subscales and over 170 items and was recently developed by Rothbart and colleagues (Reference Note). The following subscales were chosen based on their presumed relevance for social interactions and task-orientated (play) behavior:

(1) *Anger and Frustration*: the amount of negative affect displayed by the child related to interruption of ongoing tasks.
(2) *Attentional Focusing*: the tendency to maintain attentional focus for prolonged periods upon task-related channels.
(3) *Impulsivity*: the child's speed of response initiation, his or her usual promptness of reacting to a stimulus.
(4) *Inhibitory Control*: the capacity of the child to plan ahead and to suppress inappropriate approach responses under instructions or in novel and uncertain situations.
(5) *Shyness*: the tendency to withdraw from new social contacts, the child feels at unease in novel situations, and generally displays low activity.
(6) *Fear*: the child is easily frightened, is afraid of darkness and novel situations, has sometimes nightmares.

All subscales consisted of 10 to 13 items and had satisfactory internal consistencies, with Cronbach's alpha's ranging from 0.65 to 0.89.

Cognitive developmental level. To asess children's cognitive developmental level, a norm-referenced test of semantic-taxonomic and logo-mathematical concept knowledge was used (van Kuyk, 1996). The test was developed by the Dutch Educational Testing Service for use in kindergarten and is part of a widely used student monitoring system. The test consisted of 42 items and had satisfactory internal consistency, Cronbach's alpha being 0.85.

Socioeconomic Status. The socioeconomic status (SES) of the families of the children was an index based on parents' educational attainment level and the families' cultural capital. The families' cultural capital was measured by means of a questionnaire of 10 items, asking parents to rate how often they participated in a particular cultural activity. Items concerned, for instance, visiting a concert of classical music or an art museum, or reading literary books. Cronbach's alpha of the SES-index, based on the educational attainment and cultural capital scores, was 0.65.

Results

Children's and Teachers' Behavior According to Mode

Table 1 shows the mean numbers and percents of verbal and nonverbal acts by the target children, the other children playing with or physically close (parallel) to the target children, and the teachers if intervening in the child's (collaborative) play. During the video-observations, the target children were in focus, explaining why they account for most of the observed acts and utterances. The other children in the same kindergarten were only recorded and coded if they interacted with the target child or were physically close, explaining the lower numbers of verbal and nonverbal acts found for these children.

Teachers were almost absent in the free play of the target children, as Table 1 shows. Of the average total of 197.7 observed verbal and nonverbal actions, only 9.5, or 4.8%, was a teacher action. Teachers were either involved with other children who were not present in the target child's situation, or occupied by classroom managerial tasks. These findings fit well with other Dutch studies, for instance by Schonewille and Van der Leij (1995), revealing that the time kindergarten teachers spend supporting and instructing an individual child or a small group in which this child participates, averagely amounts to only 2.7% of the total time. It should be noted here that the average class size in Dutch kindergartens is large and the number of children often exceeds 30 by the end of school year.

A further finding is that in free play nonverbal behavior is quantitatively the most important action mode, although verbalisations accompanying the nonverbal play behaviors were almost always present as well. This supports the approach of the present study that an exclusive focus on the verbal behavioral mode probably does not do sufficent justice to the developing young child.

Children's and Teachers' Behavior According to Function for Cooperation

The main category function for cooperation was intended to evaluate behavioral units as to their supposed function for good cooperation and collaboration between the children and the teachers in the free play situation. Table 2 shows that, averagely, the target children were often playing solitarily (33%), that is, *not* interacting, let alone collaborating. The fact that other children seemingly played less often solitarily is due to the observation and coding procedure that focused on the target children and included other children only when they were playing parallel to or in interaction with the target children. Solitary play of other children concerned play in the target child's vicinity and, therefore, the figure of 9% solitary play by the other children may be taken as an indication of the prevalence of parallel play.

Table 2 also shows that children took initiatives towards each other — inviting other children to join in or starting a discussion on matters which may or may not have been related to the play. Furthermore, these initiatives were often followed, verbally and nonverbally, i.e. they were adequately responded to and/or coherently extended (together 54%). Explicit rejections of initiatives and breaking off ongoing

Table 1: Verbal, paraverbal and nonverbal behavior of target children and of other children and teachers interacting with the target children, based on 6 minutes observation per target child.

	Target Children			Other Children			Teachers		
	Mean (SD)	%	Range	Mean (SD)	%	Range	Mean (SD)	%	Range
Verbal Utterances	35.5 (15.3)	27.1	5–70	25.9 (20.7)	45.1	3–80	6.2 (9.4)	65.2	0–32
Paraverbal Utterances	2.1 (3.7)	1.6	0–17	0.6 (1.2)	1.0	0–5	0.0 (0.24)	0.3	0–2
Nonverbal Acts	93.2 (32.3)	71.3	39–155	31.0 (22.1)	54.0	0–89	3.3 (6.5)	34.6	0–24
Total	130.8 (40.8)	100.0	59–216	57.4 (40.4)	100.1	3–173	9.5 (15.5)	100.1	0–52

Table 2: Verbal and nonverbal behavior of target children and of other children and teachers interacting with the target children according to its function for cooperation.

	Target Children			Other Children			Teachers		
	Mean (SD)	%	%%	Mean (SD)	%	%%	Mean (SD)	%	%%
Solitary Acts	42.5 (35.4)	33.2	—	5.4 (10.9)	9.5	—	0.1 (0.4)	1.0	—
Initiating Acts	15.9 (13.3)	12.4	18.6	9.8 (5.9)	17.2	19.0	1.9 (2.7)	19.8	20.0
Immediate Responses	29.3 (17.0)	22.9	34.2	18.3 (17.0)	32.0	35.4	3.0 (6.2)	31.3	31.6
Coherent Extensions	39.7 (33.8)	31.0	46.4	22.7 (23.7)	39.8	43.9	4.5 (8.1)	46.9	47.4
Disruptive Acts	0.6 (1.2)	0.4	0.7	0.9 (1.3)	1.6	1.7	0.1 (0.3)	1.0	1.1
Total	128.0 (40.4)	99.9	99.9	57.1 (40.1)	100.1	100.0	9.6 (15.5)	100.0	100.1

Note. Not codable behavior: 2.8 (2%), 0.3 (0.5%), and 0 (0.0%) for target children, other children and teachers respectively.
%% Percents based on interactive behaviors, solitary acts are excluded.

interactions was rare in the observed play situations. When the analysis was confined to interactive behaviors only, excluding solitary play behavior, the resulting percents for target children, other children and teachers, also in Table 2 (in the column headed by %%), were remarkably similar. The lower means of the other children can be partly explained by the fact that target children sometimes were interacting with the teachers, in particular responding to or contingently following initiatives by the teachers. It is interesting to note that the profile of the teachers' interactive behavior was not very different from that of the children.

Children's and Teachers' Behavior According to Distancing Level

Table 3 shows the mean frequencies of the play behaviors in the categories that represent the underlying dimension of psychological distancing. The table reveals that on average quite a lot of children's verbal utterances were on intermediate and high distancing level, about 54% and 64% in all for target and other children respectively. It is also noteworthy that on average quite a number of utterances were thematically not related, that is, relational or procedural, almost 36% and 23% in all for target children and other children respectively. Remarkably, the teachers' behavior was less often evaluated as intermediate or high distancing, but far more often as relational and procedural (in all 62%). If teachers participated in children's activities and social interactions, it mostly concerned managing the situation (resolving conficts, instructing children to clear up, etc.).

Table 3 also gives the results of the psychological distancing level of the nonverbal behavior. Procedural nonverbal behavior —arranging the situation, fetching play materials, putting materials away, clearing up — occurred by far most. Still, almost 41% of target children's and 42% of other children's behavior was considered play-theme related, with again quite a lot of nonverbal behaviors classified as intermediate or high distancing, about 27% and 29% for target and other children respectively. Target children were more often observed to be distracted than other children. This is probably due to the observation procedure, because distracted behavior was more frequent in situations of solitary play. Solitary play of other children was as a rule not included in transcription and coding, except in cases of parallel play. The teachers' nonverbal behavior paralleled their verbal behavior. Many nonverbal actions were again coded as relational or procedural (64%). Furthermore, teachers were relatively often observed to be distracted (e.g. apparently not attending to the children or to their own work). Nonverbal involvement of the teachers in the children's play activities was rare and never on the highest distancing level.

Solitary Play Versus Interactive Play According to Distancing Level

To examine whether target children's interactive play was associated with higher cognitive distancing level than their solitary play was, the coding dimensions

Table 3: Verbal and nonverbal behavior of target children and of other children and teachers interacting with target children, according to cognitive content and distancing level.

	Target Children		Other Children		Teachers	
	Mean (SD)	%	Mean (SD)	%	Mean (SD)	%
Relational Utterances	7.2 (10.6)	19.5	2.1 (3.4)	8.3	1.2 (2.3)	19.7
Procedural Utterances	6.1 (5.8)	16.5	3.7 (5.1)	14.6	2.6 (4.8)	42.6
Low Distancing Utterances	3.8 (3.7)	10.3	3.3 (6.0)	13.0	0.2 (0.5)	3.3
Intermediate Distancing Utterances	17.4 (12.4)	47.0	13.7 (14.0)	54.2	1.9 (4.0)	31.1
High Distancing Utterances	2.5 (4.5)	6.8	2.5 (4.8)	9.9	0.17 (0.6)	2.8
Total Verbal Utterances	37.0 (16.5)	100.1	25.3 (21.3)	100.0	6.1 (9.1)	99.5
	Mean (SD)	%	Mean (SD)	%	Mean (SD)	%
Distracted Nonverbal Behavior	14.6 (13.9)	15.7	4.2 (4.3)	13.6	0.6 (1.7)	18.2
Relational Nonverbal Acts	6.5 (9.2)	7.0	3.0 (2.9)	9.7	0.5 (1.3)	15.2
Procedural Nonverbal Acts	33.7 (19.6)	36.3	10.7 (9.1)	34.6	1.6 (3.5)	48.5
Low Distancing Nonverbal Acts	13.3 (10.0)	14.3	4.2 (5.7)	13.6	0.3 (1.0)	9.1
Intermediate Distancing Acts	16.1 (18.0)	17.3	6.1 (8.1)	19.7	0.3 (0.8)	9.1
High Distancing Nonverbal Acts	8.6 (14.9)	9.3	2.7 (6.5)	8.7	0.0 (0.0)	0.0
Total Nonverbal Acts	92.8 (32.6)	99.9	30.9 (22.1)	99.9	3.3 (6.5)	100.1

Note. Not codable verbal behavior: 0.1 (0.2%), 1.2 (4.5%) and 0.1 (1.6%), and not codable nonverbal behavior: 0.4 (0.4%), 0.1 (0.3%) and 0 (0.0%) for target children, other children and teachers respectively.

cooperation and distancing level were combined. In order to reduce the number of cross-dimensional variables, distracted, relational, procedural and low-distancing verbal and nonverbal behaviors were pooled into new categories of, respectively, verbal and nonverbal *lower distancing behavior*. Similarly, intermediate and high level distancing were pooled into new categories of verbal and nonverbal *higher level distancing*. Disruptive behavior was excluded from further analyses, because of its low prevalence. The results are shown in Table 4. Note that the table reflects the earlier reported findings that most of the observed behavior was coded as nonverbal and interactive.

Taking into account that verbal behavior was less prevalent than nonverbal behavior, the results show that children when playing interactively, verbalised more and more often on higher than lower distancing level than when playing solitarily. This was particularly so when children were coherently extending the joint behavioral sequence. Immediate responses and particularly initiatives were more often on lower verbal distancing level than coherent extensions. When children were playing solitarily, they verbalized much less and if they did, it was more often on lower distancing level (e.g. especially relational and procedural). Nevertheless, a few times children who were playing solitarily were observed talking to themselves about their play in a play-theme oriented manner on a high psychological distancing level.

With respect to the nonverbal behavior, the results were reversed. When children were playing solitarily, their nonverbal behavior was more often on a higher distancing level (e.g. assembling planfully pieces in a construction play, painting planfully a picture) then when playing interactively. In solitary play higher and lower distancing nonverbal behavior was roughly in balance, whereas in interactive play lower distancing level nonverbal behavior predominated. A possible explanation is that the types of play differ. Interactive play was more often pretend or fantasy-play; nonverbal behavior associated with this type of play was rather relational (e.g. negative affective gestures as part of a dispute about roles), procedural (e.g. clearing up, arranging the play situation) or merely supporting the verbalizations (e.g. pointing, gesticulating) than a planful chain of goal-directed performative or constructive actions. Solitary play was more often constructive or creative play in which a child planned and executed a sequence of actions in order to attain a pre-set goal.

Note that within the cross-dimensional category of nonverbal interactive behaviors, coherent extensions were more than responses and particularly more than initiations related to higher distancing level.

Relating Target Children's Temperament and Social Background to Play Behavior

The possible role of individual differences in free play was further examined in a correlational analysis. Table 5 presents the Pearson-correlations of target children's socioeconomic background, temperament as rated by their parents, and

Table 4: Solitary and interactive verbal and nonverbal behavior of target children according to cognitive distancing level. Mean frequencies of observed actions, and column and cell percents.

	High Distancing Verbal			Low Distancing Verbal			High Distancing Nonverbal			Low Distancing Nonverbal		
	M	Coln %	Cell %	M	Coln %	Cell %	M	Coln %	Cell %	M	Coln %	Cell %
Solitary Actions	2.5	12.7	2.5	2.9	21.9	2.8	12.7	52.5	12.4	15.4	34.2	15.1
Interactive Actions	17.2	87.3	16.8	10.2	78.0	9.9	11.5	47.4	11.2	29.7	65.7	29.2
– Initiations	(1.6)	(7.9)	(1.5)	(2.0)	(15.1)	(1.9)	(1.3)	(5.5)	(1.3)	(8.8)	(19.5)	(8.4)
– Immediate Responses	(4.3)	(22.0)	(4.2)	(3.5)	(26.8)	(3.4)	(3.8)	(15.8)	(3.3)	(11.7)	(26.1)	(11.4)
– Coherent Extensions	(11.3)	(57.4)	(11.0)	(4.7)	(36.1)	(4.6)	(6.3)	(26.1)	(6.2)	(9.2)	(20.3)	(8.9)
Column Total	19.7	100.0	19.3	13.1	100.0	12.7	24.3	100.0	23.6	45.1	100.0	44.3

Note. Coln %: percents based on column total. Cell %: percents based on grand total.

cognitive ability as determined by a test, with the cross-dimensional play behavior scores.

SES correlated rather strongly with verbal play behavior. The higher the SES of the family, the more cooperative and the higher the distancing level of children's free play as exemplified by the rather strong positive correlations with higher distancing level responsive and coherently extending verbal behavior and the rather strong negative correlations with lower level initiating and coherently extending verbal behavior.

Table 5 also shows that children's temperament was correlated with play behavior. Children who were rated as relatively angry and easily frustrated showed less higher distancing cooperative verbal behavior. Children who were rated as impulsive and high-active were more verbally involved on a higher distancing level than other children, both when playing solitarily and interactively. These children, furthermore, initiated more often than other children higher distancing level interactions. Shy, low-active children were also less interacting and cooperating with other children on a higher verbal distancing level, but also less engaged in higher level solitary play. Children rated as relatively attentive and/or controlled were less involved in solitary play overall and tended to play on a higher verbal distancing level more than on lower distancing level. Finally, children rated as more fearful were not clearly playing differently than other children.

The correlations of cognitive ability with verbal play behavior were not overly strong. There was a clear tendency that the children with higher testscores verbalised more on a higher distancing level when playing and less on a lower distancing level. The relationship with cooperation in play was less clear.

The correlations of background and temperament with the cross-dimensional categories of nonverbal play behavior were overall weaker, less consistent and more often statistically not significant, but showed a roughly similar pattern as with verbal behavior regarding SES and angry temperament. Higher SES was associated with more cooperative and higher-distancing nonverbal play behavior, and with less lower-distancing nonverbal interaction. Angry children were observed to play less cooperatively and more on lower distancing level.

The correlations of the cognitive testscores with nonverbal play behavior did not show a clear and consistent pattern.

Effects of Other Children and Teachers on Target Children's Play

The final analysis to be reported here concerns an exploration of the possible impact of other children and teachers on target children, more in particular on the psychological distancing level of their verbal and nonverbal interactive free play behavior. It should be noted in advance that the present analysis is correlational and does not allow strong causal conclusions.

To limit the number of variables, the categories higher and lower distancing level were combined into single indexes representing the *degree of distancing* of verbal and nonverbal behavior respectively. Indexes were constructed by simple addition

Table 5: Pearson-correlations of social background and personality characteristics with target children's play behavior.

Verbal Play Behavior

	Higher Distancing				Lower Distancing			
	Solitary	Initiating	Responsive	Coherently extending	Solitary	Initiating	Responsive	Coherently extending
Family's SES	−0.01	−0.05	0.49**	0.38*	−0.17	−0.46**	−0.14	−0.43**
Angry	0.22	0.05	−0.39*	−0.32†	0.06	0.09	0.07	0.19
Attentive	−0.25	0.12	0.27	0.16	−0.40*	−0.17	0.12	−0.24
Fearful	−0.12	0.20	0.00	0.05	−0.27	−0.06	0.04	−0.04
Impulsive	0.46**	0.38*	0.11	0.26	0.14	−0.12	−0.01	−0.00
Controlled	−0.37*	−0.29†	0.02	−0.07	−0.12	−0.04	−0.12	−0.24
Shy	−0.32†	−0.15	−0.27	−0.25	0.01	0.26	−0.10	0.07
Cognitive Ability	0.19	0.27	0.31†	0.24	−0.21	−0.34*	−0.13	−0.48**

Nonverbal Play Behavior

	Higher Distancing				Lower Distancing			
	Solitary	Initiating	Responsive	Coherently extending	Solitary	Initiating	Responsive	Coherently extending
Family's SES	−0.05	−0.07	0.18	0.19	−0.18	−0.38*	−0.20	−0.29†
Angry	0.08	0.07	−0.37*	−0.34*	0.27	0.25	0.15	0.16
Attentive	−0.22	−0.01	0.13	−0.08	−0.20	−0.08	0.20	−0.12
Fearful	−0.12	−0.05	−0.26	−0.18	0.19	0.06	0.17	0.06
Impulsive	0.30†	−0.07	0.09	0.06	0.03	0.03	0.20	−0.03
Controlled	−0.05	0.01	−0.02	0.20	−0.01	−0.21	−0.19	−0.22
Shy	−0.09	0.28†	−0.31†	−0.08	0.11	0.13	−0.05	0.24
Cognitive Ability	0.03	−0.01	−0.02	0.15	−0.09	−0.35*	−0.03	−0.22

†$p < 0.10$; *$p < 0.05$; **$p < 0.01$.

Table 6: Regression analysis of the distancing level of target children's play behavior. Predicted variance (R^2), standardardized regression weights ($\square$) and zero-order correlations (r).

Target children's	Verbal Distancing		Nonverbal Distancing	
Model 1	R^2-change		R^2-change	
Step 1: Target children's social background and personality	0.48**		0.32*	
Step 2: Other children's interactive play behavior	0.25**		0.17†	
Step 3: Teachers' instruction behavior	0.02		0.06	
R^2-total	0.74**		0.56*	
R^2-adjusted	0.60**		0.32†	
Model 2	R^2-change		R^2-change	
Step 1: Target children's social background and personality	0.48**		0.32*	
Step 2: Teachers' instruction behavior	0.09		0.05	
Step 3: Other children's interactive play behavior	0.17*		0.18†	
R^2-total	0.74**		0.56*	
R^2-adjusted	0.60**		0.32†	
Regression weights	$\square$	r	$\square$	r
Distancing level of other children's verbal initiatives	0.00	0.46**	−0.40†	−0.15
Distancing level of other children's verbal responses, extensions	0.57**	0.72**	0.22	0.13
Distancing level of other children's nonverbal initiatives	0.03	0.16	−0.05	0.16
Distancing level other children's nonverbal responses, extensions	−0.05	−0.01	0.24	0.36*
Distancing level of teachers' verbal initiatives	0.04	0.45**	−0.15	0.04
Distancing level of teachers' verbal responses and extensions	0.04	0.41**	0.01	0.11
Distancing level of teachers' nonverbal initiatives	0.08	0.13	0.22	0.28
Distancing level of teachers' nonverbal responses, extensions	−0.09	0.06	0.18	0.22

†$p < 0.10$; *$p < 0.05$; **$p < 0.01$.

in which lower level distancing behaviors were given the weight -1 and higher distancing behaviors the weight $+1$. Responsive and coherently extending behaviors were also pooled into a single category.

Regression analyses were run separately for the target children's verbal and nonverbal interactive play behavior (solitary play was not included). To control for confounding influences of personality and social background characteristics, assumingly explaining at least part of the variance in the observed play behavior, these variables were entered first in the regression equation. At the next steps, in systematically varied order, interaction behavior of other children and teachers were entered. The resulting R^2-changes provided indications of the impact of other children and teachers. The results of the regression analyses are in Table 6.

The distancing level of target children's verbal and nonverbal behavior could be very well predicted by SES, personality characteristics, cognitive ability and other children's and teachers' interactive behaviors. R^2s were 0.56 and 0.74 (in the case of verbal behavior) and were statistically significant; the adjusted R^2s were smaller, but still quite substantial. Social background, personality characteristics and cognitive ability as determined by a standard test, accounted for the major part of the variance (R^2s were 0.32 and 0.48). Still, adding other children's behavior to the regression equation (both in models 1 and 2) statistically significantly increased the R^2.

Adding teachers' behavior increased the R^2 much less (and statistically not significantly). In the case of target-children's verbal distancing teachers' behavior added only to the predicted variance when other children's behavior was not taken into account (as in the second model in Table 6). The teachers' behavior apparently was less important for the cognitive quality of children's free play than other children's behavior. Based on the □-weights it could further be inferred that especially other children's *cooperative (i.e. responsive and coherently extending) verbal behavior* was important as predictor of the distancing level of target children's play behavior. Although the zero-order correlations show that other children's initiations as well as the teachers' initiations, responses and coherent extensions were moderately to strongly related to target children's verbal distancing, other children's responsive and coherent extensions correlated even stronger and accounted for almost all additionally predicted variance.

Discussion

The present study examined four-year-old kindergartners' free play from the perspective of cognitive co-construction. Co-construction was defined as the active participation of individual children in a collaborative activity marked by semantically coherent relations between each child's contribution to the joint activity. The notion of semantic coherence was derived from work in cognitive text linguistics, specifying a model-theoretical basis and a related psychological information processing theory to understand pragmatic phenomena as text comprehension and interpersonal communication.

Reviewing some of the literature on play research it was further argued that co-construction processes in social interaction could be seen as the creation of an intersubjective zone of proximal development (ZPD; cf. Musatti, 1993), but that the cognitive-educational potential of this ZPD would depend upon *what* was actually constructed in the social process. As a matter of fact, it was suggested that co-construction is essentially multi-dimensional, encompassing a social or co-operation aspect and a cognitive aspect. It was hypothesized that the developmental and educational potential of children's social interactions in free play would depend both upon the quality of cooperation and the cognitive complexity, i.e. psychological distance, of the shared underlying mental model. These notions were reflected in a multi-dimensional coding system that was used to study free play in kindergarten classrooms.

A second interest of the present study concerned the influence of children's personality characteristics, cognitive ability and social background on co-construction processes in free play. As co-construction requires a social-motivational basis —a fundamental willingness to cooperate and to abide by pragmatic ground rules — and moreover social and pragmatic skills, it was presupposed that children would differ in the quality of the co-construction processes they would get involved in and that these differences would correlate with social background, cognitive ability and personality. Based on the research literature into family socialization, the family's socioeconomic status was seen as a proxy of differences in pragmatic and cognitive socialization that would become manifest in situations of peer cooperation. As to the role of temperament in co-construction processes, a brief overview of studies suggested several possible mechanisms of the ways in which particular temperaments would fit better or worse in group educational arrangements.

The results based on an as yet relatively small sample, one measurement occasion and only six minutes observation per child, corroborated the basic starting points concerning the multi-dimensionality of co-construction — e.g. quality of cooperation and level of psychological distancing. As to the first research question stated earlier in this paper, the four-year-old children who were studied in free play situations *did* play interactively most of the time and, within their interactive play, *appeared to collaborate quite well* as was reflected by the large shares of (verbal and nonverbal) actions that were classified as responsive and coherently extending. Furthermore, the cognitive quality of play was good as was reflected by the relatively large proportions of intermediate and high distancing and small proportions of not-task-related verbal and, to a lesser extent, nonverbal actions.

Although children played solitarily during about one-third of the observation time, even this solitary play reflected aspects of co-construction when children verbalized understandably about the task or play at hand on an intermediate or higher distancing level. Based on the mental model theory it would seem that these solitarily playing children somehow internalized and mentally represented others as virtual co-participants. Solitary high level play as observed in this study was also reminiscent of Vygotsky's notion of inner speech as an advanced developmental step in the internalization of cultural knowledge and skill. Nevertheless *interactive* play, more in particular collaborative play, proved to be superior as regards the use of the verbal versus non-verbal behavioral mode and the use of higher versus lower distancing strategies. As to the second research question, whether playing together does make a difference, the answer was definitely affirmative.

The third research question concerned the influence of social background and personality on free play behavior. Social background, represented by SES as a proxy of differential socialization in the family, and children's temperament as rated by the parents, appeared to be related to differences in play behavior. For instance, SES correlated substantially with the observed frequencies of responsive and coherently extending higher distancing level utterances and negatively with initiations of interactions on a lower distancing level. Children rated by their parents as angry and easily irritated and frustrated, were playing less collaboratively and tended to play more on a lower distancing level. Particularly interesting was the case of children who were rated as relatively impulsive and hyperactive. They apparently fared relatively well in both solitary and interactive play, producing relatively many high distancing level verbal and nonverbal actions. Shy, hypo-active and impulse-controlled, perhaps over-controlled children seemed to profit least of the free play situation in terms of the socio-cognitive quality of their involvement in this activity.

The basic point that emerges is that an extravert (impulsive, active, to a lesser extent also angry) temperament fits better with the free play didactic format in Dutch kindergartens than the more introvert (shy, controlled and attentive) personality, assuming, of course, that collobaration on a higher distancing level is important for social-cognitive development. Similarly, preparation at home for higher level, largely verbal interactions is important as well, and puts children of higher SES background at advantage.

The final question addressed in this study concerned the roles of other children and teachers in target children's free play behavior, in particular with respect to the cognitive potential of the child's play behavior. This was exploratively examined in different ways. Firstly, as was already noted, the sociocognitive and educational quality of free play appeared to be overall higher when children played with other children (which occurred quite freqently) or interacted with the teacher (which occurred rather infrequently). Secondly, it was determined that the cooperative and cognitive quality of the behavior of other children and teachers mattered for the cognitive quality of the target children's behavior after controling for socioeconomic background, temperament and cognitive ability. The results supported the presupposition that the *way* (e.g. more or less collaboratively, more or less distancing) in which other children were involved in the target children's play influences the target children's play quality, but detailed sequential analyses are needed for more conclusive results as to the cause-effect relationships. The results were also in agreement with findings in intervention studies that show that improving social-relational and pragmatic aspects of young children's collaborative educational activities increases the cognitive gains (cf. Gillies, 1997; Wegerif and Mercer, 2000).

Free play provides children with relevant, development stimulating educational experiences. This is a widely advocated official ideology in the early years education and, fortunately, the present results can be interpreted as corroborating it. What happens in play interactions is in principle to be seen as actualization of cognitive potential. In view of this, it is remarkable that teachers are so marginally involved in children's free play and contribute so little in terms of higher cognitive-distancing extensions. The present findings on this matter are not exceptional, because the teachers in this research were quite average and other studies in (Dutch) kindergartens arrive at essentially the same conclusion. It is probably because of this lack of (especially, play-theme oriented, higher distancing) involvement that there seemed to be no real influence of teachers on target children's play, at least not compared to what the other children in the classroom contributed. However, a consequence may be that initial differences between children arising from different socialisation and different temperaments are reproduced and reinforced in free play.

The present study did not relate children's play behavior to cognitive development over time. So it is not possible now to be more definite about the leading question of the research whether peer-interactions really matter for cognitive development in the long run. The scope was limited to possible proximal determinants of cognitive development, such as the quality of cooperation, verbalization and cognitive distancing. New observations and measurements will be added to the present data-set in the near future, so that longitudinal analyses can be carried out. These data will concern free play at later measurement occasions but also work lessons which are a regular part of the kindergarten curriculum as well. One matter of great interest is whether children's cognitive development rate — their "growth curve' — is somehow related to their experiences in kindergarten. Another matter of interest is whether the role of the teacher, almost absent in free play, is different when work lessons are concerned.

A major theoretical interest concerns the further conceptual clarification of the notion of the zone of proximal development (ZPD), a core notion in present day social-constructivist developmental psychology. In children's social interaction research an alternative view seems imminent that places the ZPD outside the individual child, amidst concrete social activities in everyday formal as well as informal educational settings and which acknowledges that at least part of children's cognitive potential is not an individual property, for instance, gene-based, but a property of the social interactions of the individual with other individuals within "incorporating cultural systems" guided by "cultural rules" (Serpell, 1999), such as the playgroup in kindergarten.

It is too early to end with all kinds of concrete recommendations for educational practice. However, we think that the practical relevance of this study and the planned additional research activities in the near future will underscore the importance of adapting standard didactic arrangements to individual children's personality, ability and social background so as to optimize the actualization of their (cognitive) potential.

Reference Note

A unpublished version of the Child Behavior Questionnaire was made available in 1996 by Professor M.K. Rothbart of the University of Oregon.

Acknowledgement

The research reported in this chapter was supported by a grant of the Dutch Organisation for Scientific Research, project 575-90-804.

9

Activity and Interaction in Pedagogical Contexts

Judith Ireson

Introduction

This chapter focuses on the interactions taking place between adult–child dyads in educational contexts. The aim is to explore aspects of these contexts that influence the structuring of activity between the adult and the child. In educational contexts, an important aspect of teachers' work is to structure activity for children so as to promote their learning. This aspect of interaction has not been investigated extensively in research on adult–child interaction, which has for the most part been concerned with interactions during the completion of tasks that have been predetermined by a researcher and usually have clear endpoints. The theoretical orientation of the work lies in a socio-cultural approach, which views social context as integral to individual development, structuring and mediating exchanges between adults and children.

Analyses of the interactions between adults and children performing tasks outside school have drawn on Vygotskian and neo-Vygotskian theory, including the ideas of a "zone of proximal development" (Vygotsky, 1978), "scaffolding" (Wood, Bruner & Ross, 1976; Bruner, 1983) and "guided participation" (Rogoff, 1990). The analysis of adult–child interactions during the completion of a variety of tasks demonstrates that adults generally adjust their support to assist children, simplifying the task where necessary and taking over the more difficult parts. This form of assistance is found in many different cultures, although the variations in cultural norms and goals for development influence the nature of involvement of adults and children (Rogoff et al., 1993).

The majority of more detailed, controlled investigations of adult–child interaction have studied the performance of well-defined tasks with clear endpoints. In these experimental situations, the dyads have been presented with a predetermined task, worked out by the experimenter (e.g. Rogoff et al., 1993; Gonzalez, 1996; Nilholm & Saljo, 1996). Most of these tasks have been easy for the adults to perform and would not have presented difficulties when it came to deciding how to break the task into simpler components. Very little consideration has been given to more complex learning or to situations in which children are unwilling or unable to complete the tasks. Nor has much attention been paid to the analysis of the context in which the activity has taken place, even though the quality of the interaction is likely to be influenced by the adults' perceptions of the nature of their role and of the task (Wertsch, Minick, & Arns, 1984; Paradise, 1996). In educational contexts the structuring of tasks and learning activities is an important and sometimes difficult aspect of teaching, which impacts on the interactions between the teacher and the learner.

The context in which an activity takes place may be considered at a number of levels. Bronfenbrenner (1979), for example, proposed that social systems were nested inside one another, like a set of Russian dolls. In such a view, interactions between a teacher and a pupil take place in a classroom environment, which is nested in and influenced by the wider settings of the school, the local community and the national system of education. Contextual information, in the form of descriptions of cultural conventions and practices, has been used as a means of assisting in the interpretation of interactions between adults and children (Greenfield, 1984; Rogoff, 1990). Adults' educational levels and their perceptions of their part in helping children to learn appear to influence the quality of interactions (Wertsch, Minick & Arns, 1984; Rogoff, 1990; Rogoff et al., 1993; Levin & Korat, 1997). For example, mothers who are not teachers are more inclined to focus on their child's correct completion of tasks, whereas mothers who are teachers are more inclined to focus on learning and to allow children to make errors in the service of learning. The performance of most activities offers a variety of potential meanings and interpretations, and the process of interaction involves a negotiation of shared context (Wertsch, Minick & Arns, 1984; Goodnow, 1990; Nilholm & Saljo, 1996).

An important element of the context of interaction, and one that has not received much attention to date, is the learning activity itself. Recently, Wertsch (1995), has drawn attention to the centrality of action in the mediation of learning, and to a need for further analysis and development of this idea within sociocultural theory. As an example he cited the introduction of more advanced poles in the sport of pole vaulting. The use of a new fibreglass pole provoked controversy, particularly from athletes still using the older, aluminium poles. This controversy is taken by Wertsch to be a reflection of the introduction of a new mediational means into the activity of pole vaulting, and the questions at that time centred around whether the activity itself was the same or whether those athletes using the pole were actually participating in a different activity. Moreover, the users of the new mediational means had to make adjustments to their technique. Teaching methods may be viewed in a similar way in that certain activities are introduced into the interaction as a means of enabling children to learn. Activities may be thought of as mediating devices introduced by the teacher to promote the child's learning. In the teaching of reading there is considerable controversy about the most effective methods for the initial teaching of reading and programmes for the remediation of children's difficulties in reading differ strongly from one another. The interactions between the teacher and the pupil are constrained or enabled by the mediational means employed, which form part of a set of practices constituting a particular programme.

The two studies to be reported in this chapter aim to delineate some aspects of educational settings that influence the interactions between teacher–child dyads. The research investigated activity and interaction in two contrasting settings. The first study investigated a construction activity in a pre-school playgroup and the second investigated the individual tuition of reading with primary school children. The first study, which has been more fully reported elsewhere (Ireson & Blay, 1999), illustrated the part played by young children in constructing activity with adults and suggested that the adults' perceptions of the goals of the activity played an important part in structuring it. As the work progressed, it became apparent that the teachers' pedagogical beliefs and their perceptions of the goals of the activity could be considered as part of the setting. The teachers' perceptions of the goals appeared to be linked to the principles underpinning the training programmes they had followed. Pre-school Playgroup Association training is based on the principles of promoting children's growth and development through play and playgroups aim to offer informal activities which encourage children to explore, experiment, question and talk.

The second study focused in a more detailed way on the links between particular teaching programmes and teachers' structuring of activity. The teachers chosen to participate in this study were providing individual tutoring for primary school children having difficulty with reading. They used contrasting methods for teaching early literacy. Induction into a set of practices in literacy support teaching occurs through specialised programmes that differ in relation to both underlying epistemology and pedagogy. By comparing teachers engaged in different programmes, the links between the programmes, the teachers' perceptions of the programme goals and the activities became more apparent.

Constructing Activity in a Playgroup

The aim of the first study was to explore the contribution of both the adult and the child in an open-ended, naturally occurring activity. Adult–child dyads were observed and recorded during a construction task, in a pre-school playgroup (Ireson & Blay, 1999). The activity chosen to form the focus of the study was building with Lego. This activity was chosen through discussions with the leaders of the playgroups in which the research was carried out, who were asked to suggest an activity that was usually carried out as a individual activity and that formed a normal part of the playgroup day.

Two female playgroup leaders and six children, three girls and three boys, participated in the research. The children were aged between 3 years 7 months and 4 years 5 months and all had attended the playgroup for more than one term. They were described as having good or fairly good language ability. Both the playgroup leaders had pre-school play association training and extensive experience of working with under-fives, one having 18 years' and the other 26 years' experience.

Short interviews were held individually with the playgroup leaders to obtain information about their training and experience and to explore their views about the value of playgroup provision for young children and their role as a playgroup leader. The researcher also discussed possible activities to form the focus of the study. Lego building was chosen, as it represented an activity that was familiar to the children and one in which it was common for an adult to interact with an individual child. For the purposes of recording, the activity was set up in a quiet room away from the noise and bustle of the large playroom. Immediately before each of the Lego activities took place, the adults were asked what they thought each child would gain from the experience and after the session they were asked how they thought it had gone.

The Lego building sessions were recorded on audiotape and videotape by one of the researchers and transcribed for analysis (see Ireson & Blay, 1999 for details). Audio-recording was used for five sessions, and the researcher supplemented these recordings by taking notes. Three sessions were recorded on videotape. The analysis of the interactions demonstrated that the activity itself was jointly constructed by the children and the adults. Once the building was under way, the adults introduced counting, colour naming and social conversations. These were considered as topics and the analysis focussed on the transitions from one topic to another. This drew attention to the way in which the children, as well as the adults, constructed the activity itself. Some of the children resisted the adults' attempts to distract them from building with the Lego, whereas others engaged readily in these diversions or introduced fantasy and role play themselves. This analysis illustrated how both the adults' and the children's engagement in the activity influenced the unfolding and development of each session, creating opportunities for learning.

By involving the play leaders in the choice of the activity, the researchers were placed in the position of discovering the participants' meaning of the activity, initially through the interviews and subsequently through the observation and analysis. The adults referred to the task as Lego building but their interpretation of the activity only became apparent to the researchers as the activity unfolded. Indeed, the researchers were initially surprised by the small amount of building undertaken and by the simplicity of constructions produced. In naturalistic settings, the unfolding and development of activities is ubiquitous but it is an important determinant of the opportunities for children's learning. This unfolding and development is invisible when tasks are predetermined by the researcher. When activities do not have a clear endpoint, both participants are able to influence the course of the activity, in line with their own interests. It became clear that the children influenced the course of the activity in a variety of ways. With the adult's encouragement, they adopted the role of architect, making decisions about what they would like to build, selecting pieces for their constructions and deciding on the details. The children also influenced the course of the activity itself, sometimes keeping the adult focused on the task of building and sometimes diverting from it.

This study suggested that the adult's participation in the activity was influenced by their perceptions of the cultural setting of the playgroup, including their perceptions of the playgroup principles, their intentions for the particular activity and their perceptions of their role in supporting children's development. Consistent with the playgroup philosophy of "leading-by-following", the adults saw their role in terms of setting up situations for children to explore. They viewed the building activity as a vehicle for cognitive and social development and therefore entered the session with multiple goals. They did not have a pre-determined plan for the session itself; instead their aim was to be responsive to the child. Because they had several rather broad goals in mind, they responded flexibly during the sessions and created opportunities to engage with the children on a variety of topics.

To summarise, from this study we already see three aspects of the setting which impinge on and form the activity. The philosophy and pedagogical beliefs underpinning the educational provision, the selection of particular activities as means of encouraging learning and development in a way that is consonant with the educational philosophy, and the influence of both the adult and the child on the course of the activity. A second study was designed to explore these.

Individual Literacy Tuition

Background

For the second study, a context was chosen that would allow further exploration of some of the aspects of settings identified as of interest in the first study, in particular, the impact of differing pedagogies on the structuring of activities. The teaching of reading is an aspect of the curriculum that generates strong and conflicting views about teaching methods and pedagogy. For this reason, the second study took as its focus the individual tuition of children who were experiencing difficulty learning to read.

Helping children who experience difficulties in reading is a complex task and there has been much heated debate about the appropriate sequences of instruction in early literacy, stemming from differences in theories about reading development. Some theories of reading development, sometimes characterised as "bottom up" approaches, are based on a logical progression starting with the individual letters and letter sounds, then moving to simple, phonically regular words before combining words into sentences and then into longer texts. Psycholinguistic theories, on the other hand, have encouraged a "top down" approach, in which reading is seen as essentially a search for meaning, and individual letter sounds and words are learned in the context of reading longer texts, right from the start. The different epistemologies tend to be associated with different theories of learning, the bottom up approach being more behavioural and the top down approach being more constructivist (see Stanovich, 1994 for a discussion). Although some consensus is emerging about an instructional middle ground, many primary class teachers in England remain uncertain about the most appropriate methods of teaching and they adopt a variety of approaches and activities in the classroom (Ireson, Blatchford & Joscelyne, 1995). Children who do not make satisfactory progress may be offered individual tuition in reading.

The type of support offered to children identified as making poor progress in reading is quite varied. For many teachers, induction into a set of practices in literacy teaching occurs through specialised training programmes. These programmes differ in terms of their underlying epistemology and pedagogical principles. Some tutors offer very structured, phonic based programmes, while others offer programmes incorporating a mixture of phonics and text reading. One well-established training programme in England is the Reading Recovery programme developed by Marie Clay (Clay, 1985; Clay & Cazden, 1990). This programme is based on the principle that children utilise several strategies when decoding text and these strategies should be taught in the context of reading connected texts. A second well-established programme is a Literacy Programme based on a linguistic analysis of the English language, emphasising the teaching of phonics in an ordered sequence, starting with letter sounds before moving on to blending, then word reading and spelling, then sentences and finally sentences in texts. The teaching techniques are multi-sensory and designed to ensure that the pupil achieves automaticity of response, thereby reducing the load on memory. (Hickey, 1977; Hornsby & Shear, 1993). Some teachers follow a variety of other courses in literacy development, which combine features of different programmes.

The individual tutoring of reading therefore presented a useful situation in which to study the relationships between teachers' own perceptions of their teaching and the practices they adopted during teaching sessions with the children. The study focused on the structuring of teaching sessions and activities by teachers trained in different programmes. It explored evidence for the adoption of particular mediational means, through the analysis of the teaching activities used. It also aimed to draw out aspects of the setting that influenced the interactions between the teachers and the children.

Method

Participants: Five teachers participated in the study. One was an experienced reading recovery teacher, two had completed a Literacy Programme offered by the Dyslexia Institute, and two were experienced members of a learning support team who had completed specialised training in special educational needs. Each teacher was asked to select two children who would form the focus of the more detailed study. As children are taken into the Reading Recovery programme when they are aged 6–7 years, the other teachers were also asked to select children in Year 2 who were 6–7 years old. The Literacy Programme teachers were only able to identify one child each in this age group.

Procedure: Initial interviews were held with each teacher. They were asked to explain the procedures leading up to the children's referral for help with reading and the initial assessments of the children. The teachers were then asked to describe the way they generally worked with the children and this led to a

Coding categories

AFFect	Comments about the child's feelings, confidence.
ASSESS	Assessments made at the beginning, when the teacher first started working with the child.
INTERaction	Information about liaison with the child's class teacher or parents.
METHOD	Comments on how the teaching session is organised, activities, what is normally done.
PHONics	Comments about phonics teaching.
PLAN	Plans for working with individual children, including targets.
PRINCIPLE	Statement of the teacher's view of the principles of the programme, or underpinning her role.
PROGress	Comments about the child's progress.
READWRIT	Comments about the relationship between reading and writing.
SPELLing	Comments about spelling.
STRATegies	Comments about the strategies a child uses or a strategy the teacher would like a child to use, including metacognition.

Figure 1: Coding categories for the teacher interviews.

discussion about which of the children would form the focus of the subsequent research. The interviews were tape-recorded. A time was arranged for the researcher to observe the teacher working with the children. During these sessions, the researcher made field notes covering the activity structure of the sessions and the emphasis of the teaching. The teacher was asked to provide copies of the records of each child's programme. Finally, the teachers were asked if they would be willing to have one teaching session with each child video recorded.

Analysis of the Interviews

The interviews were transcribed and observation notes of teaching sessions were written up. The video recordings were also transcribed. The analysis of the interviews will be reported first, followed by an analysis of the structure and content of the teaching sessions. The interviews were coded into the broad categories displayed in Figure 1. The main topics were the assessment of the children and planning and structuring teaching. Because of space limitations, the analysis of the information on assessment will not be reported here (it is available in Ireson, 1997).

When teachers talked about their teaching, they were asked to think about one or two children in Year 2, aged 6–7 years. As part of their normal practice, all the teachers completed structured planning forms outlining their plans for each of the children and making predictions of progress over the short and long term and they referred to these during the interviews. Long term reading recovery predictions were expressed in terms of the strategies the child was expected to be using, such as self-correcting behaviour, monitoring behaviour and cross-checking, which were seen as important for the child to help her "take herself forward" when the recovery programme was withdrawn. In the short term, the teacher worked on developing the use of strategies the child was not using, often the "visual strategies" such as increasing letter knowledge and writing the child's last name, but also increasing self-correcting behaviour. Other teachers' plans were expressed in terms of a progression of the phonic aspects of reading, moving on from a few letter sounds to consonant-vowel-consonant words and then combining words into sentences.

The teachers' descriptions of how they started working with a child revealed three different structures, one based on the combination and ordered sequence of activities in the lesson, the second based on a general curriculum progression and the third based on activities which were not ordered. The description of reading recovery was based on the combination of activities in the lesson. When a child started on the reading recovery programme the teacher spent the first sessions "roaming around the known" before going "into instruction". During these initial sessions the teacher provided work to consolidate what the child already knew and this also provided an opportunity to add to the initial assessment information. Once "in instruction", lessons were described as including five activities: writing on a white board, reading familiar text, making and breaking words using magnetic letters, writing a short story which was then cut up by the teacher and reassembled and read back by the child, reading a new text.

The teacher chose the new text for each lesson and decided what to work on in the "making and breaking" but other than that, she said that "she responded to the child's behaviours". Over a period of time she checked on the strategies the child was using and tried to help him/her develop others. An indirect approach to helping the child use strategies was seen as a feature of the programme "It's very much following the child ... scaffolding and building and supporting where she needs it". The teacher referred to the programme as structured, but not in the sense of a pre-planned set of criteria or set of things to work through. The indirect approach led to some difficult situations for the teacher, for example when a child could not read the word "can". Direct teaching of phonics even in common, regular words such as "can" does not form part of the Reading Recovery programme. The teacher therefore had to consider carefully the methods she would use to encourage the child to listen to the sounds in the word and to help the child write the word.

A contrasting activity structure was described by one of the Literacy Programme teachers, who said "I have a number of things I like to do in it (the lesson), but it doesn't have a structure order necessarily". With the younger children, the lesson usually incorporated five activities: alphabet sequencing, introducing a new sound, reading cards (designed to help teach children the sounds of the letters), a spelling activity and a game. The main object of these activities was to teach letter-sound correspondence.

A second structure to emerge in the analysis was a curriculum structure for reading. The Literacy Programme programme is based on a sequence of teaching points and teachers worked through this sequence in strict order. It was described as a basic list of phonics, ordered in a sequence of teaching points of increasing difficulty. Elements of a similar structure were evident in the description provided by one of the Learning Support teachers. This started with work on the sounds of a small number of consonants, followed by the short vowel "a", and several consonant-vowel-consonant words ending in "at" and "en", also developing some work on rhymes. This teacher said that an important aspect of this work for the child was to realise that the letters make words and that the system is not arbitrary. Once the child made progress then the aim was to bring in sight words as well. The sight words were seen as falling into two groups, those that the child could read using their knowledge of phonics and those that they could not. The teachers had lists of the first 32, 68 and 100 most common words and aimed to enable the children to read these out of context in due course. The point at which a child worked on the key words was not predetermined, but for one teacher was after about one and a half terms. The next stage in reading was to increase the book level, to help children recognise the difference between fiction and non-fiction, the structure of text such as title and chapters, reading for enjoyment and reading for information.

The third framework was more fluid than the first two in that no firm curriculum or lesson structure was stated. What emerged was a set of comments on a variety of activities, which when grouped, fell into five categories: (1) work on the letter sounds through activities such as word searches and sorting games; (2) work on letter patterns, syllables, word endings and beginnings e.g. st/and/ing, rhyming words; (3) developing a sight vocabulary, working on words taken from the reading book which the child had not read correctly, practising these through a variety of activities until they were automatic; (4) dictation, the idea being that spelling supported reading; (5) reading text, choosing books, reading in groups, listening to taped stories, reading difficult texts with support.

This analysis suggests that teachers' practices are underpinned by an activity structure and a curriculum structure. These structures formed part of the particular literacy training programmes, which placed differential emphasis on the curriculum sequencing and the types and sequences of activities. Although the term "structure" has been used in relation to both curriculum and activities, it is clear that there are differences in the degree and type of structure. The Literacy Programme curriculum was highly determined and stemmed from a logical analysis of the English language, whereas the Reading Recovery curriculum was loosely structured and based on the idea of following the child. Where the structure was strongly predetermined, it mediated the steps in teaching, through the sequence of teaching points.

Observations of the Teaching Sessions

All the teachers were observed on at least one occasion and a video recording of one session was obtained. During the sessions that were not recorded, the researcher made notes of the activities. As the focus at this stage was on the activities introduced by the teachers, the video recordings were transcribed in sufficient detail to give information about the activities and discourse, but without intonation or detail of non-verbal communication.

A striking feature of the sessions was the differences in the number and type of activities included by the teachers following different programmes. The Literacy Programme teachers included up to 11 activities in a 45-minute session, which meant that the pace was very brisk and activities followed one another in quick succession. The Learning Support and Reading Recovery teachers included between four and six activities in sessions of about 30 minutes. All the teachers moved from one activity to the next with very little pause, and little time was spent explaining the next activity, suggesting that the form of the activities was familiar to the children. In addition, the type of activity differed markedly, with the Literacy Programme teachers doing work at the letter and word level for most of the session, with text reading limited to a few sentences constructed to incorporate the phonic rules already taught. This was in strong contrast to Reading Recovery sessions during which children read back their own writing and read from several texts, some of which they had read before and one which was new. The learning support teachers included some book reading and some reading from worksheets.

Some activities were common to all approaches. For example, all the teachers used plastic letters to make words and the children then changed one word into another by altering a letter at a time. This was referred to as "making and breaking" in reading recovery, where it formed a short part of the teaching session. The Literacy Programme and Learning Support teachers incorporated more work using the letters. All approaches also included work on letter names and sounds, although the emphasis differed in the three approaches and it was only in the Literacy Programme and Learning Support that teachers asked the children to set out the letters in alphabetic sequence. In many ways the learning support teachers occupied an intermediate position, combining work on phonics with text reading.

The discourse of the teachers differed, with Literacy Programme teachers doing a great deal of direction and reinforcement, praising children for working hard and getting correct answers and asking whether they remembered information such as letter sounds and procedures for the activities. The role of the child was predominantly to memorise. The other teachers also used direction and reinforcement but the directions were sometimes more indirect, taking the form of questions. In addition the teachers commented more on the children's use of strategies, such as self-correcting, reading back or looking at the picture in a book to help work out a word. In reading recovery there was quite frequent comment on the use of strategies in text reading. The role of the child was to memorise and to use a range of strategies.

Discussion

The aim of these two studies was to explore aspects of context that influence the structuring of activity between adults and children in educational settings. The strategy of including teachers and children from different phases of education and from contrasting literacy training programmes has highlighted teachers' beliefs and intentions, activity structures and participants' interpretations of activities as potentially significant influences on interaction. In educational settings, an important aspect of teachers' work is to structure activity for children so as to promote their learning. This structuring takes places within a cultural setting, which acts as an influence on teachers' views of appropriate activities and teaching goals. The structuring of activity also influences the nature of children's participation and their opportunities for learning.

The participation of novices in expert activities has been considered by Lave and Wenger (1991) to be an important means of learning out of school. Individual learning is structured and organised by opportunities for and varieties of participation. The term guided participation has been used by Rogoff (1995) to denote a process involving both the management of roles during interaction and the structuring of situations through facilitating or limiting access to participation in cultural activities. Both authors point to the significance of the structuring of activities and opportunities for learning. The analysis presented in this chapter demonstrates that further elaboration of the influences on participation and interaction in educational settings may be useful.

A tentative model of the features of the context to emerge from the studies presented in this chapter, influencing the interactions between the teacher and the learner, is displayed in Figure 2. The model is necessarily incomplete, as it is based on the analysis of a small number of dyadic interactions, but it is put forward as a framework to be extended and refined in later work. It represents an attempt to capture the dynamic and fluid nature of contextual influences on interaction. In this it differs from other models that consider context in terms of relatively stable features impinging on individuals and influencing interaction. Bronfenbrenner (1979), for example, argued that the development of human abilities depended in large part on the social and institutional context of individual activity. His work has been important in drawing attention to the influence of the context on human relationships and on cognitive processing (Ceci & Bronfenbrenner, 1985). Similarly, Saljo & Wyndham (1993) demonstrated that pupils adopted different strategies when given the same task in two different subject lessons.

In contrast, the interaction between the child and the adult is at the heart of the model presented here. A network of beliefs and intentions influences adult participation. One part of this network is a set of relations between the principles underlying particular programmes, teaching intentions and activity sequences. The second part is a set of relations between the teachers' role in controlling the activity and of the child's role in learning. Also included here is the adult's role in maintaining the child's motivation. The first part of this network is more fully articulated than the second part. Several factors influence the child's participation,

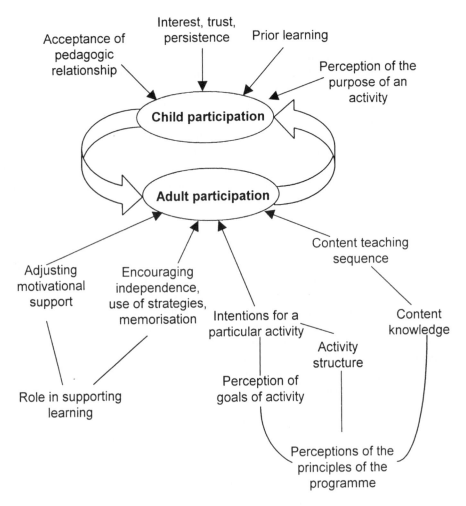

Figure 2: Model of interaction

but there is insufficient evidence from this research to do more than sketch these.

The relations between the principles underlying the teaching programmes, teaching intentions and activity sequences are complex. The contrast between adult–child interactions during the Lego building in the playgroup and the tutoring of reading illuminated relations between the teachers' intentions and activity structures. The Lego building activity probably represents one of the least structured teacher–child activities, whereas the literacy tuition was one of the most structured. The adults' intentions for the building activity were expressed in a very general way, in terms of developing children's cognitive and social abilities, whereas the literacy teachers were much more specific. The specificity of the teaching goals was one significant element, related to the structure of the activity, which was clearly defined and predetermined in the literacy sessions but open for negotiation in the Lego building activity.

Even though the literacy activities were clearly defined and directed in all the sessions, there were interesting differences between the activity structures of the literacy programmes. Certain activities were excluded from a given programme while others were required. For example, a teaching session in Reading Recovery generally included a combination of five types of activities, while the Literacy Programme required a multi-sensory approach. The activities were based on the pedagogic principles incorporated in the respective programmes. They mediated between the curriculum goals and the principles of the programme methodologies, but were not directly related to them in a simple way.

The participation of the child was also influenced by the teachers' role in controlling the activity and of the child's role in learning. The young children were encouraged to be decision-makers and architects during the building session, whereas the older, poor readers were encouraged to memorise and utilise strategies. The literacy sessions were characterised by teacher-led activity, which proceeded at a brisk pace, whereas the building activity allowed the children to be more active participants in constructing the activity itself. This difference in participation was in part a reflection of the type of learning at hand. The young children were already capable of assembling Lego blocks and the adults did not attempt to teach them to make more complex constructions, instead they encouraged the children to take control of the design, while they provided general support. In contrast, the initial teaching of literacy involved memorising arbitrary relations between letters and sounds and co-ordinating information from several sources.

The differences may also reflect beliefs about appropriate pedagogy for children of different ages. In general, pedagogy for pre-school children is less structured than for older children. The whole philosophy of the playgroups is that young children learn through play, rather than through direct teaching. This developmental aspect has been overlooked in the past, as researchers have tended to focus on children within a restricted age range, or on adult learners. There is still much to learn about the role of maturation in children's ability to benefit from direct teaching.

Pedagogical differences may also arise from beliefs about appropriate pedagogies for learners of differing abilities. The tendency for teaching programmes for low attaining pupils, or those in need of remedial help in reading, to be more structured and direct than approaches for pupils of higher attainment has been noted (McArthur, Stasz & Zmuidzinas, 1990; Barr & Dreeben, 1991). On the other hand, detailed studies of tutoring for undergraduate students demonstrates that tutors adopt a supportive, interactive role. They do not appear to see tutoring as a transfer of information but rather as a means of making visible to students the otherwise hidden activities that are the foundations of scientific and mathematical concepts (Fox, 1993). The directive nature of the reading programmes forms part of a set of beliefs about an appropriate pedagogy for these pupils. In terms of the model presented above, these beliefs influence the interactions between the adult and the learner through the adjustment of the teacher's role in supporting learning and the teacher's intentions for a particular activity. Tutors' interpretations of their role and the role of the learner may vary according to the age and ability of the learner and the particular programme being followed.

An interesting feature to emerge from the investigation of the literacy teaching was the sense that the Reading Recovery and Literacy Programmes represented different pedagogical cultures. Each required teachers to undergo an extended training, through which the cultural tools of the programme were passed on to the teachers, who were inducted into a set of practices, together with mediational means in the form of assessments, resources and activities for teaching and learning. Interestingly, both the Reading Recovery and Literacy Programme training meet the criteria for programmes that are considered by Guskey (1986) to be successful in changing practice. Both combine the teaching of theory with closely supervised practice and extended feedback on performance. The Learning Support teachers did not follow a common training programme before starting to work with individual children and they had more autonomy in deciding on the approach to take with each child. They were, however, part of a group serving a particular borough, which had an ongoing programme of professional development activities for the group. In this case the pedagogical culture was less strongly framed by adherence to a particular method and the teachers were more open to ideas and practices from other literacy programmes. The views of the literacy curriculum, the assessments, activities and resources differed markedly in the programmes, resulting in quite different types of learning experience for the pupils.

It is important that all concerned are aware of the influence of the pedagogical culture and are able to assess its impact critically. For teachers, this means that they must have an understanding of the theoretical basis on which programmes are designed. Without such an understanding, an analysis of practice will be limited to the implementation of practical aspects of the teaching method, rather than an evaluation of the methodology itself and a rational decision about the form of provision to be offered to a child needing support in reading. A rational view would be that the child's needs should determine the provision. Contrary to expectation, the type of provision for a child experiencing difficulty in reading may be decided on the basis of what is available in a particular school or area, rather than on the specific needs of the child. Certain schools or boroughs opt in to programmes like reading recovery or the literacy programme and this is what is on offer for all children experiencing difficulty. The programme may then be adapted for each child, but the underlying principles and methodology are the same for all. This should not be taken as a criticism of the schools or the teachers themselves, but simply a reflection of the current situation. It may be that teachers who are highly experienced in using a particular programme are able to adapt it to meet the needs of children with a variety of difficulties. Those who are less experienced are likely to find this problematic.

The model presented in this chapter represents a starting point, which sketches tentative relationships that will need to be substantiated in further research. It is clear that the process of structuring in educational contexts is highly complex, involving teachers' pedagogical culture, their choice of learning activities for children and their structuring of engagement in the activities. The work demonstrates the need for models that incorporate the wider pedagogical context and the social interaction within one dynamic analytic system.

10

Mapping the Dynamics of Peer Group Interaction: A Method of Analysis of Socially Shared Learning Processes

Kristiina Kumpulainen and Mika Mutanen

Introduction

A central question around which recent research on learning and instruction has concentrated is how social interaction mediates the construction of knowledge in classrooms. There exists research which has explored the ways in which meanings are socially constructed in classroom interactions (Lemke, 1990; Wells & Chang-Wells, 1992; Edwards, 1993; Bergqvist & Säljö, 1995; Mercer, 1995). There are also research studies which have investigated teachers' use of discursive strategies to scaffold students' learning (Palincsar, 1986). Other studies of social interaction and learning have focused on students' contributions to classroom conversation and the learning outcomes of these (Barnes & Todd, 1977; Sharan & Shachar, 1988; Teasley, 1995; Webb, Troper & Fall, 1995). Research on language socialization and classroom learning has looked at the primary discourses of children's home and community lives and the ensuing impact of differences in these on children's learning across the curriculum (Delamont, 1976; Cazden, 1988; Phelan, Davidson & Cao, 1991). In the light of current research it is clear that classroom interaction is seen as a valuable tool for learning which should be studied from different perspectives in order to deepen our understanding of the practice of learning in and through social interaction.

The reasons for the growing interest towards classroom interactions and, more generally, towards the processes of learning in social activity reflect a theoretical shift in perspectives to learning and instruction which have started to emphasise the social and contextual nature of human learning (Brown, Collins & Duguid, 1989; Lave & Wenger, 1991; Greeno, 1997). Post-Vygotskian notions of teaching and learning as an assisted performance (Tharp & Gallimore, 1988) or as a process of guided participation (Rogoff, 1990) suggest that learning arises both as the result of deliberate guidance of the learner by a more capable other or, incidentally, through participation in activities within a community of practice. In the light of these views, learning is not only a construction process that takes place in the mind of an individual but also an enculturation process embedded in the sociohistorical and sociocultural context of activity (Salomon, 1997).

Contemporary views of learning and their pedagogical applications are affecting traditional classroom interaction patterns modifying the roles of the teacher and students as communicators and learners. Student-centred learning activities, collaborative working modes, authentic learning contexts, and technological innovations are giving students more opportunities to participate, observe, reflect on, and practice socially shared ways of knowing and thinking. Although teacher–student interaction also plays an important role in today's instruction, peer to peer interaction has increased in many classrooms. Consequently, it has become important to understand better how meanings and knowledge are constructed between students whilst working in small groups or teams under various leaning activities. Furthermore, it has become important to understand what kind of opportunities do particular interaction patterns and social activities give to students' learning and what are the possible obstacles that may hinder effective problem solving and peer group learning. Analyses of the social and cognitive dynamics of peer group interaction can reveal important information about the enabling conditions for effective interaction and learning.

In this paper we introduce a descriptive system of analysis for investigating the situated dynamics of peer group interaction. The method takes a dynamic and process-oriented perspective to peer interaction which is seen as socially and situationally developed in students' evolving interactions. Of particular importance are the mechanisms of social and cognitive dimensions of peer group activity. In addition, the forms, patterns and relationship of peer group interaction with socially mediated problem solving and learning are considered.

The analysis method has emerged as a result of a number of studies we have conducted of primary-aged students' classroom interactions on various educational tasks in Greece, Britain, and in Finland (Fourlas & Wray, 1990; Kumpulainen, 1996; Kumpulainen & Mutanen, 1998; Kumpulainen, Kaartinen, & Mutanen, 1998). The main goal in these studies has been to investigate the nature of students' social interaction, particularly verbal interaction in different learning situations. The initial development of the method concentrated on the functions of students' verbal interaction as a basis for investigation of students' roles as communicators and learners in teacher-centred and peer-group centred classrooms (Fourlas & Wray, 1990). The functional analysis method was later piloted, modified and applied by Kumpulainen (1996) in a study which investigated students' verbal interactions during the process of collaborative writing with a word processor. Due to its fine-grained categorizations, the functional analysis method was considered to give a structured overview of the nature and quality of students' verbal interaction in this learning context. Despite the potentials of the analysis method, in our recent studies of peer group learning we found the functional analysis inadequate to unravel the complexities of socially shared learning processes. Firstly, there seemed to be a need to develop a descriptive system of analysis which takes a more holistic and multidimensional perspective to interaction. Consequently, the analysis of the communicative functions of verbal interaction alone seemed not to serve this goal. Secondly, it seemed important that more attention be paid to the moment-by-moment character of interaction to highlight the situated processes of knowledge construction within peer groups. Thirdly, it seemed important to take the individual and the group as units of analysis in order to investigate the types and forms of participation within peer groups and how they mediate individual learning. In addition to methodological developments, there seemed to be a need to develop more efficient models of interaction data presentation.

In the following sections, we shall firstly outline the theoretical background of the method. This is followed by an introduction to the analysis method highlighted with an empirical example. The paper ends with a reflective analysis of the method and considers its possible research applications.

Theoretical Overview

Social Interaction and Learning

Recent views of learning emphasize its social and situated nature regarding the construction of knowledge both as an interpersonal and intrapersonal process. Learning is seen to be mediated by the individual's active involvement and participation in situated social practices and not as the result of knowledge transmission. Views originating from socioconstructivist theories of learning emphasize the importance of social processes in the individual's knowledge building (Piaget, 1970; Tudge & Rogoff, 1989; Perret-Clermont, Perret & Bell, 1991; Teasley & Roschelle, 1993). According to this line of thinking, learning involves interpretation whilst learners relate new information to their pre-existing knowledge and personal experience (Resnick, 1989). The fact that knowledge construction relates to prior knowledge makes learning in social contexts particularly beneficial since the diversity in learners' prior knowledge can be utilized during the interaction so that the contribution of each team member is accumulated to provide a large base of resources for the group's knowledge construction. Cognitive conflicts created by divergent points of view and their resolution in peer interactions are seen as affecting intrapersonal processes (Doise & Mugny, 1984). Moreover, social learning contexts are found to promote explaining to others and self-explanations often leading to cognitive gains (Schwartz, 1995). Consequently, social modes of working are regarded as creating effective learning situations for students to express, discover and construct their knowledge structures at a more abstract level than whilst working on the same problem alone (Light et al., 1994).

The sociocultural perspectives, which view learning from the cultural point of view, emphasize the role of social interaction in the movement from interpersonal to intrapersonal functioning (Vygotsky, 1962, 1978; Wertsch, 1985; Wertsch & Stone, 1985; Van der Veer & Valsiner, 1994). In sociocultural perspectives on learning particular emphasis is put on the mediation of action through tools on the development of the mind (Wertsch, 1991; Harré & Gillett, 1994). Semiotic artifacts are defined as cultural amplifiers which are central to the appropriation of knowledge through representational activity by the developing individual (John-Steiner & Mahn, 1996). Although language is seen as one of the main sources of mediational means, they also include various other cultural artifacts such as different symbol systems and schemes, maps and works of art (Cole & Wertsch,

1997). By stressing the interdependence of social and individual processes in the co-construction of knowledge, sociocultural approaches view semiotic tools as personal and social resources, and, hence, mediating the link between the social and the individual (Vygotsky, 1962, 1978).

The importance of considering the interdependency between social interaction and context has been pointed out by a number of researchers working within the socioconstructivist and sociocultural framework (e.g. Wertsch, 1985, 1991; Rogoff, 1990; Light & Perret-Clermont, 1991; Anderson, Reder & Simon, 1997). According to these views, the nature of the individual's activity and cognitive performance cannot be isolated from its social and cultural contexts. The considerations of the dialogical and dynamic relationship between individual and environment have led to the situative view of learning (Brown, Collins & Duguid, 1989; Lave & Wenger, 1991; Greeno, Smith & Moore, 1993; Greeno, 1997) which focuses on the development of participation in valued social practices and on learner identity rather than on individuals' knowledge and contexts of performance.

The notion of context should not only be limited to the physical environment. Instead a more dynamic approach is necessary. It holds that contexts are actively created in situated interactions: They are continuously shaped by social and interactional meanings as well as by participants' perceptions and interpretations of the situation (Lemke, 1990; Edwards & Potter, 1992; Grossen, 1994). Schubauer-Leoni and Grossen (1993) highlight the multidimensional nature of contexts by identifying three different levels: the socio/cultural, institutional and interindividual contexts. They argue for their recognition in the analysis of the complex relationship between the individual's activity and social context, both at theoretical and methodological levels.

Peer Group Interaction

Research has already provided convincing evidence of the positive effects of collaborative small group work activity on students' cognitive and social development (Cohen, 1994; Rosenshine & Meister, 1994). The diversity in learners' prior knowledge and experience appears to provide a large base of resources for the group's knowledge construction, giving opportunities for self-reflection and joint meaning making (Teasley, 1995). Although peer group activities can offer students extended opportunities for active participation, not all kinds of interactions will lead to joint meaning making and knowledge construction. The quality of learning in small groups is strongly associated with the quality of interactions and collaboration learners engage on academic tasks (Fisher, 1993; Webb, Troper & Fall, 1995; Mercer, 1996).

For effective learning interaction it is necessary that participants have a shared understanding of the task and its goals (Forman & Cazden, 1985; Edwards & Mercer, 1987; Rogoff, 1990). In order to create a common understanding, participants also need to have established ground rules for their interaction. These are constructed over the course of a shared history between the participants (Mercer,

1995). Other features identified to be conducive to effective learning interaction in peer group situations are a joint appreciation of the purpose and goals of the task, sharing of tools and activities, an acceptance of educational agenda over a social one, and a willingness to speculate, make hypotheses and use valid evidence (Fisher, 1996). Instructional conditions that seem to encourage such activities are found to include elements that foster joint task-involvement and interdependence between group members (Cohen, 1994).

The dynamics of peer group interaction are complex and do not automatically lead to collaboration and joint understanding. Complex processes are present in peer group activity which are linked to the sociocultural context of the activity as well as to the evolving interpretations and meanings created in the immediate context (Lemke, 1990; Edwards & Potter, 1992). The dimensions of interaction are also related to the participants' socio-cognitive and emotional processes, including their interpretations and perceptions of the aims of the activity in question (Grossen, 1994). Vion (1992) when characterizing the complexity of interaction situations introduces the concept of heterogeneous interactive space. This refers to the social, cognitive and interactive roles and contexts which interactors have to negotiate in order to achieve a joint understanding (cf. Grossen, 1994). Consequently, studies of social learning need to approach interactional phenomena from multiple view points and via multiple levels of analyses which take account of the evolving and dynamic nature of interaction (Kumpulainen & Mutanen, 1999).

Introduction to the Method

The theoretical grounding of the method introduced in this paper is informed by the sociocultural and socioconstructivist perspectives to interaction and learning (Wertsch, 1985, 1991; Bruner, 1990; Resnick, Levine & Teasley, 1991), whereas the methodological solutions presented are strongly influenced by the work of Barnes and Todd (1977, 1995), Mercer (1994, 1996) as well as by interactional ethnographers (Green & Wallat, 1981; Green & Mayer, 1991; Tuyay, Jennings & Dixon, 1995). A closer analysis of the analytical methods that have contributed to the development of the present method can be found in Kumpulainen and Mutanen (1999).

In the present method, learning is viewed as an interactional process that requires an understanding of language and other semiotic tools as both personal and social resources (Halliday & Hasan, 1989; Wertsch, 1991; Harré & Gillett, 1994). Social interaction is treated as a dynamic process in which language and other semiotic tools are used as instruments of communication and learning. Interaction is seen as a complex social phenomenon which is composed of non-verbal and social properties in addition to its verbal characteristics. social interaction is not treated as representing a person's inner cognitive world, nor even as descriptive of an outer reality, but rather as a tool-in-action shaped by participants' culturally-based definitions of the situation (Edwards & Potter, 1992; Edwards, 1993).

In the analysis method, the dynamics of peer group interaction are approached from three analytic dimensions. The first dimension of the analysis, entitled *the functional analysis*, investigates the character and purpose of student utterances in peer group interaction. It characterizes the communicative strategies used by participants in social activity. The second dimension, *cognitive processing*, examines the ways in which students approach and process learning tasks in their social activity. It aims at highlighting students' working strategies and situated positions towards learning, knowledge and themselves as problem solvers. The third dimension of the analysis, *social processing*, focuses on the nature of social relationships that are developed in students' social activity. This includes examining the types and forms of student participation in peer groups.

The application of the method is realized with a microanalysis of evolving peer interactions by focusing on three analytic dimensions, namely the functions of verbal interaction, cognitive processing and social processing. Whereas the functional analysis concentrates on students' verbal language, the analyses of students' cognitive and social processing focus on interactive dynamics as they occur across the participants. Consequently, a group is taken as a unit of analysis. The three dimensions are treated separately for analytic purposes. In actuality they cannot be separated since each dimension gives meaning to all the others and simultaneously obtains meaning from them.

Dimension 1: Functional Analysis of Verbal Interaction

The functional analysis of students' verbal interaction focuses on the purposes for which verbal language is used in a given context. It investigates and highlights the communicative strategies applied by individual students whilst taking part in interaction (Halliday & Hasan, 1989). Analysis of this nature often concentrates on the illocutionary force of an utterance, that is, on its functional meaning (Austin, 1962; Edwards & Westgate, 1994). The functions for which students use their oral language are closely linked with the topic of discussion as well as with the individuals' expectations and evolving interpretations of the situation shaped by the sociocultural context of the activity. The functions of language used in the course of interaction serve both intra- and interpersonal purposes: On the one hand, the purposes and intentions carried by means of verbal language serve an ideational, i.e. cognitive function. On the other hand, they serve an interpersonal function relating to the personal and social relationships between the interactors (Halliday & Hasan, 1989).

The identification of language functions in peer interaction takes place on the basis of implicature, that is, what a speaker can imply, suggest or mean may be different to what the speaker literally says. Consequently, the functions are not identified on the basis of linguistic form. Rather, they are identified in context in terms of their retrospective and prospective effects on the actual discourse both in terms of content and form. Data gathered by means of observations and student interviews also give understanding to the functions for which students use their verbal language in interaction. The functions of peer interaction are the minimum units analysed in the system. They are identified on an utterance basis and defined in terms of source, purpose and situated conversational meaning. An utterance is viewed as a meaningful unit of speech, i.e. a message unit. The boundary between each utterance is linguistically marked by contextualization cues. Given that an utterance may serve multiple functions, more than one function can be recorded for each utterance.

Examples of language functions we have often identified in peer group interaction across learning situations are *the Informative, Expositional, Reasoning, Evaluative, Interrogative, Responsive, Organisational, Judgmental (agrees/disagrees), Argumentational, Compositional, Revision, Dictation, Reading aloud, Repetition, Experiential,* and *Affectional functions.* Some of these functions describe the nature of interaction more from the activity point of view (e.g. dictation, reading aloud), whereas others take a more interpretative/cognitive (e.g. informative, reasoning, evaluative) or social perspective (e.g. affectional, responsive, judgmental) on the analysis of verbal interaction. However, none of the functions could be clearly seen as only reflecting one of these dimensions. Consequently, each function in the framework is regarded as reflecting the social-cognitive-discursive actions of the participants as they verbally interact in their social activity. The functions in the system are defined further in Table 1. The language functions used in the course of joint problem solving often differ across situations and contexts, thus these functions presented in the analytic framework should not be understood as fixed, pre-defined categories. Instead, the functions must be situationally defined for each interaction situation on a post hoc basis.

Dimension 2: Analysis of Cognitive Processing

The analysis of cognitive processing examines the ways in which students' approach and process learning tasks in their social activity. It aims at highlighting students' working strategies and situated positions towards knowledge, learning and themselves as problem solvers. In the method, cognitive processes are seen as dynamic and contextual in nature, being socially constructed in students' evolving interactions in the sociocultural context of activity.

In the analytical framework we have distinguished three broad modes to characterize the nature of students' cognitive processing in peer group activity: *Procedural processing* refers to the routine execution of tasks without thorough planning or thinking. Ideas are not developed, rather they are cumulated or disputed without constructive judgments or criticism. The students' activity is often product-oriented and concentrates on procedural handling of information. *Interpretative* or *exploratory processing*, on the other hand, refers to a situation during which thinking is made visible through language or other tools and the whole activity is focused on strategies, planning, and hypothesis testing. The students' activity reflects their deep engagement and interest in the problem solving task. *Off-task activity* refers to a situation during which the students' activity does not focus on the task, e.g. playing around, discussing break time activities, "absent minded" activity. It is important to recognize that these three broad analytical modes are used as heuristic devices rather than distinct categories in which students' cognitive processing can be easily coded. Rather, the modes are reflected in different ways in different contexts and situations and, hence, require situational definitions.

Dimension 3: Analysis of Social Processing

The analysis of social processing aims at characterizing the social relationship and types of participation in peer groups. The different modes in which social processing is often constructed in peer group interaction are *collaborative, tutoring, argumentative, individualistic, dominative, conflict,* and *confusion modes.* The latter characterizes interaction during which there is an obvious misunderstanding or lack of shared understanding between the children. The conflict mode reflects disagreement, usually at a social level. The dominative mode reflects the distribution of power and status in the peer group. The individualistic and dominative modes are contrasts to collaborative interaction. The individualistic mode implies that students are not developing their ideas together but rather working individually in the group. The dominative reflects imbalance in students' social status and power. The argumentative and tutoring modes of interaction characterize the nature of collaboration between the participants. In this sense they can be regarded as sub-modes of collaborative activity. The argumentative mode implies constructive interaction in which students negotiate their differing understandings in a rational way by giving judgments and justifications. This often leads to a shared understanding of the situation. The tutoring mode shows students helping and explaining for the purpose of assisting the other to understand the matter at hand. In addition, collaboration includes interaction in which participants attempt to achieve a mutual understanding of the situation, ideas are jointly negotiated, and discourse is coherent. In collaborative interaction participants often create bi-directional zones of proximal development assisting one another (Forman, 1989).

It must be noted that, apart from the functional analysis of peer group interaction, the unit of analysis for the different modes of cognitive and social processing is not defined by distinct rules, such as an utterance basis. Instead the units of analysis for the modes of cognitive and social processing are based on their development in peer interaction on a moment-by-moment basis (see Table 2 on pp. 156–157). In other respects the three dimensions on which the analytical framework concentrates, all emerge from the data as the result of the researchers' and, when possible, also the interactors' interpretations of the situation. The analysis method is summarized in Table 1 shown below.

An Empirical Example

In the following, the method will be highlighted with an empirical example. The example is derived from our current research project which investigates the social

Table 1: Analytical framework of peer group interaction

Dimension	Analytical Categorization		Description
Cognitive processing	exploratory/ interpretative	EXPO	critical and exploratory activity which includes planning, hypothesis testing, evaluation, and experimenting
	procedural/ routine	PROC	procedural on-task activity which focuses on handling, organising, and executing the task without reflective analysis
	off-task	OFF	activity not related to the task
Social processing	collaborative	COLL	joint activity characterized by equal participation and meaning making
	• tutoring	TUTO	student helping and assisting another student
	• argumentative	ARGU	students are faced with cognitive/social conflicts which are resolved and justified in a rational way
	individualistic	INDI	student(s) working on individual tasks with no sharing or joint meaning making
	domination	DOMI	student dominating the work, unequal participation
	conflict	FLCI	social or academic conflicts which are often left unresolved
	confusion	FUSI	lack of shared understanding, student(s) do not understand the task or each other, often includes silent episodes
Language functions	informative	I	providing information
	reasoning	RE	reasoning in language
	evaluative	EV	evaluating work or action
	interrogative	Q	asking questions
	responsive	A	answering questions
	organizational	OR	organizing or/and controlling behavior
	judgmental		
	• agrees	Ja	expressing agreement or
	• disagrees	Jd	disagreement
	argumentational	AR	justifying information, opinions or actions
	compositional	CR	creating text
	revision	RV	revising text
	dictation	DI	dictating
	reading aloud	RE	reading text
	repetition	RP	repeating spoken language
	experiential	E	expressing personal experiences
	affectional	AF	expressing feelings

and cognitive dynamics of peer group interaction and learning in heuristic instructional settings located in mathematics, science and language (Kumpulainen, 1997). The empirical example consists of data of one pair working on a design task located in geometry. The students were 12 years old from one Finnish primary school classroom. In the design task, the students were asked to construct three-dimensional objects pictorially represented on a plane with the help of two-dimensional objects. The construction was realized with cards representing different faces of objects. The faces were numbered and after the students had constructed the object they had to write down the relating numbers on paper. The pictures of the geometrical objects could be visualized in different ways and, hence, there were many solutions.

The present example should be understood as prototypical. The main goal in this paper is to demonstrate the application of the method to empirical data as well as to define and justify the three analytical dimensions on which the analysis focuses. It is hoped that the micro analytical maps, figures and summaries of the dynamics of peer group interaction give new ideas for data reporting and also highlight the different opportunities the analysis framework provides for investigating and interpreting the dynamics of peer group interaction and learning.

Data Collection

The learning situation was arranged in a classroom of the Learning Research Center of Kajaani Department of Teacher Education. The classroom is equipped with multiple technical instruments to provide effective data collection (Suortti & Atjonen, 1995). Each data collection session was videotaped as a whole and supplemented with the researchers' field notes. The videotapes included real-time information of the students' working processes. Each session lasted between 25 and 45 minutes. After finishing the task, the students were asked to fill in a question-naire which aimed at shedding more light onto their collaboration, attitudes towards the tasks and perceived goals. Stimulated recall-interviews were also held for each student individually in order to clarify the students' orientation, working strategies and understanding of the concepts dealt with within the task, as well as to increase understanding about the nature of their collaboration and interaction. The stimulated recall-interviews were audio-taped. The triangulation of research methods was considered necessary to increase the validity of interpreting the dynamics of social activity within peer groups.

The data were analysed in several phases. In the first phase, the video material of the students' social activity was examined together with the field notes written down during observations. Next, the verbal interaction of the pairs was transcribed, the questionnaires encoded, the students' work assessed and interviews sum-marized. After that, the interaction and behaviors apparent in the videotapes were analysed by taking account of the real-time information as well as by following the written transcripts. Particular attention was paid to the nature of students' verbal interaction, and cognitive and social processing. The other features observed and analysed involved the students' use of the instructional tools available in the problem solving situations (e.g. texts, computers, cards, etc.) and the students' construction of time and task within their activity. The data analyses were reflected upon in the light of the contextual knowledge acquired through observations, stimulated recall interviews and pre-study teaching experiences in the classroom. The data were collected and analysed by two researchers together. Disagreements concerning the analysis of peer interaction were negotiated until joint agreement was established.

Analytical Maps

In the present method, the dynamics of peer group interaction are illustrated with the help of analytical maps which have been created for each peer group under investigation. The product of the analysis is a series of situation-specific analytical maps that describe the sequential evolution of peer group interactions as they are constructed by students interacting with and acting on each other's messages. In addition to highlighting the dynamics of peer interaction, the maps show the construction of time in the students' activity as well as some contextual information necessary for the interpretation of the social activity in question. Although a structural map is always a simplification, it gives a coherent and temporal picture of a complex situation making comparisons across educational contexts, peer groups and students possible. Moreover, the maps help one return easily to the original data to check the validity of interpretation. In addition, when presenting extracts from the data, one is able to investigate the co-text, that is, the data context to which the extract belongs.

Selected Results

Table 2 describes the social activity of a pair, Joni and Kimmo, working on the design task. The social interaction of this pair reflects imbalance in the students' collaboration and joint problem solving. As the extract below shows, Joni seems to dominate the activity in social and cognitive terms. Although at the beginning Kimmo is eagerly involved with the task, Joni's domination gradually affects Kimmo's working processes and participation, leading to the signs of a "free-rider effect".

In this extract Joni asks Kimmo to find a large triangle. Kimmo seems to agree with this with an affectional statement, although his attention is directed to holding the cards the students have already constructed. Joni continues his orders but does not explain what he is actually trying to do. Kimmo tries to ask Joni to clarify his thinking and strategies but Joni seems to be thinking aloud rather than aiming towards joint problem solving or understanding. The lack of shared understanding can also be noticed in the pair's incoherent verbal interaction (e.g. conversational turns 152–155, 158–161). The lack of argumentation and explaining episodes in peer interaction further demonstrates the imbalance in the students' social activity.

The analysis of the whole data of the dynamics of Joni's and Kimmo's social interaction shows that at the beginning the students were task-oriented and interested in the design task. Both students started the activity eagerly. Soon, however, Joni started to dominate the task, for example, by handling the cards and giving orders, and did not give Kimmo much space. Kimmo did not seem to notice this at first but gradually started to be a bit restless since his ideas or suggestions were not taken up by Joni. Interestingly, Kimmo soon accepted his role and started to withdraw from the activity, letting Joni do most of the problem solving. From the data it appears that Joni was rather thinking aloud than trying to solve the design task collaboratively. Only in those instances when Joni regarded the task as difficult to solve did he start to seek confirmation of his ideas from Kimmo. The quality of the pair's work was average, 7 out of 12 points.

The functional analysis of students' verbal interaction shows that the pair's interaction was mostly characterized by the reasoning, organizational, questioning, and affectional functions. As with the other pairs investigated in the study, reasoning and organizational episodes reflect the nature of the design task, which seemed to encourage exploratory activity (Kumpulainen, Kaartinen & Mutanen, 1998). Figure 1 highlights the communicative strategies used by Joni and Kimmo in their social activity.

Figure 1 demonstrates differences in the students' communicative strategies and the nature of their participation. The data show that Kimmo expressed more affectional statements than Joni (AF; $f = 31/10$). Kimmo also posed more questions (Q; $f = 18/9$). Joni, on the other hand, organised the activity (OR; $f = 43/11$) and reasoned (RS; $f = 68/42$) more frequently than Kimmo. The differences in the students' communicative strategies and types of participation demonstrate further the imbalance in the students' social activity. In addition, they highlight differences between the students' subject knowledge and social behaviour. Kimmo's subject knowledge in mathematics was assessed as being much lower than that of Joni by the classroom teacher.

The data gathered by means of student questionnaires and interviews give slightly different interpretations of the nature of peer collaboration and joint problem solving than those made by the researchers. According to the students, their collaboration was good and pair group work made problem solving easier. Yet, the students expressed the view that they had not learned anything from each other and that they would have needed some help from the teacher. There were also differences between the students in their interpretations of the task goals. Kimmo considered the goal of the design task to be related to the development of concentration skills, whereas Joni thought they were related to mathematical thinking. The differing interpretations of the goals of the exercise may reflect the students unfamiliarity of working in the instructional setting devised for the study.

Table 2: An analytical map of peer interaction: The case of Kimmo and Joni

SESSION: 1.1.2 Mathematics
PUPILS: Kimmo and Joni
WORKING TIME: 11:05–11:30

Time	Participation		Transcribed peer interaction	Language functions	Cognitive processing	Social processing	Contextual notes
11:16	147	JONI	where is the large triangle? *missä täältä on iso kolmio?*	asking for information Q(I)	looking for a face	slight domination from Joni's side	students are trying to find correct faces to construct the geometrical object
	148	KIMMO	oh, yeah ... *outeeh ....*	affectional utterance (AF)	Kimmo is holding the construction students have already made		
	149	JONI	take those away *otapa pois nuo ete*	organising (OR)			
	150	KIMMO	hahah ... what are you looking for? *hähä ... mitä nää niiku etit?*	affectional utterance (AF) and asking for information Q(I)		Kimmo initiates collaboration	
	151	JONI	a kind of a triangle to the center ... these tasks are a bit too difficult ... *jotaki kolomiota tuohon keskelle ... on nää vähän liika vaikeita nää tehtävät ...*	answering A(I) and evaluating the task (EV)	explaining		
	152	KIMMO	how about this one then? *ei se mikkään tämmönen sitte?*	reasoning in a question form Q(RS)	speculating		
	153	JONI	it might be ... perhaps two of these there ... *se voi olla ... jos vaikka kaks tämmöstä sinne ...*	reasoning (RS)			
	154	KIMMO	basically no *ja periaatteessa ei*	reasoning (RS)			
11:17	155	JONI	show me ... hmm ... let's turn to the next exercise ... let's solve that one since it's easier ... it is what one sees ... hey, could it be these ... *näytäppä ... hm ... hy ... hy ... vaihetaan tehtävää ... ratkassaan tuo, ko tuo on aika heleppo ... se on nimitään miten sen näkkee ... onko nämä hei ... katoppa ... onko nämä ...*	organizing (OR), evaluating (EV), and reasoning (RS)	organizing working, speculating	slight domination from Joni's side	

156	*KIMMO*	do you mean these small ones? *tämmösiä pieniä vai?*	reasoning in a question form Q(RS)		Kimmo initiates collaboration
157	*JONI*	these *tämmösiä*	answering A(RS)		
158	*KIMMO*	what about these big ones, I think they look big ... like this ... *vai semmosia isoja ... minusta ne näyttää niiltä isoilta ... tämmösiltä näin ...*	reasoning (RS)	speculating	
159	*JONI*	I think ... (indistinct) *minusta ...*	—		
160	*KIMMO*	I don't know ... *en tiiä yhtään ...*	informing (I)		signs of "a free rider effect" starting to appear
161	*JONI*	that's a bit too thick that one there ... that's there ... rather small ... *tuo on vähän liika paksu tuo osa tuossa ... se oli siinä aika lyhlyitä ...*	reasoning (RS)	comparing cards	
162	*KIMMO*	that's not it ... heheheh ... *se ei ole siite sen enempäähähäh*	reasoning (RS)		
163	*JONI*	It's all the same really *se on ihan sama oikeastaan*	reasoning (RS)		
164	*KIMMO*	let's try both *no kokkeillaan kumpiakin*	organising (OR)		
165	*JONI*	let's take ... this is there below, isn't it? ... bigger one ... hold it *no otetaan ... tämmönen on siinä alla, eikö ookin ... isompi ... tämmönen ... noni piä sitä*	organizing (OR), reasoning (RS), and organizing (OR)	organising working	
166	*KIMMO*	no, I don't want to *enkä piä*	disagrees (Jd)		social conflict

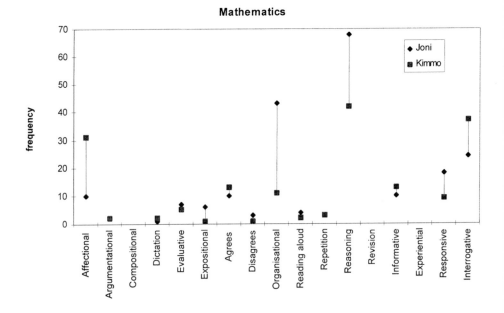

Figure 1: Communicative strategies and types of participation in the light of the functional analysis of students' verbal interaction.

Discussion

The importance of understanding the mechanisms underlying social interaction and learning has become an important topic for current research on learning and instruction. More attention is paid to the practices, processes and conditions leading to the social construction of knowledge in different learning situations. The focus of analysis is being extended from cognitive, acquisition oriented view of individual learning to situative, participatory conception which emphasizes interaction, forms of participation and social meaning construction in sociocultural settings (Salomon & Perkins, 1998). In the midst of these changes in emphasis, new methodological questions concerning the analysis of social activity, context and learning have arisen. Questions to which researchers try to find answers are, for example: How to take account of the complex and dynamic nature of interaction? How to highlight qualitative differences within and between interactive activities across learning contexts and arrangements? Upon what criteria should such judgments be made? and How applicable are the methods used? (Westgate & Hughes, 1997). It is clear that the recent focus has challenged the methodological approaches used to investigate collaborative peer group interactions and learning processes. It is evident that the methodological tools developed should take a more dynamic and process-oriented account of social interaction and learning. In addition, they should recognize the role of physical and psychological tools in shaping the nature of social activity. On the whole, there is a need for multi-layer analyses which support one another and which enable investigations of the relationship between and within them. Analyses of this nature are likely to increase current understanding of the social conditions and practices of collaborative learning and how they mediate individual growth.

To investigate and interpret the dynamics of social activity and learning is extremely complex. In every interaction situation there is a close interplay between the different dimensions of which social activity is composed. Furthermore, the mechanisms of social activity are not static in nature but evolve over time in social interactions (Edwards & Potter, 1992). In our analytic framework we have concentrated on the social and cognitive dimensions to unravel the mechanisms of peer group interaction and learning. We have also been concerned with the differing demands of learning tasks and situations on students' evolving interactions and consequent learning opportunities. In this method, we have tried to take a synchronic as well as a diachronic view of peer group interaction: On the one hand, the method investigates peer group interaction across different analytical dimensions, on the other, the method investigates the processes of meaning making, characterizing the evolution of peer group interaction over time. The different levels of analysis support and complement one another by giving a holistic and structured picture of the complex phenomena.

In our empirical studies of peer group interaction, we have used multiple data collection methods by employing video-recordings, field notes, direct observations, stimulated recall interviews and questionnaires. The data gathered through these triangulated means has been re- and cross-analysed in order to obtain an in-depth understanding of peer group activity and of those meanings underlying it. The methodological principles that guide the present method draw from constructivist, interpretivist approaches to human inquiry (Schwandt, 1998). These approaches see learning as a social and individual construction process which is situationally embedded in the sociocultural context of activity. Instead of investigating cause and effect relationships typical of the positivistic research tradition, the interpretative approaches aim at unravelling the mechanisms and dynamics of social activity. In this line of research, human interaction is investigated from different dimensions with multiple methods, with the aim of constructing an in-depth and holistic understanding of the phenomena.

The dynamic nature of peer interaction is acknowledged in the system by focusing on the whole interactive spaces created by the students in their verbal and non-verbal interactions on a moment-by-moment basis. These interactive spaces are viewed from three analytic dimensions by concentrating on the functions of peer interaction, and the nature of cognitive and social processing. The different categories identified within the analytical dimensions should not be seen as pre-defined or hierarchical in nature. In the present method, we do not want to suggest that there are only certain ways of interacting that indicate that quality learning is taking place. The "quality" interaction conducive to students' learning must always be defined in context. The need for situational definitions also applies to the development of analytical categories that aim at describing the social activity under investigation. Consequently, the whole analytical method introduced should be understood as an analytical lens or a flexible framework through which social activity within peer groups can be studied and highlighted.

The method introduced in this paper can be applied and modified to different studies of peer group interaction and learning. On the one hand, the method can be used to highlight the dynamics between social and individual learning. On the other hand, it can be used to investigate how cognitive and social aspects of learning interrelate and interact in synergistic ways. The patterns and mechanisms of peer group interaction can be investigated in the light of students' subject knowledge, goals, interpretations of the learning situation, motivational orientation, age, gender, social background, or of the effects of certain pedagogical arrangements and learning tasks on students' social practices and learning opportunities. The method can also be applied to cross-cultural studies of peer group interaction in a variety of classrooms and curriculum areas as well as to investigate relationships between particular interaction patterns and learning outcomes. Knowledge of these matters can provide valuable information about the mechanisms and dynamics of peer group work interaction and learning, and pedagogically, for the organization of effective small group learning and the design of powerful learning environments.

Despite the potentials of the analytic framework, it still needs further clarification and development. The analytical categories need critical examination and the sociocultural context and history of social activity should receive more profound consideration. In the future it also seems important to consider how to include instructional guidance offered by expert tutors into the interaction analysis. Nevertheless, we firmly believe that the current method offers one analytical tool to investigate the dynamics of peer group interaction and learning and will hopefully stimulate new ideas and developments in relation to collecting, interpreting and reporting data of socially shared learning processes.

Acknowledgement

The research reported in this paper was supported by the Academy of Finland (Project no: 132925).

11

Deep Processing in a Collaborative Learning Environment

Carla van Boxtel, Jos van der Linden and Gellof Kanselaar

Introduction

Conceptual understanding implies that a person can communicate the meaning of a certain concept, can relate the concept to other concepts within the domain and can use the concept adequately in explaining an object or phenomenon in a scientific way or in performing an action. Students need to build an integrated conceptual framework, because incomplete and fragmented knowledge hinders the adequate use of science concepts in problem-solving tasks. However, developing an integrated conceptual framework that corresponds with scientifically accepted conceptual models is problematic for several reasons. Scientists not only use concepts to describe and order the reality we experience, but they also give a theoretical reconstruction of that reality. Students have to understand concepts in their scientific meaning (Lijnse & De Vos, 1990). Therefore, they have to understand the *theory* in which the concepts are used to describe and explain phenomena (Caravita & Halldén, 1994). This also explains the difficulty in changing misconceptions when it concerns concepts also used in everyday life, such as "force", "energy" and "current".

The learning of concepts can be described as the improvement of conceptual knowledge through refinement, (re)structuring and expansion of concept knowledge or as the development of the ability to make use of the scientific concepts in different situations (e.g. Rumelhart & Orthony, 1978; Eylon & Linn, 1988; Ferguson-Hessler & De Jong, 1993; Elshout-Mohr & Van Hout-Wolters, 1995). In particular deep processing strategies are believed to improve conceptual understanding.

Most of the research on the learning of (science) concepts describes deep processing as an "individualistic" learning activity or strategy. In this chapter we focus on deep processing in a face to face collaborative learning environment that aims at the improvement of conceptual understanding within the domain of physics. Two general questions are considered in this chapter. First, what can be considered as indicators of deep processing in student interaction? Secondly, how do characteristics of the task influence the appearance of deep processing in student interaction? In the following section deep processing strategies are described and illustrated with respect to the domain of physics. Subsequently, we describe the potential of collaborative learning in stimulating students to engage in deep processing activities. We report the results of our experimental study that was set up to investigate the influence of some task and student characteristics on the appearance of deep processing in student interaction.

Deep Processing

In the literature the following strategies are considered as deep processing strategies:

- the active use of prior knowledge
- the recognition and acknowledgement of problems
- attempts to look for meaningful relations

The Active use of Prior Knowledge

The activation of prior knowledge is important for the assimilation of new information. But within the domain of physics the fact that some of the preconceptions can be considered as misconceptions or naive conceptions, makes the use of prior knowledge problematic. New information can be assimilated in naive conceptions (Joshua & Dupin, 1987; Pintrich, Marx & Boyle, 1993). It is important that students understand that their prior knowledge is not adequate in explaining or manipulating certain phenomena (Schmidt *et al.*, 1989; Eylon & Linn, 1988).

Different instruction models stress the importance of a phase of prior knowledge activation to achieve conceptual change. Licht (1990), for example, designed a learning environment in which students first had to formulate expectations on the base of their preconceptions and intuition. Afterwards, students were confronted with conflicting evidence through hypotheses testing or demonstration. Biemans (1997) designed a strategy for students working in a computer environment stimulating the activation of relevant prior knowledge and the validation of this knowledge through explicit comparison with new information. This strategy resulted in significant improvement of the learning results.

Recognition and Acknowledgement of Problems

Krapp, Hidi and Renninger (1996) describe the recognition of problems and the attempt to solve these problems as an important deep processing strategy. Two kinds of problems are important concerning the learning of concepts. First, students can experience knowledge gaps or a lack of understanding. When students are confronted with this problem, we would like them to make it explicit through formulation of a question. In classroom settings students hardly ask (high level) questions, whereas question asking is at the heart of active learning and deep comprehension (Graesser, Person & Huber, 1993). Questioning can elicit elaboration. Some instruction models focused on stimulating and improving questioning (Brown & Palincsar, 1989; King, 1990; Webb, 1989).

Another problem students can experience, is being confronted with information that conflicts with their own knowledge. Chinn and Brewer (1993) stress that students need to be motivated to understand conflicting information and alternative theories. Because it is well known that many students incorporate new information in their naive theories, they consider it as an important condition for reaching an adequate understanding of science concepts.

Look for Meaningful Relations

A third important deep processing strategy is the attempt to look for meaningful relations. Within the domain of physics three types of relations can be distinguished. First, students have to be able to relate different concepts. For example, they have to understand how current strength is related to resistance and voltage. Secondly, students must be able to connect theoretical concepts to concrete phenomena. Within the domain of electricity, for example, a bulb has to be considered as a resistor. Finally, within the domain of physics students also have to be able to associate concepts with different forms of representation.

Physics is a bilingual subject; not only textual forms of representation are used, but also specifically mathematical forms of representation, such as tables, formulas and diagrams (Alexander & Kulikowich, 1994). Many students have problems with interpreting these different forms of representation and with making appropriate connections and associations among them. Students find it difficult to understand what exactly is represented in a formula (Perkins & Unger, 1994). A lack of understanding of the qualitative relationships of the terms impedes real understanding.

The Potential of Collaborative Learning

Collaborative learning has a strong potential in stimulating students to be actively involved in deep processing. Collaborative learning can be defined as a learning environment in which students coordinate their activities and try to achieve a common goal through verbal interaction and is focused on communal knowledge building (Webb & Palincsar, 1996). Especially verbalisation, elaborated help and conflict are believed to explain positive results of collaborative learning (Cohen, 1994; Doise & Mugny, 1984; Damon & Phelps, 1989; King, 1990; Webb, 1991).

When collaborative learning aims at improvement of conceptual understanding, student interaction should be characterised by deep processing. First, we would like students to use the language of science (Lemke, 1990), to talk about relationships between different concepts, relationships between scientific concepts and concrete phenomena and other forms of representation. Secondly, we want them to make problems explicit, to ask questions that can evoke elaborated explanations and to elaborate conflicts. Finally, we want students to build on each other's ideas and to draw new ideas into a common conceptual frame. However, it is not guaranteed that such a student interaction will appear. Research shows that both characteristics of the instruction and of the students are important factors influencing the amount of deep processing during learning activities. Most of this research is done with participants who work individually on a task. Less is known about the influence of such factors in a collaborative learning environment.

Recently, researchers on collaborative learning have shifted their attention to the question how student interaction mediates knowledge construction (Dillenbourg *et al.*, 1995; Webb & Palincsar, 1996). Salomon and Perkins (1998) suggest that from a constructivistic perspective there exists a spiral of reciprocal relations between socially distributed understandings and individual cognitive ones. The effects *with* are to be found in the process, while students are engaged in collaboration. Effects *of* are the cognitive, social, metacognitive and affective residues of these activities, which will affect learning and behaviour in new situations, either of individual students or of the group. Deep processing activities can be considered as the desired "effects with", and improvement of conceptual understanding reflected by an improvement of the behaviour in new situations as the desired "effects of" when focusing on concept learning.

In this chapter we do not report individual learning outcomes and the relation between these outcomes and student interaction. This subject was partly reported on and discussed in Van Boxtel, Van der Linden and Kanselaar (1997). We will focus on the influence of some task characteristics on the quality of student interaction. O'Donnell and Dansereau (1992) and Cohen (1994) state that task characteristics will influence the type and amount of processing and will, consequently, affect the outcomes of collaborative learning. Kumpulainen (1996) and Bennett and Dunne (1991) found that the quality of pupil's talk was closely linked with the nature of the task. In the next section we describe task characteristics in general and also in relation to the tasks we have chosen in our experiment.

Collaborative Learning Tasks

We chose a form of group work that can be described as completely collaborative. In completely collaborative peer-work groups students try to reach a common goal and share both tools and activities (Webb & Palincsar, 1996). Shared goals and tools can strengthen a positive interdependence between students (Cohen, 1986). There is no instruction that imposes a task division. Participants are on a comparable prior knowledge level. We decided to work with completely collaborative dyads, because we expected this form was most likely to create maximum opportunities for all students to communicate about the concepts. A larger group may encourage asymmetric participation or could possibly lead to cognitive overload.

Although we chose a collaborative learning task, such tasks still can differ from each other in: the kind of product that is asked for; the tools that are available and the script that is given to structure interaction. We describe and illustrate these task characteristics and we also present the tasks we decided to use in our research.

Product

Products can be concrete or verbal. Students can be asked, for example, to reach agreement about a statement that serves as input in a discussion in the classroom. Concrete products can facilitate interaction, because students can refer to parts of the product in the process of formation. However, making such a concrete product can also hinder a more conceptual oriented discourse.

When a lot of concrete actions are needed to construct the product, activity-related utterances can dominate student talk at the cost of abstract talk (Bennett & Dunne, 1991). Carter and Gail Jones (1994) concluded that when groups are engaged in making experiments this group work may lead to "hands-on-science" without "minds-on-science". Cohen (1994) suggests that products with answers not fully predetermined are more suitable for collaborative learning.

Within the subject we chose the domain of electricity. Students in the upper level of secondary school are supposed to have developed some initial understanding of concepts such as energy, voltage, current and resistance. To follow successfully the new course about electricity, it is important to activate prior knowledge and to improve the quality of this knowledge. We chose a concept mapping task and a poster task to achieve this learning goal. Concept mapping has been shown to help students in meaningful learning.

A concept map is a network in which nodes represent the concepts and labelled lines between concepts represent the relationships. We considered this task suitable, because it especially stimulates talk about meaningful relations. Roth and Roychoudhury (1993, 1994) conclude that concept mapping as a *collaborative* activity promotes communication and negotiation about meaning. We extended the concept map by asking students to integrate multiple representations, thus also the symbols, formulas and diagrams they associate with the concepts and relations.

We expected the concept map to be less powerful in provoking talk about relations of concepts with concrete phenomena. Therefore we chose the poster task. This task consisted of making a poster in which the working of an electric torch had to be explained using given concepts such as current and resistance. As both tasks require the making of a visible representation on one large paper it is not easy to divide the task into parts and strengthens interdependency between the collaborating students.

Tools

Concrete tools, such as schoolbooks, simulation programmes or materials to make an experiment, can offer students exploration and manipulation possibilities or can structure and sustain communication. The way tools represent information (words, graphs, pictures, animation) and the way this information is organised can affect the discourse of students. For example, diagrams can be social tools for achieving convergence of meaning in discourse, because they can support individual reasoning and facilitate negotiation of meaning (Roschelle, 1992).

We wanted students to make maximum use of their prior knowledge, consequently giving them no other tools, except for the cards with the electricity concepts on them and paper and pencils. The fact that students could only use one another as a source of information and feedback, we also believed, contributed to positive interdependency.

Script

A script describes the nature and sequence of activities the group has to be engaged in and can specify the roles played by the members of the group (O'Donnell et al., 1987). Structuring interaction can stimulate positive interdependency and can result in higher learning outcomes (Yager, Johnson & Johnson, 1985; O'Donnell et al., 1987). However, Cohen (1994) and Salomon and Globerson (1989) think that in case of concept learning, interaction should not be structured too much. To stimulate conceptual understanding, a free exchange of ideas, hypotheses and strategies is needed. Task division can hinder such a conceptually oriented interaction.

A collaborative learning task implies a common task therefore we did not script a task division. We expected that role division would be very artificial and probably less necessary, in the case of dyadic learning. We only scripted interaction by imposing the sequence of activities. Because it was some time since the students had worked with the electricity concepts, we thought it would be useful to let students prepare individually, before starting collaborative activities. We asked students to make an individual design for the concept map or poster.

Palincsar, Anderson and David (1993) used the same kind of script with a collaborative problem solving task. They report that this sequence was meant to activate prior knowledge and to stress the expectation that each student would make a contribution to the solution of the group. However, Palincsar, Anderson & David (1993) did not investigate the effect of this phase of individual preparation on student interaction. We expected that individual preparation could stimulate communication of personal understanding of the concepts and would increase the appearance of questioning (as students become aware of knowledge gaps or misunderstanding during individual preparation) and conflict (as students want to defend their personally constructed design).

Method

Subjects and Design

An experiment was carried out in order to investigate the influence of some task characteristics on the quality of student interaction. Subjects were 40 students of two physics classes of two different schools. We chose a pretest post test design. We taped student interaction on video. However, one dyad could not be videotaped.

The tenth grade students within each class were randomly assigned to sex-homogeneous dyads. The same number of dyads was randomly assigned to one of the following four conditions, containing five dyads per condition:

- concept map with individual preparation;
- concept map without individual preparation;
- poster with individual preparation;
- poster without individual preparation.

Instruments and Procedure

A pre-test about electricity had been administered five weeks before students carried out the task in dyads. The *Electricity Test* consisted of three units. The problem-solving unit contained six multiple-choice items, but students also had to account for their answers. The second unit was an essay question in which the working of an electric torch had to be described and explained. In the last unit students were asked to give a definition, in their own words, of six electricity concepts. We excluded the concept electric circuit from this unit, because students confused this concept with a switch (in Dutch the two words are almost the same). The test's reliability was 0.64 (Cronbach's alpha).

Next to prior knowledge, interest may also be considered an important student characteristic affecting the quality of learning processes and outcomes (Alexander & Kulikowich, 1994; Hidi, 1990; Krapp, Hidi & Renninger, 1996; Pintrich, Marx & Boyle, 1993; Tobias, 1994). A focus on understanding, which often goes together with interest, will probably influence the amount of engagement and persistence. To explore the influence of affective factors such as interest and anxiety, we administered the *Attitude Towards Physics Questionnaire*. This Likert-scale questionnaire was an adaptation of a questionnaire on mathematics (Cito, 1987). Items focused on interest in physics, the amount of pleasure taken in working within the domain of physics and the perceived relevance and difficulty of physics. A higher score on the questionnaire implied a more positive attitude towards physics. The Cronbach's alpha reliability was 0.92.

Students also received instruction about making a concept map and a poster two weeks before students worked together in dyads. The experiment was carried out in a separate room in school under the guidance of the experimenter in a session that lasted for a maximum of 45 minutes, depending on the time that students needed in order to complete the task. The post test took place during the following physics lesson. The pretest and post tests were parallel tests. Cronbach's alpha of the post-test was 0.66. The correlation between the tests was 0.75 (Pearson).

Coding of Verbal Interaction

The videotapes of the 19 dyads were transcribed in detail. The utterance was the basic unit of analysis. An utterance is distinguished from another utterance through a "perceptible" pause, comma or point and has a singular communicative function. The coding scheme to identify communicative functions was developed in a study by Erkens (1997) and was adjusted on the basis of a pilot study (Van Boxtel, 1997). This coding scheme contained the following communicative functions: statements, arguments, evaluations, questions, requests, proposals, confirmations, nonconfirmations, repeats, orders and off-task utterances. We categorised different types of arguments and questions. We described these subcategories in more detail elsewhere (Van Boxtel, Van der Linden & Kanselaar, 1998).

As we were also interested in the content of the discourse, we added categories that were content-related. We distinguished different proposition categories. A proposition was defined as an utterance in which the student makes a statement about the meaning or a relation of an electricity concept. The coding scheme contained propositions about one concept, propositions in which students relate a concept to another concept, to a concrete phenomenon or to another form of representation. We considered the amount of talk about relations of concepts as an important indicator of deep processing in collaborative learning. Inter-rater agreement (Cohen's Kappa) between two judges for the communicative functions categories reached 0.89 (353 utterances, from a transcript chosen at random, were coded by two judges) and for the proposition categories 0.83. A total of 302 propositions (from two transcripts chosen at random) were judged by a second person to identify incorrect propositions. Inter-rater agreement reached 0.87 (Cohen's Kappa).

Coding the protocols on this utterance level has its limitations. It does not give a description of the dynamics of the discourse, such as the way students constructed a reasoning or resolve a conflict. It fails to give insight in meaningful sequences. The contingencies of the actions of both partners also need to be categorised (Grossen, 1994). We were most interested in the contingencies reflecting deep processing.

Next to the amount of talk about relations among concepts, we identified three other indicators of deep processing. We made a distinction between three episodes on the basis of the codings of the utterances: question episodes, conflict episodes and reasoning episodes.

Question-episodes were identified by selection of the questions that were related to the meaning or the relations of the given concepts and which were coded on the local level of utterances as disjunctive questions, verification questions or open questions. We categorised no answers, short answers, and elaborated answers. Not answering a question may be the result of not hearing the question, ignoring the question or of a lack of knowledge. Elaborated answers are answers that contain more information than only "yes", "no" or a certain alternative and can consist of several sentences. To avoid overlapping categories, we decided to exclude questions that were part of a conflict or a reasoning episode.

Conflict episodes are identified on the basis of the following communicative functions: non confirmations, counter arguments and critical verification questions. A conflict is elaborated when one student explains or justifies his or her statement (individual elaboration) or when the students argue about the solution (collaborative elaboration). Resolution of a conflict can also be reached without elaboration.

For example, when a student immediately accepts the counterargument of his or her partner.

We describe reasoning as a sequence of utterances in which definitions, observations or hypotheses about electricity concepts are related. Reasoning contains at least one utterance of which the communicative function was coded as an argument. Besides reasoning that appears in answering a question or elaboration of a conflict, students can also construct a reasoning apart from questions and conflicts. Only these episodes were coded as reasoning episodes. Reasoning episodes with arguments constructed by only one of the participants were coded as *individually* constructed. A *co*-constructed reasoning is a reasoning that is constructed by contributions of *both* participants.

Four transcripts, chosen at random, were coded on the episodic level by a second coder (a total of 1553 utterances). The proportion of agreement was 0.79.

Research Questions

In the next section we report the results of our analyses of the transcripts and we present examples of the indicators of deep processing in student interaction. We shall try to answer the following questions:

(a) To what extent do indicators of deep processing (talk about meaningful relations of concepts, answering of questions, elaboration of conflict and construction of reasoning) appear in student interaction and can we distinguish between interactions that are more or less characterised by deep processing?
(b) How do the product that is asked for (concept map or poster) and the script that is given (imposing individual preparation or not) affect the appearance of deep processing? Is appearance of deep processing also influenced by prior knowledge and attitude towards physics?

Results

Indicators of Deep Processing

We expected that students would activate their prior knowledge about the electricity concepts and especially that they would talk about meaningful relations. Table 1 shows the amount of talk about the electricity concepts.

The average intensity of talk about concepts was three propositions per minute. There was a moderate variance; the intensity of talk ranged from a minimum of half a proposition per minute to a maximum of 6.2 propositions per minute. Most conversation was about relations between concepts. A further examination of these propositions revealed that a part was characterised by imprecise language. Usually, the formulation of relations became more precise and specific during the accomplishment of the task. "*Resistance and current strength are related*" is an

Table 1: Proposition categories ($N = 19$)

Categories	M	SD	Min	Max
Total number of propositions	79.32	46.21	14.00	153.00
Proposition – intensity*	3.13	1.42	0.51	6.23
— one concept	0.19	0.15	0.00	0.50
— relation between concepts	1.38	1.24	0.00	4.05
— relation with concrete phen.	0.79	0.73	0.00	2.78
— relation with other form of repr	0.77	0.63	0.05	2.08
— incorrect proposition	0.35	0.21	0.07	0.86

*Total number of propositions (all categories) divided by the time student interaction lasted (in minutes).

example of a proposition with low specification. A proposition with high specification is *"if resistance is small, the current strength is large"*. The proposition categories did not distinguish between descriptive and explanatory propositions about relations. We had the impression, however, that students did not talk much about the underlying microscopic mechanisms: the level of moving electrons. For example, students stated that a higher voltage results in a higher current strength, but most students did not talk about how this relation could be explained.

Students also formulated incorrect propositions. An average of 11% was incorrect of all propositions that a dyad formulated. Somewhat more than a third of the participants (37%) of all erroneous propositions were corrected during interaction. Another third (34%) was followed by an explicit confirmation or was further elaborated. The rest was not explicitly confirmed but also not corrected.

Question Episodes

In each dyad an average of 11% of all utterances consisted of questions. We distinguished between verification, disjunctive and open questions. Especially verification questions were frequent (59% of all questions). An example of such verification question is: *"an electron transports energy, doesn't it?"* These questions are important in monitoring common ground (Graesser, Person & Huber, 1993). The relatively high proportion of verification questions may also be due to the main goal of the task: prior knowledge activation and elaboration. To complete the task students could only use their prior knowledge, because no other information resources were available. As it was some time ago since they were confronted with these concepts, most students did know something about the meaning of the concepts but were very uncertain about their knowledge. The asking of verification questions suggests that students actively reflect on their prior knowledge. They assert their belief and at the same time check whether this belief is shared by the

Table 2: Means, Standard Deviations and Minimum and Maximum of Episodic Categories in frequencies and ratio* (N = 19)

Category	M		SD		Minimum		Maximum	
	f	*ratio*	*f*	*ratio*	*f*	*ratio*	*f*	*ratio*
Question Episodes	12.79	0.55	7.71	0.36	1	0.05	29	1.57
Answered questions	9.53	0.40	6.24	0.25	1	0.05	23	0.92
— elaborated answer	3.26	0.13	2.58	0.08	0	0.00	10	0.29
— short answer	6.26	0.28	4.41	0.21	1	0.02	18	0.83
Not answered	3.16	0.14	2.43	0.15	0	0.00	8	0.67
Conflict Episodes	4.68	0.18	3.61	0.15	0	0.00	11	0.67
Elaborated conflicts	3.26	0.12	2.64	0.08	0	0.00	8	0.26
— collaborative	1.68	0.05	1.83	0.06	0	0.00	5	0.18
— individual	1.58	0.06	1.46	0.06	0	0.00	5	0.25
Not elaborated	1.37	0.06	1.38	0.08	0	0.00	4	0.33
Reasoning Episodes	5.16	0.21	4.19	0.16	0	0.00	15	0.50
— individual	1.79	0.07	2.02	0.07	0	0.00	6	0.23
— co-constructed	3.37	0.14	2.43	0.10	0	0.00	9	0.35

*Ratio: frequency divided by the time during which the students worked at their task.

other. Table 2 shows the appearance of indicators of deep processing in the 19 dyads.

Question episodes were more frequent than conflict and reasoning episodes. A quarter of the question-episodes contained elaborated answers. Almost a quarter (24.7%) of the questions was not answered at all. However, it must be taken into account that, especially in the case of verification questions, it is possible that not giving an answer was perceived as a confirmation.

The next fragment contains an example of a question episode about the relation between resistance and the cross-section area of a resistor. In this episode an open question is followed by an elaborated answer. The same problem is discussed for a second time a couple of minutes later (not in the example). This may imply that the second student did not completely understand yet what her partner meant or did not yet agree with it. Apparently she is motivated to understand the relation.

Example of an Elaborated Answer in the Condition:
Poster with Individual Preparation.

Student 1: we can use this one, cross-section area of a resistor
Student 1: but I don't know what to write about it

Student 2: of a resistor, **but what do you mean**?   (open question)
Student 2: I didn't understand it
Student 1: look, there is a resistor
Student 1: if the resistance is high, then U is
Student 1: then something is smaller, but I don't know what it is
Student 1: it is something like this, resistance, when you compress it (gesticulates) then it is more dense, more molecules
Student 1: when you enlarge it, the molecules are further away from each other and the current can go more easier through it
Student 1: it's something like that
Student 2: oh, oh yes.

Conflict Episodes

Most conflicts were elaborated. Out of a total of 89 conflicts 29% were not elaborated. As shown in Table 2, individual elaboration occurred almost as frequently as collaborative elaboration (argumentation). The next example of an elaborated conflict comes from the interaction of a dyad in which conflict was very frequent. This conflict is about whether a wire is a resistor or not. The conflict was elaborated through argumentation: both students justified/explained their point of view. Finally the first student agrees with the proposal of his partner. He says that the wish to finish the task in time is the reason he agrees. He is not really convinced. The conflict already had taken considerable time. Thus, although the students resolved the conflict, they did not reach a common understanding. In such a case, good time-management can be in conflict with the construction of (a shared) conceptual understanding through a serious engagement in conflict.

Example of a Collaborative Elaboration of a Conflict in the Condition: Concept Map with Individual Preparation.

Student 1: look, current strength has to do with sort of material (points), length (points) and cross-section (points)
Student 1: I am sure about it
Student 2: the length of what? (points)?
Student 1: the length of sort of material (points)
Student 2: yes
Student 1: of the wire
Student 2: yes a wire is a resistor too
Student 1: **a wire is not a resistor, a copper**   (nonconfirmation)
Student 2: because it has to go through it
Student 1: a copper wire is not a resistor
Student 2: of course it is
Student 2: copper is resistance

Student 2: it has to go through it
Student 1: copper is not a resistor, it is a conductor
Student 2: a conductor also is
Student 2: when I connect a copper plate with two wires, what is it, according to you?
Student 1: a conductor
Student 2: a resistor, the current has to go through it, it has difficulty in going through it, even if it conducts
Student 1: to go through copper?
Student 2: yes because some materials conduct better than others, because when I have iron, for example, I don't know it, but when it conducts better than copper, then it is easier for the current to go through it and consequently there is a smaller resistance
Student 1: yes (indignant)
Student 2: resistance only hinders current in going through it
Student 2: that is only what current means
Student 2: thus actually a wire too
Student 1: but you can also say it the other way around
Student 1: there are conductors, conductors of different current strength
(further explanation of student 1)

Reasoning Episodes

Arguments are the basic units of reasoning episodes. An average of 23% of the utterances in student interaction consisted of arguments. However, there was a large variance; the percentages ranged from a minimum of 8% to a maximum of 39% of all utterances. Table 2 shows that collaborative reasoning was more frequent than individual reasoning. The following example illustrates the process of co-constructing reasoning. Both students contribute to the reasoning. The first student relates the voltage source to the electric circuit. Then, the second student relates the concept of voltage to the voltage source and consequently to the concepts energy and current. Finally, the first student relates the concept of current to the concept of energy.

Example of Co-constructed Reasoning in the Condition: Concept Map Without Individual Preparation.

Student 2: an electric circuit has got a voltage source too, hasn't it?
Student 1: yes, actually it has
Student 2: (draws)
Student 2: and it consists of (writes)
Student 2: the voltage source has, gives, gives
Student 1: the voltage source gives voltage   (argument continuation)

Student 2: and energy   (argument continuation)
Student 1: yes also
Student 2: and current isn't it?   (argument continuation)
Student 2: the voltage source also gives current
Student 1: and due to this current, there is energy   (argument conclusion)

Coherence between Indicators of Deep Processing

Reasoning implies talk about relations. We pooled the data across the conditions to explore whether indicators of deep processing were correlated, due to the small sample size in each condition. Talk about relations between concepts was significantly correlated with reasoning episodes ($r = 0.85$, $p = 0.00$, $n = 19$). Talk about relations was also related with elaboration of conflict ($r = 0.60$, $p = 0.01$, $n = 19$). Question episodes (ratios) correlated with the appearance of conflicts ($r = 0.73$, $p = 0.00$, $n = 19$). Elaboration of conflict was not significantly related with answering questions ($r = 0.28$, $p = 0.24$, $n = 19$). However, not answering questions was statistically significantly related with *not* elaborating conflicts ($r = 0.88$, $p = 0.00$, $n = 19$). This strong correlation may indicate the presence of dyads in which problems are not acknowledged, in which students do not ask, answer questions, and avoid conflicts or resolve conflict without elaboration. In such interactions there appears hardly any deep processing. The variance in the appearance of deep processing may be due in part to task characteristics and learner characteristics such as prior knowledge and attitude toward physics. The influence of these factors will be discussed in the next section.

Factors Influencing Deep Processing

The Influence of Task Characteristics

Analyses of variance were conducted to test for effects of the product that was asked for (concept map or poster) and the script that was given (imposing individual preparation or not) on the appearance of indicators of deep processing. We expected that scripting individual preparation would result in more question asking and conflict. There was an effect of the script on the percentage of utterances that was identified as verification questions. Dyads in which students prepared individually, asked more verification questions ($F(1, 15) = 6.46, p = 0.02$). However, the analyses of variance revealed no significant effect on the number of conflicts ($F(1, 15) = 0.51, p = 0.50$).

In 10 dyads students prepared individually by making a design for the concept map or poster. When and how were the designs used during interaction? Individual designs were used in an average of eight times. We identified five general ways of using the designs during the accomplishment of the common task (see Table 3). The designs were mostly used during the first phase of collaboration. In this phase

Table 3: Examples of the use of individual designs in the conditions with individual preparation ($N = 10$).

Use of individual designs	Example
Exchanging ideas (mostly at the beginning of the task)	*I put the electrons among these (points at his design)*
Supporting a proposal	*Shall we do it this way? (points at her design)*
Supporting a confirmation	*Yes I am sure it does, because I wrote exactly the same (shows her design)*
Supporting a statement in case of a conflict	*(consults her design) I think this (points) is the electric circuit*
Opening a new topic	*What shall we do with the rest? (looks at his design) What do they mean by length?*

students show and explain their own work. The designs were further used as an extra tool during interaction to support proposals, confirmations and criticism and to choose new topics that have to be dealt with.

Regarding the product, we expected differences in the kind of propositions that are formulated. We found that students who made the concept map, talked more about relations between different concepts ($F(1, 15) = 19.18$, $p = 0.00$), whereas students who made the poster talked more about relations of the concepts with concrete phenomena ($F(1, 15) = 9.07$, $p = 0.01$). We also found some unexpected product effects: students who made a concept map talked more about relations of concepts to other forms of representation ($F(1, 15) = 5.59$, $p = 0.03$). How can we explain the fact that students who made a concept map, talked more intensely about concepts (all proposition categories taken together and divided by the number of minutes students worked on the task) than the students who made a poster ($F(1, 15) = 6.90$, $p = 0.02$)?

A closer examination of the protocols, revealed that there appeared more and longer phases in which students were writing or drawing in the dyads that were working on a poster. Some students wrote short stories near the concepts linked to parts of the electric torch and spent considerable time drawing an electrical circuit inside the electric torch. The concept map, however, did not ask for those kind of drawing activities, and only asked for short sentences to describe the relations between the concepts.

Further, student interaction of dyads who made a concept map, contained more conflicts ($F(1, 15) = 4.99$, $p = 0.04$) and more collaboratively elaborated conflicts ($F(1, 15) = 5.28$, $p = 0.04$). It is possible that the need to resolve a conflict is felt stronger by students who made a concept map. Talking mostly about relations between certain physical quantities, these students almost always have to choose between two opposite directions. For example, the current strength is either directly or inversely proportional to resistance. And voltage has something to do with resistance or not. The product is asking for a clear answer. On the poster, students can write a short story about each concept, whereby it is much easier to combine different points of view. It seemed that students who made a poster could more easily ignore a conflict.

The Influence of Prior Knowledge and Attitude Towards Physics

Due to the small samples in each condition ($n = 5$) we only explored the effects of prior knowledge and attitude towards physics on the quality of interaction on the *individual level* of utterances ($n = 38$). We pooled the data of the four conditions and investigated if there were significant correlations between the pretest score and the score on the attitude questionnaire, and the number of propositions about relations of concepts, questions and arguments. These categories were important basic elements of the indicators of deep processing. There were no significant differences on the pretest and the questionnaire between the four conditions. We found a significant correlation between pretest scores and the numbers of arguments ($r = 0.34$, $p = 0.04$). Students with higher scores on the pretest formulated more arguments (all subcategories of arguments taken together). Scores on the attitude questionnaire were only significantly related to one subcategory of arguments: arguments that students continue a previous proposition with ($r = 0.40$, $p = 0.02$). A positive attitude towards physics also went together with the formulation of more propositions with which concepts were related to one another or to another form of representation ($r = 0.38$, $p = 0.02$; and $r = 0.43$, $p = 0.01$).

Conclusion and Discussion

We showed that indicators of deep processing, such as activation of prior knowledge, the recognition of problems and the attempts to look for meaningful relations can also be described in the context of collaborative learning. We suggested that deep processing is reflected in talk about relations, construction of reasoning, answering questions and elaboration of conflict. In general, the tasks that were used in this research elicited such activities. However, although students mostly talked about relations, these relations hardly touched the explanatory level. Therefore, it may be useful to make a distinction between different levels of deep processing.

To engage students in talk about explanations it may be necessary that the product that is asked for requires talk at this level. We have seen that the product that is asked for influences the kind of talk during collaboration. Although the concept map and poster were very much alike, the concept map elicited more talk about the electricity concepts, especially talk about relations of concepts. The concept map may be extended, by asking explicitly for explanations. In our present research we investigate the effects of such concept mapping task.

We also showed some evidence that individual preparation affects student interaction. The results show that imposing individual preparation did affect the number of verification questions and gave students an extra tool that supported the exchange of ideas and the recognition of conflicts. Question asking and answering turned out to be the most frequent indicator of deep processing. A possible explanation for the fact that elaborated answers appeared less frequent than short answers is that most of the questions were verification questions. On the other hand, some verification questions were followed by more explanatory answers. As has already been mentioned, verification questions are not only important as possible opportunities to elaborate, but are also important to monitor and construct a common conceptual framework.

The fact that we did find some significant correlation between the presence or lack of talk about relations, answering questions and elaboration of conflict suggests that these characteristics of student interaction often appear together in the case of collaborative learning. Additional research, with a larger number of subjects working on different kinds of collaborative tasks, is needed to specify more precisely the relations between the presumed indicators of deep processing.

We think that deep processing in a collaborative learning environment especially implies activities that can be considered *constructive* and *collaborative*. Constructive interaction is reflected by the appearance of talk about relations, the answering of questions, elaboration of conflict, construction of reasoning and probably also correction of incorrect propositions. Collaborative interactions are characterised by a *common* focus on understanding, that is not only reflected in a large symmetry in participation, but also in a high number of co-constructed answers, co-constructed reasonings and collaboratively elaborated conflicts. Then, *both* students are at the same time actively engaged in deep processing activities.

Sizmur and Osborne (1997) analysed the verbal interaction of primary school children, working together on a concept map, and made a comparable distinction between elaboration that was achieved individually or collaboratively. He found that the collaboratively elaborated exchanges were more likely to result in incorporation of a scientifically valid proposition in the concept map. It would be interesting to investigate if collaborative elaborations are also related to individual learning outcomes.

To stimulate deep processing in student interaction we have to know why some students do not elaborate on each others' statements or do not answer questions or elaborate conflicts. In particular the kind of product that was asked for influenced the quality of student interaction. The concept map seems to be a stronger task for eliciting talk about concepts, conflict and elaboration of conflict. The results of the correlational analyses suggest that prior knowledge and the attitude towards physics also have an influence on the indicators of deep processing in collaborative learning, indicated by talking about relations and elaboration through reasoning. These findings are consistent with results of research on the effects of prior knowledge and motivational factors on deep processing with students learning individually.

In our present research we try to gain more insight in the way students use textbooks as an extra tool during a concept mapping task. Are the books used when students are not able to answer a question or to resolve their conflict (due to lack of appropriate knowledge)? Do they enhance the correction of erroneous propositions? We expect that scripting the use of such tools is needed, because the students may trust these resources too much.

Finally, the increasing interest in the processes that take place in collaborative learning environments has heightened the need for instruments to analyse these processes. We tried to develop a valid and reliable instrument that focuses on the identification of indicators of deep processing, regarding tasks that aimed at improvement of conceptual understanding. A challenging task for further research is the development of instruments to analyse student interaction, not only to identify the amount of deep processing but also the appearance of, for example, activities that are important for learning certain skills. We can only gain insight into the relation between characteristics of the collaborative learning environment and student interaction, and between student interaction and learning outcomes, if we analyse this interaction in an appropriate way.

12

Language for Thinking: A Study of Children Solving Reasoning Test Problems Together

Rupert Wegerif and Neil Mercer

Introduction

This chapter investigates the language of effective reasoning. We focus on the talk of a group of three nine year old children working together on the problems that make up a test of reasoning. This group were part of a larger study in which sixty children were taught the ground rules of "exploratory talk" — a type of talk in which reasoning is made explicit. The design of this study enabled us to compare the talk of children before and after our ten week intervention programme. Our analysis shows some of the ways in which the language of those children changed, from which we draw conclusions about the use of language as a tool for constructing shared understanding.

Overview of Theme and Research Question

Influenced by Habermas's concept of communicative rationality (Habermas, 1991, p. 89; White, 1988; Habermas, 1995) and the arguments of other philosophers and communication theorists (for example Rorty, 1991, p. 39; Burbules & Rice, 1992), we have argued elsewhere that reasoning is dialogical and can be characterised through inter-personal orientations and associated ground rules (Wegerif & Mercer, 1997a). By calling our description of reason "dialogical" we mean that it is not a model of reason drawn from the outside, after the event, as if reason was a closed and finished system. Instead, we have tried to give a description of discursive rules and orientations that inform a free and open encounter between different perspectives and ideas. This "dialogical" description of reason contrasts with more "monological" descriptions — notably those associated with Piaget (e.g. Piaget 1971/47).

We have combined this conception of reasoning embodied in discourse with a neo-Vygotskian view of individual cognitive development as induction into a social practice. This leads to the notion that learning to reason can be described as induction into that social practice that best embodies reasoning. This definition of reasoning in terms of pragmatic orientations and ground-rules of communication is very different from more established descriptions of reasoning found in educational psychology. The idea of learning to reason as induction into a situated social practice of this kind questions the role given by others to "decontextualisation" (Donaldson, 1992; Wood, 1988) and also that given to literacy and to a literate mode of communication (e.g. Olson, 1986). The argument explored in this study is that most of what has traditionally been meant by the idea of "learning to reason" can be understood as learning to use language in a particular way.

Exploratory Talk and Reasoning

If it is to be taught, then reasoning as a social practice has to be specified rather more closely than has been done by philosophers such as Habermas and Rorty. To do this, we have used the concept of "exploratory talk", a concept whose origin lies in empirical studies of classroom interaction. Here is our own recent definition of exploratory talk:

> *Exploratory talk* is that in which partners engage critically but constructively with each other's ideas. Statements and suggestions are sought and offered for joint consideration. These may be challenged and counter-challenged, but challenges are justified and alternative hypotheses are offered. In exploratory talk, *knowledge is made publicly accountable* and *reasoning is visible in the talk.* (Adapted from Mercer, 1995, p. 104.)

As with Habermas's dialogical approach to characterising reasoning, exploratory talk involves a fundamental orientation. It contrasts with *disputational talk*, in which participants defend their self-identity and show little interest in mutual understanding and *cumulative talk* in which participants establish mutuality or intersubjectivity but in an uncritical way. Like cumulative talk, exploratory talk involves a positive orientation towards the other person but with the ground rule that critical challenges are allowed and are to be responded to with reasons. (This characterisation reflects Habermas's characterisation of communicative rationality in his Theory of Communicative Action; Habermas, 1991). Our interpretation of these three types of talk as representing fundamental orientations to the other in dialogue is discussed and illustrated in Wegerif and Mercer (1997a).

We have attempted to represent exploratory talk as a list of ground-rules which participants in dialogue most follow. In doing so, we were influenced by three factors: conceptual considerations, particular those raised by Habermas (Wegerif, 1999), the literature on research on effective collaborative learning (see review in Mercer, 1995: pp. 90–95) and our experience in classrooms working closely with teachers (see Dawes, 1997). Out of this combination of sources the following ground rules for generating exploratory talk are provisionally proposed:

1   all relevant information is shared
2   the group seeks to reach agreement
3   the group takes responsibility for decisions
4   reasons are expected
5   challenges are acceptable
6   alternatives are discussed before a decision is taken
7   all in the group are encouraged to speak by other group members

The first three rules in the list are ground rules that are shared with cumulative talk; rules that serve to bind the group, share information together and construct knowledge together through seeking agreement. Rules four and five focus on the explicit reasoning that characterises exploratory talk as opposed to other types of talk. The role of challenges is important in distinguishing between cumulative, disputational and exploratory orientations. In exploratory talk challenges stimulate joint reasoning, while in cumulative talk they are experienced as disruptive and often lead to a loss of cooperation and a switch into disputational talk. In disputational talk participants may still offer arguments but are in fact focusing on "winning" rather than on understanding or solving a problem together.

Ground rule six, that alternatives are discussed, reflects the findings of research on collaborative problem solving, particularly that of Kruger (1993) who found that groups which performed best were those which considered alternatives before deciding on solutions or courses of action. In contradistinction to some researchers (e.g. Howe et al., 1992) we argue that this generation of alternative views does not necessarily imply that there must be different initial conceptions of the problem held by collaborators. In our view, alternative perspectives on a problem can be generated by joint intellectual activity as people talk together. The last rule, ground rule seven, was a product of empirical experience working with groups of children. We found that specifying the abstract right to participate (a feature of Habermas's characterisation of the ideal speech situation Habermas, 1990: p. 87), was not sufficient. In practice some children needed to be actively encouraged by their peers to speak and to put forward their views for joint consideration. These ground rules again emphasise our focus on the generative power of the interaction as opposed to an emphasis on the prior dispositions and views of the participants.

Aims

One aim of the study as a whole was to test the hypothesis that children learn to reason individually, in situations such as that of individual non-verbal reasoning tests, through prior participation in social reasoning. To do so, we looked for relationships between the kind of language children used when jointly tackling reasoning problems and their success (jointly and individually) in solving them. That is the part of the study that we focus upon in this paper. We approach this through an open-ended exploration of the changes that occurred in the talk of one group of children who learnt to reason together more effectively.

Methods

Experimental Design

The design of the study allowed for a systematic comparison to be made between Year 5 children (eight and nine years old) in target classes (who followed the TRAC programme) and Year 5 children in control classes (who did not). 60 children in three middle schools in Milton Keynes were matched with control classes, of 64 children of similar social backgrounds in three other local schools. We gathered two main kinds of data: video-recordings of the discussions of focal groups in all the classes and scores on Raven's tests for all the children.

The Intervention Programme

The programme consists of a series of nine lessons. Each lesson is designed to last for about one hour and focuses on one or more of the ground rules of exploratory talk. The first few lessons also deal with skills such as listening, sharing information and co-operating, while later lessons encourage children to make critical arguments for and against different cases. The children are given opportunities to practise discussing alternative ideas, giving and asking for reasons and ensuring that all members of the group are invited to contribute. Some computer-based group activities are included, using specially-designed software.

Discourse Analysis

In each of the four target classes, one "focal group" of three children was video-recorded as they worked on the Raven's SPM test, before and after the intervention. In conjunction with qualitative discourse analysis of the kind developed and described by the present authors and associates (Edwards & Mercer, 1987; Mercer & Fisher, 1993; Mercer, 1996b; Wegerif & Mercer, 1997b) a computer-based text analysis concordancer was used to search for pre- and post-intervention differences in the talk of these focal groups. This method (described in more detail in Wegerif & Mercer, 1997b) involves integrating qualitative analysis of the full transcript with the abstraction of "key words in context" in order to generalise significant features and compare different transcripts. This approach thus combines qualitative and quantitative analyses of discourse.

Results

Findings of the Study as a Whole

Our findings provided support for the claim that exploratory talk helps children to reason together. Two further claims were also supported by the findings of the study: that children's use of exploratory talk can be increased by structured intervention; and that individual scores on a standard non-verbal reasoning test are significantly increased for children who take part in the intervention.

Evidence for the claim that the intervention encouraged more exploratory talk was provided by a computer-based comparison of post-intervention and pre-intervention talk. Initial analysis had shown exploratory talk to be associated with the use of certain key terms ("because", "agree" and "I think"), and by the occurrence of much longer utterances (over 100 characters in transcription). The incidence of the key terms and long utterances was found to be four times greater in post-intervention talk of target focal groups, while no such increase was found in the talk of control focal groups.

Evidence to support the hypothesis that children learn to reason individually through prior participation in joint reasoning activity was provided by statistical analysis of the results of individual reasoning tests. An analysis of covariation (with post-test scores as the dependent variable and pre-test scores as covariate) revealed that the gains made by the individual target class children were significantly greater than those made by children in control classes ($F = 3.141; p = 0.04$). These results are reported in more detail in Mercer, Wegerif and Dawes (1999) and Wegerif, Mercer and Dawes (in press).

Findings in Relation to Effective Reasoning

The overall results showed that teaching the ground rules of exploratory talk led to changes in the talk of the children and to improved reasoning. To find out more about that talk, which was associated with successful reasoning, we carried out the following interpretative analysis.

We took one of the target groups for closer analysis, because that group (George, Susan and Trisha) showed the greatest pre/post-intervention change in score on the Raven's SPM test, from 39 to 47 (The SPM test consists of 60 test items and so is scored out of 60). For that group we also had the scores of individual members on the other version of a similar test, the Raven's CPM (which has 36 items and so is scored out of 36). Both sets of scores were then converted to a common 36 point interval scale, following the procedure described in the Raven's test manual (Raven, Raven & Court, 1995: p. 64). It was then noted that in the pre-intervention tests the group score was *lower* than the highest individual score (31 to 32). In the post-intervention tests, however, the group score was slightly *higher* than the highest individual score in the group (34 compared to 33). This suggested that the striking improvement in group score after the intervention could not be accounted for by a change in the quality of reasoning of one individual in Group 1, but was a product of a change in the way the group reasoned together. In other words the overall design of our study gave us a means to avoid the confusing variable of individual reasoning ability in order to focus on improved reasoning that occurred through a change in group process.

We initially focused our discourse analysis on the talk of George, Susan and Trisha when they worked on eight problems of the Raven's SPM test. These eight problems were chosen because they were problems that had been answered incorrectly before the intervention, but had been correctly solved by the group after the intervention. Here, for illustration, is an example of the group's pre-intervention talk (Transcript 1, which failed to produce the correct answer) and also of their post-intervention talk (Transcript 2, which led to them finding the correct answer). On both occasions, they are dealing with the same problem (B12, shown in Figure 1 below).

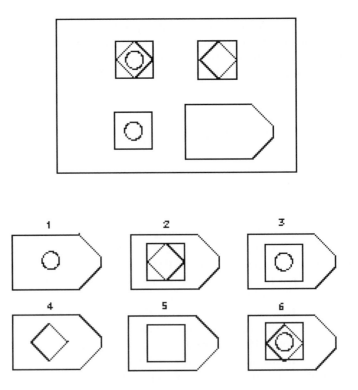

Figure 1: Problem B12. Raven's SPM

Transcript 1: Pre-intervention Talk in Group 1 School A1 on Raven's SPM Problem B12

(Note: for the sake of intelligibility, punctuation has been added to all transcripts. Contextual information is presented in parentheses)

George:	B12
Susan:	We haven't done that.
Trisha:	(*giggles*) this is where your Mum can see what you're really like at school George.
Trisha:	Square and diamond, it's 2
George:	No it's not
Trisha:	It is 2
George:	No it's not
Trisha:	It is
George:	No it's not
Susan:	It's that one 6
Trisha:	It is
George:	No it's not it's got to be a square and a circle
Trisha:	It's that, it has to be that, it has to be that, it has to be 6 because look they've only got that (*pointing to the pictures*)
Susan:	Look first they are starting with one of them things over (*pointing*) and then it has to be black
George:	Right, 6
Susan:	No it isn't George
Trisha:	That's number 2 because it goes bigger and bigger and bigger (*Trisha is looking at the next question*)
Susan:	It isn't George look at that one, no it isn't George (*George is writing "6", which is the wrong answer. Susan pushes him*)
George:	Susan! All right someone else be the writer then
Susan:	Me (*forcibly takes paper*)
Trisha:	No, Susan you have to sit in this chair to be the writer (*Trisha takes pen*)
Trisha:	Give it to George because he's quicker at it
Susan:	Give me the pen (*takes the pen*)
Susan:	Are we finished on that one, are we on that one now
Trisha:	You're not allowed to do it
George:	Let Trisha have a go when we get up to E (*Turn to next exercise*)
Susan:	Well what do you think it is you dur brain? (*addressed to George*)

Transcript 2: Post-intervention Talk in Group 1 School A1 on Raven's SPM Problem B12

Susan:	Set C
Trisha:	No we ain't done B

Trisha: That has got to be a diamond, a square with a diamond with a circle in that one, number 6, do you agree?
George: No, what do you mean?
Trisha: OK no it's got to be square
Susan: I think it's number 6, that's the one
George: No it ain't
Susan: I think it's number 6
Trisha: No 'cause it's got to swing round every time, so there is a circle in it
Susan: Yes but it hasn't got a circle in there has it and that one has (*indicating*)
          (*3 sec pause. Concentrated faces*)
George: I think it's number …
Trisha: I think it's number 4 to be honest
George: I don't I think it's number 6
Trisha: I don't, I think it's number 3 look because that one (*pointing*) has that in the middle and it's got a half one in the middle
George: Complicated ain't it?
Susan: No because that one is that, I think it's that one
George: No because look at that and look at that (*pointing*) they are the same, you can't have two the same and it's got that one on, look Sue, it's got that one on and it's got that one on so it's out of them three.
Susan: That one, one, 'cause that's a …
George: Yes but it's got to be that
Susan: It's that because look that's got a square so it's just got to be empty
George: With no circle in so it's just got to be an empty square
Susan: No they are just normal boxes
Trisha: Look that's got a triangle, that's got a square, look that's got a square with a diamond with a circle in, that's got a square with a diamond in and that's got a square with a circle in so that's got to be a square
George: I don't understand this at all
Trisha: Because look on that they've taken the circle out yes? So on that you are going to take the circle out because they have taken the circle out of that one
George: On this they have taken the circle out and on this they have taken the diamond out and on this they have put them both in, so it should be a blank square because look it goes circle square
Susan: It's got to be a blank square. Yeah it is. Mrs Dawes is coming. (*inaudible whisper*)
George: Do you agree on number 5, do you agree on 5? (*George writes "5", which is the correct answer*)
George: Who is doing C? Susan, right let's have these here, C1

Commentary

In the pre-intervention talk of Transcript 1, George challenges Trisha's first suggestion ("It is 2") without giving a reason. Trisha offers no further justification for her suggestion. This leads into a series of exchanges typical of the type of talk we call "disputational", in which participants simply assert their opposed views without reasoning. Susan then suggests "It is that one 6" and this is taken up by Trisha, and both she and Susan offer reasons. "6" is apparently agreed upon, and George writes it down. However, Susan then appears to change her mind without saying what her new opinion is (or she may be objecting to him writing the answer down before checking properly with her and Trisha: no reason is made explicit). There is then a dispute about who should be writing the answers on the answer sheet.

Measurable Differences in the Talk

Transcript 2 illustrates some ways that the talk of the same children changed after doing the intervention programme. Compared with their pre-intervention talk, there are more long turns at talk, as more elaborate explanations are given. Again, Trisha is the first to propose an answer, but this time she does this not as a statement ("it is 2") but as an elaborated hypothesis with a question encouraging debate ("That has got to be a diamond, a square with a diamond with a circle in that one, number 6, do you agree?"). George asks for more explanation. This time his challenge prompts Trisha to attempt to be more explicit. Through this effort Trisha appears to see that she is wrong and changes her claim. George and Susan again engage in a "disputational" exchange but this is short-lived. After a pause (perhaps for individual thought) the children return to using language to think explicitly together about the problem. They come to agree that it is a kind of subtraction problem, ("taking the x out of y") and so find the correct answer.

Many more of the essential features of exploratory talk — as represented by our "ground rules" — are evident in the post-intervention talk than in the pre-intervention talk. Explicit reasons for claims are given, challenges are offered with reasons, several alternatives are considered before a decision is reached, and the children can be seen seeking to reach agreement together. Explicit reasoning may be represented in talk by the incidence of some specific linguistic forms, and we can see here some "key features": the hypothetical nature of claims is indicated by a preceding "I think", reasons are linked to claims by the use of "because" or "cause" and agreement is sought through the question "do you agree?" Explicit reasoning requires the linking of clauses and leads here to the incidence of more longer utterances in the post intervention talk. This group solved a total of eight new problems in the post-test which they had failed to solve in the pre-test. When we compare talk that led to the group solving these problems correctly with talk which led to wrong answers, we find that there is a clear association with the relative incidence of these key linguistic features. This can be seen from Table 1 (below) which compares the number of long utterances (where "long" is defined through taking an arbitrary cut-off point of being 100 characters in length or more when transcribed), and the incidence of "because", "agree" and "I think".

Table 1: Incidence of key features: comparing talk leading to correct answers with talk leading to incorrect answers for Group 1

Key linguistic feature	Incidence in talk leading to incorrect answers	Incidence in talk leading to correct answers
long turns at talk	0	11
"Because" and "cause"	6	26
"I think"	1	24
"agree'	3	18

Constructing Shared Verbal Context

A computer-based concordancer is useful for making quantitative measures of the incidence of key words in recorded talk but it is not limited to this role. By making access to the context of key words easier it can also help to explore changes in the way in which words are being used. We used a concordancing programme to pull out a list of all the utterances containing our chosen key words in order to explore how the context of the use of these words changed. We found that words such as "because", that is words introducing a reason clause, were used to point to verbal context in the more successful talk whereas in less successful talk "because look" frequently occurred on its own pointing at the physical context. This different way of using "because" is illustrated in the transcript extracts already given:

Trisha: It's that, it has to be that, it has to be that, it has to be 6 because look they've only got that (*pointing to the pictures*)
(Unsuccessful talk. Pre-intervention)
Trisha: Because look on that they've taken the circle out yes? So on that you are going to take the circle out because they have taken the circle out of that one.
(Successful talk. Post-intervention)

In comparing these two ways of using because we see a shift in the talk from pointing to the physical context to pointing to a verbal context which the children construct together. This shift is also apparent in the far greater number of long turns at talk found in the more successful talk.

   In our analysis of discourse, long turns of talk turned out to be the most reliable indicators of the incidence of exploratory talk. Both disputational and cumulative talk do not encourage long turns. Reasoning, however, requires longer turns, as claims have to be backed up by sufficient support, which in practice means linking clauses together in a single utterance. We found over one hundred long turns at talk in all our data and only three of these did not include explicit reasoning — these three were all off-task stories about incidents in the lives of the children.

Creating Tools to Think With

The construction of shared verbal context can be seen in the long turn we have just quoted and George's response to it.

Trisha: Because look on that they've taken the circle out yes? So on that you are going to take the circle out because they have taken the circle out of that one

George: On this they have taken the circle out and on this they have taken the diamond out and on this they have put them both in, so it should be a blank square because look it goes circle square

Here Trisha uses language to construct something new that cannot be pointed to in the physical picture. She constructs a relationship between the parts of the picture, which she describes as a process of "taking the circle out". If we turn back to picture B12 we can see that recognising this relationship is the answer to the problem. Now that Trisha has named this relationship it can be pointed to but only using language. It can now be pointed to in the shared verbal context that has been created within the group. And this is what we see George do in the next utterance where he echoes Trisha's words. The process of "taking x out of y" is a version of the more abstract idea of subtraction. Subtraction cannot be seen directly in the physical world but it can be constructed in language. In these transcripts we can see the children apparently led to create (or to re-discover) this idea for themselves through the application of social ground-rules which support reasoning. Applying the ground-rules of exploratory talk leads them to shift their focus of attention from the physical context into the context of shared language. This new context can contain a new kind of entity, words referring to relationships or processes linking physical objects. In the talk we see one of these new entities being constructed together and used as a tool to solve a problem.

The creative ways in which a concordancer can be used to explore differences in transcripts can be illustrated by focusing on the word "out". Before looking in detail at the construction of meaning in the talk of the group of children we did not think that the word "out" would prove significant. Having found "out" being used in collocation with "take" in a way that helped the children understand the Raven's problems we explored other collocations of out to see if they too were significant. We first looked to see if the way in which the word "out" was used was affected by the intervention programme teaching exploratory talk. On a simple count of words "out" is used more in the less successful talk of the group before the intervention programme. But it is not used to refer to processes. In the more successful post-intervention talk it is mainly used to refer to processes. In eight of the ten occurrences "out" is collocated with "take", "taking" or "going" to refer to an abstract relationship found in the problem.

Contexts of Occurrence for OUT for Group 1

Pre-intervention
1   in it out and you'll find out,
2   out and you'll find out, number 1 (pointing)
3   5 because that goes out there
4   has that half cut out so it is number
5   just cross it out, put a cross in
6   had to cross it out.
7   You've been out the lines, that's it
8   we had to read out our Rainforest poems, I made
9   look the circles right out, the circles out here,
10 right out, the circles out here, the circles in
11 right, the squares right out here so it's got

Post-intervention
1   then they are going out aren't they?
2   That would be going out fat, they are going
3   fat, they are going out fat but all that
4   and you will find out
5   one on so its out of them three.
6   they've taken the circle out yes? so on that
7   to take the circle out because they have taken
8   have taken the circle out of that one.
9   have taken the circle out and on this they
10 have taken the diamond out and on this

This use of language to make relationships and processes visible was generally found in the more successful post-intervention talk of all the groups. Expressions such as "the same", "getting fatter", "that and that make that" or "add that to that and you get that" were all used.

Discussion

The study reported here demonstrates the effectiveness of the ground rules of exploratory talk for supporting shared reasoning. It also sheds light on three contrastive issues raised in prior research on learning to reason. We will consider each in turn.

The first issue concerns *dialogical vs. monological conceptions of reasoning*. In the talk of the group of children given above we can see the verbal construction of an abstract relationship, subtraction or "taking x out of y", such that the children are able to see this abstract relation directly and so solve the problem. However they are only able to construct this abstract understanding because of a shift in the way in which they orient towards each other. Our teaching programme did not teach how to recognise abstract structures; it taught ground-rules such as listening with respect and responding to challenges, not with anger but with an attempt to share perspectives. In the transcripts we can see how applying these social rules leads to the construction of shared understanding. The debate between these two conceptions of reason will continue but our study at least suggests that the dialogical approach, focusing on orientation and ground rules, is useful in education and that dialogical reasoning precedes the development of monological structures.

The second issue is whether the development of *reasoning is a process of "decontextualisation" or one of "recontextualisation"*. Our findings could be used to support the "decontextualisation". But, paradoxically, the decontextualisation that we found was heavily contextualised. It was a product of the induction of children into reasoning as a social process defined by shared social rules, which were communicated by a teacher and constantly, referred to in the talk. When, for example, they asked each other what they each thought and if they agreed, they were implicitly referring back to lessons in which these ground rules had been emphasised. The notion that the shift from a shared perceptual context to shared verbal context is a process of "decontextualisation" implies that language is somehow not real or is transparent to the researcher. In fact the children use language to construct together very specific new contexts. Trisha, George and Susan understand the solution to problem B12 not by creating a pure abstraction but by using the words "taken out" in a shared way as a tool to think together. So when George says:

> "On this they have taken the circle out and on this they have taken
> the diamond out ... so it should be a blank square"

Both Trisha and Susan know that the "taken the diamond out" refers to the same process as the "taken the circle out" and that applying this process again gives them the correct answer, which is the blank square. This process of "taking out" is not physically visible but it has a concrete reality in the actual words used and through this it can be a shared context for the children. This development should therefore not be seen as "decontextualisation" but as a "re-contextualisation" from a perceptually-based context to a more linguistically-based context.

The third issue concerns the extent to which *reasoning is embodied in particular modes of language use and language practices*. Halliday (1987) used the word "nominalisation" to refer to the way that nouns are used to refer to relation-ships or processes which would otherwise take many other words to describe. Nominalisation is something he and others have used to characterise the difference between writing and speech. In the talk of these children which we analysed we found the beginning of something like nominalisation as they used new combina-tions of words to refer to more general processes and relationships. This beginning of nominalisation has nothing to do with writing but appears to result from the application of the ground rules of exploratory talk which put them under an obligation to explain, understand and build shared verbal context together. This suggests that nominalisation, and other features which have been used claims that writing is a powerful tool for rational thinking, may have more to do with the needs of reasoning in any mode than with literacy. The finding of our study lend weight to those who argue that what is important in reasoning is not the mode of communication but what people are doing, or trying to do, when they are communicating.

The successful reasoning that this paper focused on took place within a larger study that attempted to demonstrate a link between social interaction and individual reasoning. The statistical findings of the study suggest that target children became better at solving the problems of the Raven's test, without having any special training (or more experience than the control children) in solving such problems. We therefore infer that children's training in using language to reason influenced their non-verbal problem-solving. This finding provides support for the claims of socio-cultural theory that language and social experience play an important role in cognitive development. Our demonstration of the effectiveness of the ground rules of exploratory talk has significance not only for understanding how groups think together but also for understanding individual cognitive development and how that development may be supported by structured educational activity.

13

Guided Participation, Discourse and the Construction of Knowledge in Mexican Classrooms

Sylvia Rojas-Drummond

Introduction

In this paper I will summarise two strands of research on the nature of guided participation taking place inside some Mexican classrooms. The first strand deals with the relationship between guided participation and pre-school children's capacity to solve logical and arithmetic-word problems competently and independently. The second strand analyses the relationship between guided participation and primary students' capacity to deal with functional literacy activities (comprehension, production and learning from texts).

The two strands of research were analysed using very similar methods. At the same time, however, they involved students of two different educational levels working on various knowledge domains and under two curriculum programs. These contrasts were selected to test the generality of results across different populations, knowledge domains and educational contexts.

In terms of theory, the studies contribute to our understanding of the dynamic relationships holding between interactive and discursive classroom practices, on the one hand, and developmental and learning processes in childhood, on the other. At the same time, the studies offer some methodological tools to carry out fine-grained analyses of guided participation practices. Lastly, the studies contribute to educational practices by offering a detailed account of the types of interaction and discourse which, across two developmental levels, two curriculum approaches and various knowledge domains, were associated with better learning outcomes. This account can serve as a guide to help improve the quality of teaching-learning processes in the classroom.

This research has been greatly influenced by a sociocultural perspective. Thus, I will start by reviewing some key developments in the field which have influenced our work. Secondly, I will outline the methodological framework used in both strands of research to analyse interactive and discursive practices in the classroom. Thirdly, I will summarise the main findings of each of the two strands of research and the generalities that emerged by considering them in conjunction. And lastly, I will discuss the theoretical, methodological and educational implications of the studies presented.

Theoretical Background

Guided Participation

According to the sociocultural perspective, during development social interaction between experts and novices and among various members of a community leads to the joint construction of zones of proximal development. This construction takes place through guided participation (Vygotsky, 1978; Rogoff & Wertsch, 1984; Rogoff, 1990). In this apprenticeship, children actively engage in cultural practices where adults initially model, guide and help regulate performance, while creating temporary scaffolds which provide bridges from the old to the new and support children's emerging abilities (Wood, Bruner & Ross, 1976; Brown & Reeve, 1987; Rogoff, 1990). Guided participation allows novices or "newcomers" to move from an initial "legitimate peripheral participation" (Lave & Wenger, 1991) to gradually increasing command and responsibility over the diverse activities and artefacts involved in particular cultural practices. As novices become more competent and independent in particular domains, they re-construct and appropriate the regulative functions that occurred socially. Progress towards competence and expertise results from a complex interplay between social factors (among others) and each child's own developmental processes and constructions. Thus, the child plays an active, constructive role in the overall process of guided participation, even as a novice (Saxe, Guberman & Gearhart, 1987; Rogoff, 1990; Elbers et al., 1992).

The Role of Scaffolding

One key question when trying to understand how does guided participation lead to development of expertise refers to the nature of the interactions taking place between experts and novices, or among the various members of a community, and how does this nature affect the emerging processes and outcomes. In this respect, the seminal work of Bruner and associates on the nature of scaffolding and its role in promoting development has contributed importantly to our understanding of Vygotsky's original conceptions of the dynamic interactions between learning and development. Similarly, this work has provided important insights for understanding how guided participation between adults and children can be pivotal in promoting progress when it is organised around zones of proximal development (Wood, Bruner & Ross, 1976; Vygotsky, 1978; Rogoff & Wertsch, 1984).

Bruner's pioneering work in the late 70s generated a wealth of literature on the nature of scaffolding and its role in promoting learning and development in various sociocultural settings. These settings include experimental situations (Wertsch et al., 1980), home environments (Saxe, Guberman & Gearhart, 1987), a wide variety of informal apprenticeship contexts (Rogoff & Lave, 1984; Lave & Wenger, 1991) and more formal educational contexts (Brown & Palincsar, 1989; Newman, Griffin & Cole, 1989; Moll, 1990; Nicolopolou & Cole, 1993; Brown & Campione, 1996). In the school context, several studies have focused on scaffolding as it takes place between adults and children (e.g. Hedegaard, 1996), among peers (e.g. Cowie et al., 1994) and through the mediation of artefacts such as computers (Wegerif & Scrimshaw, 1997). The literature describes how the patterns of relations between interactive practices and developmental and learning processes and outcomes are shaped by the specific contexts in which the practices take place. In spite of this specificity, studies consistently highlight the central role scaffolding plays within guided participation, and how it can foster development and learning when it is shaped to work within zones of proximal development. It is important to stress, however, that we conceive of scaffolding as a co-constructive process where novices and experts actively contribute to its unfolding, rather than as a uni-directional one shaped mainly by the adult (Elbers et al., 1992; Renshaw & Brown, 1999).

Discourse and Knowledge Construction

Another key factor in understanding how guided participation gradually leads to increasing competence and independence is the role played by cultural artefacts in general, and linguistic signs, in particular, as mediators of activity. Sociocultural theory has highlighted the central role played by cultural artefacts, and particularly language, in mediating social interaction and cognition throughout development (e.g. Vygotsky, 1962; 1978; Bruner, 1990; Bronckart, 1992; Wertsch, 1991, 1998; Wertsch, Del Rio & Alvarez, 1995; Cole, 1996). Through discursive interactions meanings are negotiated, allowing for increasing intersubjectivity, which is crucial for working in the zone of proximal development and towards appropriation of cultural practices (Rogoff, 1990). Similarly, social communication is gradually re-constructed as internal speech or voices of the mind (Wertsch, 1991, 1998), contributing importantly to problem-solving, knowledge construction and self-regulation, among other central cognitive functions.

Recently, the study of the role of language in mediated action has been extended by important work on the function of discourse in social interactions within various educational contexts and in diverse cultural groups (e.g. Wertsch, Del Rio & Alvarez, 1995; Coll & Edwards, 1996; Hicks, 1996). This work has highlighted the key role of discourse as "a social mode of thinking", which can facilitate the guided construction of knowledge (Mercer, 1995). This work also reflects a growing tendency within sociocultural theory to consider encompassing units of analysis centred on mediated action in its sociocultural context (Wertsch, 1998). Similarly, recent efforts have been increasingly directed towards understanding how participants in learning communities engage in the social construction of knowledge and the re-creation of culture. In addition, recent studies have addressed the role of interaction and artefact mediation in weaving the course and outcomes of these cultural activities (e.g. Wertsch, Del Rio & Alvarez, 1995; Brown & Campione, 1996; Cole, 1996, 1998).

In conclusion, the literature highlights the importance of guided participation, and particularly the nature of the interactive and discursive practices taking place between experts and novices, as key factors to help understand the course and outcomes of development and learning. This research has been carried out in a great variety of sociocultural settings, and represents samples of situated practices from diverse developmental levels, knowledge domains, learning contexts and cultural groups. However, in the educational context, although the literature is abundant with very enlightening accounts of how guided participation and discursive practices take place in classrooms and other learning environments, the studies do not necessarily make links between the nature of these practices and the developmental and learning outcomes associated with them. At the same time, we need more fine-grained empirical accounts of how guided participation actually evolves in the everyday classroom activities. We also need more research on which particular aspects of expert-novice interaction and discourse can be associated with particular developmental and learning outcomes in the students, to understand these dynamic interactions more fully. The field has also lacked adequate methodological tools to carry out these fine-grained analyses in situated learning contexts. The studies reviewed below attempt to contribute theoretically, methodologically and practically to understanding and promoting these processes in educational settings.

Methodological Scheme for Analysing Classroom Interaction and Discourse

In order to analyse interaction and discourse in the classroom, a methodological scheme was developed in conjunction with Neil Mercer from the Open University in the UK, and has since been refined and used in several studies of Mexican and British children, including the Mexican studies reviewed here. The scheme is concerned with analysis of interactive and discursive practices, particularly the function of talking and joint activity that take place between adults and children. Similarly, it focuses on the use of discourse as a "social mode of thinking" (Mercer, 1995). Analysis of joint talk and activity in turn allows us to make inferences about what is taught and learned, as well as about the ideology of education enacted by the teachers and students through their routine talking and action. Thus, we analyse interaction at three interrelated levels: 1. the actual discourse taking place among the participants, 2. the actions and interactions accompanying these exchanges; and 3. the educational ideology or beliefs about the teaching-learning process which might be embodied in the participants' talk and actions. We consider this ideology in terms of five dimensions within which we can characterise some aspects of the teaching-learning process, and which are of particular interest to our work: (a) the extent to which learning is treated as a social, communicative process; (b) the extent to which teachers and students actively engage in the joint construction of knowledge; (c) the extent to which teachers focus on the processes of problem solving and reasoning and not only on fact acquisition; (d) the extent to which teachers give priority to the processes for learning and not only to products (task completion) and (e) the extent to which teachers help children achieve understanding and competence through scaffolding. This methodological framework is based on the considerable resources of prior relevant research, including our own. Our primary aim is to characterise teaching-learning practices and to distinguish, in the most concise way possible, between the educational style of a teacher who provides more of a social-interactional, co-constructive, scaffolding, approach to teaching and learning and one who enacts a more conventional, directive and transmissional approach. We can then relate these patterns to developmental and learning outcomes in the students.

In order to develop our methodological scheme, we originally drew on our own experience of qualitative analysis of classroom interactions and the findings of other researchers in many countries. This enabled us to generate a list of observable teacher and students' behaviours or Actions which might represent or embody each Dimension of interest. We also sought agreement within the research team on the pragmatic function(s) of each Action. The result of this iterative process was a tentative matrix of a variety of Actions which could be associated with each of the five Dimensions considered.

The next part of the procedure centred around a series of qualitative measures on the discourse taking place. These measures involve detailed analysis of discourse features, using methods developed by ourselves and colleagues in related research (e.g. Edwards & Mercer 1987; Mercer, 1995; Wegerif & Mercer, 1997; Wegerif, Rojas-Drummond & Mercer, 1999; Rojas-Drummond, Mercer & Dabrowski, in press). Attention is given to the ways language is used, in context, as a means of pursuing classroom activities. This involves close consideration of video evidence and transcriptions to establish how the teacher and children engage in joint tasks. These activities enabled us to test and refine our hypotheses about the supposed functions of each Action and discursive feature considered, leading to some revision and refinement of the Dimension/Action matrix. The version of the matrix which emerged from the procedures described above is presented in Table 1.

To implement this methodology for analysing actual interactive episodes, we start with video-recordings from the episodes of interest. We transcribe them, adding notes on relevant contextual features. Then we carry out various qualitative analyses of the data in the fashion described above, and also examine the types of Actions and discursive exchanges displayed by the participants, guided by our methodological scheme. For this examination we identify, characterise and count the occurrences of all Actions and discursive exchanges in our complete set of recorded data, on the basis of our Dimension/Action matrix (attempting all the while to achieve satisfactory levels of inter-observer agreement). Reference to our detailed video transcriptions enables us to check the pragmatic function(s) of the Actions and discursive patterns under analysis.

The frequencies of Actions and discursive patterns obtained are inserted into the matrix appearing in Table 1. This enables us to draw a "profile" for each particular set of participants, after weighing the tendencies evident in all the quantitative and qualitative measures obtained during the interactive and discursive episodes observed over time. These tendencies are then analysed for each of the five Dimensions considered in our scheme, in order to draw inferences about the pedagogical ideology embodied in the talk and actions of the participants. These

Table 1: Dimensions and actions for describing how teachers and students enact the process of teaching and learning

---

Dimension I. Learning is an individual process vs. learning is a social-communicative process

A. Using pupils as a resource or social-cognitive support for the activity of other pupil(s).
B. Building knowledge from one to another in a chain, using the responses of previous pupils to direct the interactions with subsequent pupils.
C. Organising group-work activities so that there are interchanges of viewpoints between pupils and/or sharing of responsibility in solving problems.
D. Promotion of interactions between experts (teachers or pupils) and novices where they both participate in the task.

Dimension II. Knowledge must be transmitted by a teacher or discovered by individual learners vs. knowledge can be jointly constructed

A. Using "Spiral" Initiation-Response-Feedback (IRF) exchanges (take up on student's response to higher levels of understanding and/or performance), vs. only "Loop" ones (simply close the interchange).
B. Using reformulations, elaborations and/or recaps.
C. Cued vs. direct elicitations of information/responses.
D. Asking questions which explore pupils' levels of understanding.
E. Promoting semiotic challenge to guide pupils towards higher levels of understanding.
F. Negotiating meanings with pupils
G. Making explicit the "ground rules" or demands of a task.
H. Explicitly linking prior knowledge (from outside or inside the classroom) to the current activity.

Dimension III. Becoming educated essentially means acquiring facts vs. becoming educated includes learning ways to solve problems

A. Using "why?" questions to get pupils to justify answers or to reason and reflect.
B. Using open questions.
C. Eliciting problem solving strategies (e.g. analysing goals, planning, monitoring, error-correction, etc.) from the pupils.
D. Eliciting goals and varied ways of solving problems from pupils.
E. Constructing knowledge jointly with pupils.

Table 1: *Continued*

Dimension IV. Priority is given to task completion (product) vs. emphasis placed also on the process of learning

A.   Recapping or reviewing learning with pupils.
B.   Emphasising the meaning or purpose of tasks.
C.   Emphasising or elaborating the process of arriving at a solution.

Dimension V. Learning is solely the responsibility of the learner vs. learning can be nurtured by a teacher

A.   Promoting the active participation of pupils.
B.   Exploring the initial level of pupils' understanding of tasks and materials.
C.   Reducing degrees of freedom to allow pupils to concentrate on certain key aspects of the task when the task is difficult.
D.   Using "retreat and rebuild" exchanges (repair processes where pupils' mistakes are used by the teacher to reconstruct knowledge).
E.   Modelling of desirable actions, strategies and outcomes.
F.   Providing elaborated feedback on a pupil's response/approach to a problem.
G.   Gradually withdrawing expert support when pupil demonstrates competence.
H.   Making pupils' achievements explicit to them and/or other pupils.

pedagogic beliefs are derived from the overall interactive patterns observed, and are conceived of as flexible tendencies within continuums, rather than fixed dichotomic styles. Our characterisations allow various comparisons among teaching and learning practices. At the same time, the complementary use of qualitative and quantitative analyses enables us to make categorical comparisons without decontextualising the talk and action, thus overcoming a well-recognised weakness of most "systematic observation" categorical schemes.

I will next provide a glimpse of what some of the Actions and discursive patterns look like when actually enacted, by offering four representative excerpts from teacher-student exchanges, extracted from each of the two lines of research to be presented in the next section (see Table 2). Each example includes a brief contextual description, the actual dialogue which took place (translated from Spanish) and the Dimensions and Actions coded for these exchanges according to our methodological scheme. The codes include a Roman numeral for the Dimension concerned, followed by a letter for the particular Action identified. (Please refer to Table 1 for identification of numerical and letter codes).

Notice that the discourse in both Official pre-school and primary examples (control groups) is mostly characterised by Initiation-Response-Feedback (IRF) sequences, of the type we term "Loop IRF's". These tend to close the exchange

Table 2: Excerpts of adult-children dialogues from preschool and primary strands of research

---

A. Excerpts from Official and H/S Preschool Curricula in Arithmetic Reasoning Activities

(1) Excerpt from Official Curriculum

Sequence 1. Counting vegetables

Context: Teacher in front of blackboard. Pupils in U-shaped table. Teacher has two sheets of paper on blackboard, one with sets of vegetables, the other with numbers. She is pointing at different sets with different number of vegetables and asking for corresponding number ...

Code: Discourse	Action	Dialogue:
II A Loop		Teacher: Here is a set of what? (points at set of 1 vegetable). Students: Of 1. Teacher: Of one item.
II A Loop		Teacher: Here is a set of how many? (points at set of 2). Students: Of 2 items. Teacher: Of 2 items.
II A Loop		Teacher: Here? (points at set of 3). Students: 3. Teacher: Of 3 items.
II A Loop		Teacher: (Points at set of 4). Students: 4 Teacher: Of 4.
II A Loop		Teacher: (Points at set of 5). Students: 5
	V H	Teacher: And of 5. Good.
II A Loop		Teacher: Now, do you all know what these are called? (points at numbers). Students: Numbers.
	V H	Teacher: Numbers, right? Good. ...You're going to relate the sets according to the number appearing on the right. OK? ... Nobody start yet. Nobody helps each other. Work on your own.

Table 2: *Continued*

---

(2) Excerpt from High/Scope Curriculum

Sequence 2. Gathering apples

Context: Teacher and group of students playing a game with a dice, boards with a tree and ladder, and small toy apples. They have just finished taking turns in climbing up the ladder and bringing down certain number of apples each, according to numbers on dice …

Code: Discourse	Action	Dialogue:
II A Spiral	I C	Teacher: Let's see, let's see. Who brought down more apples? Omar: I did.
II A Spiral	II D	Teacher: How many did you get down? Omar: 2.
II A Spiral	II E	Teacher: And how many were left in the tree? Gina: 4.
II A Spiral	I B/ III C	Teacher: 4. Let's see, count them, Omar, to see if there are 4. Omar: 1,2,3,4,5.
II A Spiral	V D	Teacher: Let's see. Count them again. Omar: 1 …
II A Spiral	V C V H IIIB/ IVA	Teacher: Ah-huh (pointing). Omar: … 2, 3, 4. Teacher: Yes, you see? 4 apples were left. That's it! … Fine, … Let's see, now, what did we learn in this game?

(continued)

Table 2: *Continued*

B. *Excerpts from Primary Control and Cooperative Learning groups in reading comprehension activities*

(1) Excerpt from Control Group

Sequence 3. Identifying main characters from a story

Context: Teacher standing in front of class, with book on hands, students with books opened. Students have just finished reading silently a story about "Yacub Magrebi", a rich arab who had a dream about a treasure ...

Code: Discourse	Action	Dialogue:
II A Loop		Teacher: Who are the characters? And then we are going to reach some conclusions. For you, Aurelio, who are the characters of this story? Of this text?
		Aurelio: Ah ..., Yacub Magrebi, The Judge, ...
	V F	Teacher: Let's see ... Yacub Magrebi, he is the arab,
	V H	right? Very good.
II A Loop		Teacher: Who else?
		Aurelio: The Judge ...
		Teacher: The Judge.
II A Loop		Teacher: ...
		Aurelio: The thieves ...
		Teacher: The thieves ...
II A Loop		Teacher: ...
		Aurelio: and the policemen.
	V H	Teacher: Very good.
II A Loop		Teacher: And you, Pilar, for you who are the main characters there?
		Pilar: Yacub and The Judge.
	V H	Teacher: Yacub and The Judge, only two, fine.
II A Loop		Teacher: And you Ernesto?
		Ernesto: Yacub, The Judge, and the thieves, that's it.
	V F	Teacher: The Judge, The Arab, and that mysterious character that he saw in his nightmare, his dreams, right? ...

(continued)

Table 2: *Continued*

(2) Excerpt from Cooperative Learning Group

Sequence 4. Clarifying ideas from a summary

Context: The group guide and the students are sitting in a circle. The students, in pairs, have written a summary of part of a text about characteristics of Vertebrates. The guide is reading aloud to the group a summary produced by one pair of students, and stops in one section …

Code: Discourse	Action	Dialogue:
II A Spiral	II D	Guide: Let's see, this is a difficult word. Who knows what metamorphosis is? Daniel: An illness.
II A Spiral	I A/ II F	Guide: (To all): Do you think that metamorphosis is an illness? David: No. Alejandro: No.
II A Spiral	I D	Guide: What is metamorphosis? … David: The development of a frog.
II A Spiral	II E	Guide: The development of a frog; yes. But, what does metamorphosis mean? Students: … (no response from students).
II A Spiral	III C	Guide: Listen and pay attention to something. You all read the word "metamorphosis", and why, if no one understood it, did no one ask for clarification?
	IV C	Remember that it is very important when we read to be checking if we understand or don't understand.
	V H	When we don't understand, what do we do?
	V H	Alejandro: Clarify it.
	V F	Guide: Clarify it, ask for help, right? Very good.
	II B	So, then, what is metamorphosis? You told us well, David, it is how the frog develops, and the amphibians, right? But do you know what "metamorphosis" means? That there is a *change* in development

without necessarily taking the child's response much further. In contrast, the discourse of both High/Scope (H/S) and Cooperative Learning exchanges is characterised by "Spiral IRF'S", which carry students' responses to (potentially) higher levels of understanding and/or performance. Spiral IRF's are typically accompanied by a variety of co-constructive and "scaffolding" strategies, and the H/S and Cooperative Learning excerpts exemplify several types. Loop IRF's, on the other hand, are associated with a less co-constructive and scaffolded interactive style, as is apparent from contrasting both sets of excerpts. As will become evident from the studies to be presented, we have found the types of IRF observed (Loop versus Spiral) to offer a particularly sensitive and reliable indicator to help discriminate between the styles of teaching-learning practices under study.

In the next section I will present the two strands of research on preschool and primary school children respectively. After each presentation I will discuss results from each strand of research. Then, in the final section, I will provide an overall discussion of both strands of research in combination.

Summary of Two Strands of Research

High/Scope (H/S) vs. Official Pre-school Curricula

Method

In this strand of research we set out to analyse further some original findings from a previous longitudinal study on the development of independent problem solving capacities in Mexican pre-school children (Study 1: Rojas-Drummond & Alatorre, 1994). We carried out a follow-up study of the same children and teachers (Study 2: Rojas-Drummond, Mercer & Dabrowsky, in press) to analyse more directly the nature of the guided participation taking place in the classroom that might have contributed to our original findings, using the methodological scheme outlined above.

The children and teachers (same for both studies) came in equal numbers from two pre-school settings: the H/S Curriculum (Hohmann, Banet & Weikart, 1979) and the official state curriculum. Both pre-school groups were equivalent in relevant socio-economic and educational measures, and included 5–6-year-old children and their respective teachers.

In essence, results of Study 1 had shown that at the end of the academic year the H/S children's performance on two dynamic assessment tests (arithmetic word-problems and figure-matching puzzles) was significantly more competent and more independent than that of their peers in the official curriculum. Further qualitative analysis of the arithmetic test revealed that at the end of the year the H/S children were able to solve most of the problems without any type of aid. In contrast, the official school children still relied mostly on the experimenter providing concrete and tangible representations of the elements involved in the problems, to achieve success. These patterns suggested that by the end of the year the H/S children had moved faster from potential to real levels of development, displaying appropriation of more sophisticated and self-regulated (that is, more independent and competent) problem-solving strategies.

Which factors can account for the differences found? Given the apparent homogeneity of the two populations, we argued that at least some aspects of the type of curriculum in operation were partly responsible for the H/S children's superior performance. Furthermore, on the basis of the sociocultural literature in the field, we speculated that part of the explanation might reside importantly in the nature of guided participation, particularly daily interactions and discourse between children and teacher, since it is these exchanges that actually enact the educational proposals of each curriculum.

In Study 2 we investigated this hypothesis in more detail. During Study 1 and parallel to the dynamic assessment, we had videotaped teacher-children interactions in activities around arithmetic reasoning for each of the four classes under study (two each for H/S and official curricula) several times throughout the year. This source of data became the focus of Study 2, in which we applied the methodological scheme described above to analyse all the exchanges recorded. Inter-observer reliability from a random sample of 6 representative sessions yielded an overall average score of 89.8%, with a range of 86–93%.

Results

Systematic comparisons between curricula for each Action were carried out after pooling frequency distributions across teachers and sessions for each curriculum. Statistical comparisons between curricula were performed for each of the 24 Actions allowing for quantitative comparisons. Most of the significant comparisons favoured the H/S curriculum (63%), while none favoured the official curriculum (Table 3).

An analysis of the Actions which yielded more highly significant results ($p < 0.001$ and $p < 0.01$) indicated that, in comparison with the official curriculum, the H/S teachers and students engaged significantly more frequently in the following types of interactions:

(a) At the discursive level, they displayed significantly more often Spiral IRF's (47% of all exchanges), which potentially take the students to higher levels of understanding and/or performance. In contrast, only 8% of Spiral IRF's were evident in the exchanges from the official surriculum (the other 92% were Loop).

(b) At the level of Actions, Spiral IRF's were translated into a variety of social-constructivist and scaffolding strategies, which also appeared significantly more often in the H/S exchanges: H/S teachers more frequently elicited problem-solving strategies in their students; reduced degrees of freedom, thereby allowing students to concentrate on certain relevant aspects of the activity; displayed "retreat and rebuild" exchanges; modelled desirable actions; provided elaborate feed-back; used other students as a social-cognitive support for learning; explicitly linked prior knowledge to the current activity; emphasised the processes for arriving at solutions and made students' achievements explicit to the group (see Table 3).

Discussion

Besides the quantitative analyses carried out, we observed many interesting qualitative differences between the styles of teacher-student interactions between the two curricula. Overall, these observations qualified and reinforced the quantitative results obtained. In general, they revealed that the H/S teachers tended to be more consistent, explicit, systematic and comprehensive in the acting out of the strategies and behaviours considered under Actions in the system of analysis. At the same time, the specific tasks that the H/S teachers chose to promote mathematical reasoning tended to be more clearly directed towards advancing in that direction, and appeared to convey more functionality and meaningfulness, involving many more adequate games and group-work activities. Likewise, their scaffolding strategies, besides being much more prominent, tended to be more varied, sophisticated and more attuned both to the individual child and to the mastery of the tasks at hand.

Taken together, the quantitative and qualitative results of Study 2 suggested that H/S teachers and students, in comparison with those of the official curriculum, engaged in a style of interaction that synthetically could be characterised as follows: (a) it tended more towards the social construction of knowledge through interac-

Table 3. Comparisons between curricula that yielded significant results

Favouring	Comparisons	
	Number	**%**
H/S	15*	63
Official Curriculum	0	0
Neither	9	37
Total	24	100

*The 15 Actions which differed significantly (Chi Square tests for independent samples[1]) were: II A, III C, V C, V D, V E, V F ($p < 0.001$); I A, II H, IV C, V H ($p < 0.01$); II B, II D, II E, II F, III B ($p < 0.05$) (Table 1 for Dimension-roman and Action-letter codes).

[1]The nature of interactive data does not meet the requirements of independence of observations of the Chi Square Test. However, given the nominal level of measurement, we did not encounter adequate alternative statistical tests within the non-parametric ones to deal with comparisons of this type of data. We decided to apply the test in spite of this limitation, to offer extra support to the claims made about the many apparent qualitative and quantitative differences we observed in the data.

tion and discourse among all participants; (b) it was more oriented towards the promotion of various processes of learning, problem solving and domain-specific strategies and (c) teachers actively encouraged the above processes through a scaffolding style of guided participation. This style, which we term social-constructivist, was quantitatively and qualitatively more prominent in the H/S teachers and students than in the official curriculum ones. In contrast, the latter exhibited a style of interaction which entailed a more conventional, directive, transmissional, hands-off and product-oriented approach (termed directive-transmissional).

On the basis of the pooled results from Studies 1 and 2, we argue that at least part of the explanation for the H/S children's more developed and independent problem-solving strategies (Study 1) may lie in the differential amount, and quality of interaction and discourse taking place in each curriculum (Study 1). In particular, the more social-constructivist, scaffolding style of interaction apparent among the H/S teachers and students might contribute to the children's faster movement from potential to real levels of development, and towards the appropriation of more competent and independent problem-solving and learning strategies. This, of course, is likely to occur in conjunction with some or all of the other components of the H/S curriculum. But we believe, based on the sociocultural literature previously reviewed, that the guided participation practices actually taking place between adults and children played a key role in this dynamics.

I will next move to the second strand of research mentioned in the Introduction, to provide further evidence for the relationship between particular styles of guided participation and certain developmental and learning outcomes. This research focuses on primary school children and the development of functional literacy.

Cooperative Learning and Promotion of Functional Literacy in Primary Classrooms

Method

Our line of research on the development of functional literacy has consisted of a series of longitudinal studies of teachers and children in Mexican primary schools (see review in Rojas-Drummond, Dabrowsky & Gomez, 1998). Two of these studies are the focus of the present report.

Here too, we undertook to analyse further some original findings from a previous longitudinal study on the development and promotion of functional literacy in Mexican primary school children (Study 1: Rojas-Drummond et al., 1998). We set to analyse in more detail the nature of guided participation taking place in the classroom which might have contributed to our original findings (Study 2: Rojas-Drummond et al., in press).

Briefly, study 1 entailed an investigation of 4th-graders (9 years old) and teachers from two equivalent public primary schools in Mexico City, assigned to an experimental or control condition. Experimental groups were exposed to a series of training sessions, following a socio-instructional program for promoting functional literacy. Our program was adapted from the cooperative learning or "reciprocal teaching" methods developed by Brown and her collaborators (see Brown & Palincsar, 1989; Brown & Campione, 1996), and included cooperative learning teams working with a guide-experimenter in place of a teacher. Control groups followed their regular lessons from the Official curriculum.

In general, results from this first study showed that cooperative learning procedures were highly effective in promoting students' appropriation of declarative and procedural knowledge for comprehension, production and learning of narrative and expository texts. Further, qualitative analysis showed that the improvement in the experimental groups reflected more developed strategies to organise, synthesise and produce more cohesive and elaborated texts. These abilities did not seem to be dealt with directly or successfully within the regular classroom, since control groups did not show evident progress throughout the year in any of the discursive and learning parameters analysed.

We hypothesised that the above findings were at least partly due to the nature of the guided participation practices taking place during the cooperative learning sessions, in comparison with those commonly occurring within the regular classroom (the official curriculum). Therefore, we carried out a follow-up study of the same children and teachers, again in collaboration with Neil Mercer, to explain further the sources of our original findings (Study 2: Rojas-Drummond et al., in press). Here, we analysed more directly the styles of interaction and discourse taking place in the classrooms of each experimental group, using the methodological scheme presented previously.

As part of our general method, all experimental sessions applying cooperative learning with expository texts had been videotaped, together with some regular control classes. These videos provided the basic source of data for Study 2. In particular, one team of 6 students and their guide were followed throughout 9 sessions of cooperative learning in which work centred around expository texts from a natural science text-book. At the same time, control teachers and students were videotaped during regular classes, working around reading and learning activities.

All video transcripts were analysed systematically in qualitative and quantitative terms, using the methodological scheme described in the two previous sections.

Results

Similarly as in the pre-school strand of research, we carried out statistical comparisons between the frequency distributions of Actions obtained for the two experimental groups, for each of the 24 Actions allowing for quantitative comparisons. Most of the comparisons (71%) were significant in favour of the cooperative learning group, while none favoured the control group (Table 4).

An analysis of the Actions which yielded more highly significant results ($p < 0.001$ and $p < 0.01$) indicated that participants in the cooperative learning groups engaged significantly more frequently in the following type of exchanges, in comparison with the control groups:

(a) At the discursive level, they displayed Spiral IRF's much more often (89% of all exchanges). In contrast, Spiral IRF's were almost non existent in the control group (only 2% in the total sample; the other 98% were Loop).

(b) At the level of Actions, Spiral IRF's were translated into a variety of social-constructivist and scaffolding strategies; these appeared significantly more often in cooperative group exchanges than in control group exchanges. Participants of the cooperative learning groups more often engaged in: using other students as a resource to support the ongoing activity, asking questions to explore a student's level of understanding, presenting challenges, negotiating meanings, making ground rules explicit, eliciting various problem-solving strategies, using "retreat and re-build" exchanges, using reformulations and elaborations, emphasising a variety of strategies for arriving at solutions, revising a student's learning, emphasising the meaning or purpose of activities, reducing degrees of freedom to allow students to concentrate on key aspects of the task and providing elaborated feedback.

Discussion

A qualitative analysis similar to the one applied to pre-school data qualified and reinforced the quantitative results (as it did for the pre-school data). Overall, the style of interaction and discourse which emerged as typical of the cooperative learning activities could be characterised as follows: (a) It tended more towards social construction of knowledge; (b) it was more oriented towards guiding the construction of knowledge through a wide variety of supporting strategies; and (c) It tended to emphasise the acquisition of different types of strategies for problem solving, reasoning and learning in students.

Table 4. Comparisons between experimental groups that yielded significant results

	Comparisons	
Favouring	**Number**	**%**
Cooperative Learning	17*	71
Control Group	0	0
Neither	7	29
Total	24	100

*The 17 Actions which differed significantly (Chi Square tests for independent samples) were: I A, II A, II D, II E, II F, II G, III C, V D ($p < 0.001$); II B, III D, IV A, IV B, V B, V C, V F, V H ($p < 0.01$); V E ($p < 0.05$) (Table 1 for Dimension-roman and Action-letter codes).

In contrast, the typical interactive style of teachers and students of the official curriculum (control groups) tended to be more directive although less supportive: (a) teachers provided most of the information and dominated most of the talk; (b) however, their supportive strategies tended to be scarce and less varied, and (c) teachers tended to emphasise fact acquisition and task completion, at the expense of underlying problem-solving and other learning processes. This more "directive-transmissional" approach is typical of primary practice in several official Mexican schools, as found in various studies (Mercado, 1997; Mercado et al., 1997).

Taken together, the quantitative and qualitative analyses of interaction and discourse in each experimental setting suggest an overall pattern. The cooperative learning procedures tested seemed to foster a social-constructivist, scaffolding style of interaction, as previously defined. In contrast, as in official pre-school classrooms discussed previously, official primary teachers and students exhibited a style of interaction which tended more towards a directive-transmissional approach.

Combining results from the two cooperative learning studies reviewed, we suggest that success of cooperative learning in promoting students' declarative and procedural knowledge (Study 1) is partly due to the differential amount and quality of the interactive and discursive practices taking place in each setting (Study 2). In particular, the more social-constructivist, scaffolding style of guided participation observed in the cooperative learning groups may partly account for the more competent performance displayed by the experimental students in declarative and procedural knowledge around functional literacy.

Taking the two strands of research together (involving pre-school and primary students respectively), the differences found between groups in each strand clearly reveal specific patterns, which result from the nature of the particular activities, educational program and developmental level involved in each setting. At the same time, however, looking at both strands in combination there were consistencies in many of the Actions that resulted in a significant difference between curriculum groups in both strands. In particular, in comparison with the respective official curriculum groups, both the H/S and the cooperative learning groups engaged more significantly in the following types of Actions and discursive patterns: I. Actions which capitalise on other students to support learning; II. Discoursive patterns which emphasise the joint construction of knowledge; III & IV. Actions which promote problem solving and learning processes; and V. A variety of scaffolding strategies to support these processes. (The specific Actions which yielded significant results across the two strands of research were: I A, II A, II B, II D, II E, II F, III C, V C, V D, V E, V F and V H. See Table 1). These types of Actions therefore are the best indices in the reviewed studies for distinguishing between social-constructivist and directive-transmissional styles of interaction. At the same time, the occurrence of Loop vs. Spiral IRF's turned out to be a particularly sensitive discursive feature for discriminating between these interactive styles. Importantly, many other Actions rest upon these basic discursive structures.

The above findings corroborate some previous studies (see Mercer, 1995) where Spiral IRF's and various accompanying supportive strategies have been found to be key indicators of a social-constructivist, scaffolding interactive style. Mercer further argues that Spiral IRF's represent central discursive structures which can play a key role in promoting the guided construction of knowledge.

Our overall analyses further suggest that the social-constructivist practices observed in both strands of research, including those for the H/S and the cooperative learning participants, represent a substantial change from the typical styles of interaction and discourse in many Mexican official curriculum classrooms. This change can improve students' competence in activities related to problem solving and functional literacy.

Wertsch's (1991) analysis of cooperative learning within a Bakhtinian perspective further supports the present interpretation. He argues that in cooperative learning children gradually internalise the dialogic structure of the interaction. This process involves adopting the privileged role of asking questions and a more active interanimation of reader, writer, text and audience. Adopting these roles in turn results in a fundamental shift in the arrangement of voices that ventriloquate the speech genre of formal instruction. We believe similar changes went on in our cooperative learning groups in comparison with the typical interactions that prevail in many Mexican official primary classrooms. Also, related changes of roles, dialogic structures and arrangement of voices can be assumed to have taken place in the H/S groups in comparison to the typical practices of the official curriculum classes.

General Conclusions on the Two Strands of Research Reviewed

Our analyses showed that the practices found in pre-school and primary settings differed in many respects related to the unique context under study. Nonetheless, consideration of the patterns emerging from both strands of research, which concerned various domains and two educational programs (H/S and cooperative learning), yielded an array of interesting consistencies. In particular, the two strands suggest that a social-constructivist, scaffolding style of guided participation, as actually enacted in the everyday classroom practices of adults and children, can be associated with significant enhancement of various learning and developmental outcomes. These include the promotion of competence and independence in domains such as problem solving and functional literacy (that is, a tendency towards appropriation and self-regulation of general problem-solving strategies and domain-specific ones in the students). It is possible that students from the H/S and cooperative learning groups acquired not only better knowledge, but a different type of knowledge than their respective official curriculum peers (see Rogoff, 1994).

Our findings provide empirical support for certain sociocultural claims. Our research has highlighted some of the mechanisms involved in key sociocultural constructs related to the nature of guided participation. These mechanisms include how social-constructivist and scaffolding interactive and discursive practices promote learning and development. Our findings also allow to underpin empirically, in situated educational contexts, some of the actual interactions and discursive patterns that comprise some of these constructs.

Our results in general confirm and expand findings from previous studies of the relations between expert-novice guided participation and development of children's competence and independence (Wood et al., 1976; Brown & Palincsar, 1989; Moll, 1990; Rogoff, 1990; Mercer, 1995; Wertsch et al., 1995; Brown & Campione, 1996; Cole, 1996; Hedegaard, 1996). The studies also contribute to current sociocultural research by offering detailed accounts of how participants in learning communities achieve the social construction of knowledge through discursive exchanges.

Regarding our methodological approach, we offer a practical tool for carrying out fine-grained analyses of everyday interactive and discursive practices in the classroom. I trust the presentation of data also conveyed some of the advantages which can arise from combining an array of quantitative and qualitative analyses. Here, the array yielded a fuller explanation of sociocultural phenomena related to interaction and discourse, in the context of teaching and learning practices (cf. Hammersley, 1994).

A weakness of this methodology, however, is that, although it deals with adult-student(s) interactions, analysis centres more fully on the adult. To address this limitation, in current studies we are adopting a more comprehensive approach which considers adult-child and child-child interactions and discursive exchanges in conjunction, and which takes fuller account of children's active contributions to the dynamics of the interaction. It thus analyses the role of all participants in weaving the course and results of the teaching-learning process (Rojas-Drummond et al., 1999).

The studies presented can also point up techniques for improving the quality of the teaching-learning process taking place in the classroom. For example, teachers can be encouraged to reflect on their current practices and participate in designing and implementing new educational activities that benefit from a social-constructivist approach. Also, our methodological scheme includes actions that can be adapted to particular teaching contexts. We are at present involving primary school teachers and students in such experiences, with very promising results.

In addition, based on these and related findings, we are at present implementing educational programs that capitalise on styles of interaction and discourse to promote learning and development. For this, we are creating complementary spaces within schools where participants of learning communities can engage in a diversity of social-constructivist practices. These practices include ludic and functional activities mediated by a variety of cultural artefacts. Our findings have led us to design and implement an ongoing project in primary schools. "Learning Communities for the Social Construction of Knowledge" (Rojas-Drummond & LCC, 1998) was inspired by numerous educational developments emanating from sociocultural theory and practice, including the "Fifth Dimension" proposal (Nicolopoulou & Cole, 1993; Cole, 1996; Cole & Brown, 1996–1997). As part of this current enterprise, we are implementing a "double system of guided participation" which fosters social-constructivist, scaffolded and exploratory styles of interaction and discourse among all participants, including children, teachers and researchers (Rojas-Drummond et al., 1999). So far, these types of programs are offering valuable educational experiences which have shown to promote significantly learning and development of participants (e.g. Blanton et al., Cole & Brown, 1996–1997).

In conclusion, the studies offer theoretical, methodological and practical contributions to sociocultural theory and educational practice. Along with many other researchers in the field, our contributions have resulted from our attempts to understand how participants of learning communities construct knowledge socially. We have also attempted to empower these participants with tools for enriching the course and outcomes of their cultural activities.

Acknowledgements

Preparation of this manuscript was supported by Grants 25399H from CONACyT (National Council for Science and Technology) and IN309397 from DGAPA-UNAM (Office of Academic Affairs, National Autonomous University of Mexico). We are deeply grateful to the administrators, teachers and children from the public schools which enabled us to conduct the research reported here. We also greatly appreciate the very insightful and thorough comments made by Hugh Drummond, Ed Elbers and James Hipps to several versions of the manuscript. Highly professional technical support was also provided by Keith Prior.

14

Overview and New Perspectives

Geerdina M. van der Aalsvoort, Helen Cowie and Neil Mercer

Introduction

In this chapter we look retrospectively at how the various studies reported in this book relate to the book's subtitle "The meaning of discourse for the construction of knowledge". Every chapter deals in some way with the process of knowledge construction through discourse. There is a general recognition of the interdependency of social and individual processes in this constructive process, and of tasks as situation-dependent, socially constructed activities in which individuals may take on particular, culturally influenced discursive roles as "teachers" and "learners". There is also an implied recognition of the temporal or historical dimension of the process of teaching and learning, as an activity inevitably draws on, and builds on the past relevant experiences of all concerned. Adopting such a socio-cultural perspective to learning and instruction requires that researchers use methods that recognize the specific contributions of child, task and contextualizing environment in the construction of knowledge.

Chapters 3 to 13 presented investigations into the meaning of discourse for social interaction in learning and instruction, and represented the authors' decisions regarding relevant concepts and suitable methods. As Van der Aalsvoort and Harinck suggested in chapter 2 of this volume, the "multi method" approach seems the most appropriate for studying the process of knowledge construction through discourse. In the following paragraph the various contributions will be related to conceptual and methodological quality issues as set out in chapter 2. Our aim is to provide a comparative, constructive evaluation of these contributions, which we hope, will contribute to the development of future research. We have therefore set out these issues as a set of evaluative questions addressed to each research study. We will conclude the overview with suggestions for new perspectives on the role of discourse in the construction of knowledge.

Answers to the Questions Regarding Qualitative Standards when Investigating Social Interaction

Are the researchers' assumptions about how knowledge is constructed made explicit, and hypotheses about processes clearly stated?

This question implies that a sound theoretical conception of social interaction and the role of discourse in it should be used to formulate research questions and plan data gathering. Moreover, it implies that the researcher should be able to demonstrate that data have been gathered concerning theoretically relevant parameters of processes of teaching and learning (Creswell, 1998). Gee and Green (1998) propose four groups of elements that may be included in framework (MASS-system) for studying social interaction. These elements are:

— *Material aspects*: actors, place, time, object present or referred to during interaction;
— *Activities*: specific social activities or interconnected chains of activities in which participants are engaging (sequences of actions);
— *Semiotic aspects*: situated meanings and cultural models connected to various "sign systems" such as language, images, gestures or other symbolic system;
— *Sociocultural aspects*: personal, social and cultural knowledge, feelings and identities, relevant in the interaction, including knowledge of the preceding three aspects.

In the case of research into the social process of teaching and learning, it may be appropriate to add "output" elements to this conceptual frame (which might be framed as the question: "Does the research demonstrate that new knowledge or skills have been gained as a result of participants' involvement?"). Gee and Green (1998) suggest that the theoretical relevance of a study will be greater if several of the MASS elements are included. However, as they admit, it is neither necessary (nor feasible) to deal with all elements for any particular study to claim some theoretical value. In fact, by taking different perspectives in a series of related studies, researchers may gradually develop parts of the MASS-system work into a more coherent, holistic account.

We can relate to the contents of chapters 3 to 13 of this volume to these matters as follows. The sociocultural approach to adult-child interaction in teaching and learning is the main theoretical framework for all contributors to this volume. Some of the authors highlight the original ideas from Vygotsky (Kumpulainen & Mutanen, and Rojas-Drummond: this volume), while others elaborate more recent, emerging perspectives in sociocultural theory, such as Grossen who explores how adults frame the situations in which teacher and student act, and how this affects the negotiation of the participants' identities during completion of a shared task.

Learning through social activity when performing a shared task in small groups is the focus of Brown and Renshaw's work. They created communicative spaces in primary classrooms in order to encourage argumentation (which they see as an important element in the construction of zones of proximal development). Van Boxtel et al. speak about "deep processing", and Wegerif and Mercer describe how individuals can learn and develop in their reasoning capability through using "exploratory talk" during collaborative activity. Leseman et al. view social learning from the perspective of co-construction and draw attention to how young children's play activities can create zones of proximal development. In school-based research, Ivinson sees the curriculum as embodies in social practices, and shows how classroom activity and curriculum are integrated by classroom talk. From a rather different angle, Ireson argues that teachers' perceptions of task influence how they initiate social interaction with first grade students.

Sociocultural theory is used by many authors to explain how the negotiation of meaning leads on to the joint construction of knowledge. Collaborative problem solving is often used as a source of data for studying this phenomenon. Several authors (Brown & Renshaw; Leseman et al.; Van Boxtel et al.; Rojas-Drummond; Wegerif & Mercer) test hypotheses about processes that underlie knowledge construction. Others include in their reports descriptions of collaborative activities and transcribed extracts of speech. In doing so, some include transcripts as typical examples of changes in teaching and learning (Naylor & Cowie; Elbers & Streefland), while others present them as examples of specific or intriguing patterns of discourse (Ivinson; Kumpulainen & Mutanen).

Despite some common theoretical foundations in sociocultural theory, there is, then, some considerable methodological diversity amongst the research described here. A comparative consideration of the assumptions about how knowledge is constructed during the social process of teaching and learning represented in the studies reported in this volume could be of great value to future research on discourse and the joint construction of knowledge. (Some similar comparative views can be found in Littleton and Light (1999) in their overview of studies of interaction between students when working with computers. See also Kazdin (1992) for an overview regarding the structural analysis of clinical research in case studies and small sample research.)

Is the research based on continuous engagement and observation of relevant practice?

Are contextual features given adequate recognition?

It is convenient and appropriate to consider the two questions above together, because they both refer to the ways in which data gathering and analysis deal with the contemporaneous and historical context of any activity being researched. All research methods for studying human behaviour should be expected to deal in some way with the physical, interpersonal and cultural context of that behaviour. While this requirement has often been ignored or treated only superficially in laboratory-bound experimental research, to researchers who are concerned with the observation and analysis of real-life teaching and learning interactions, this requirement is usually treated as obvious. In practice, however, such recognition of the importance of "context" is hard to achieve.

In the studies included here we can point to the following ways in which researchers have tried to deal with this requirement. All contributions deal with the dynamic enterprise of social learning in relevant practice and several authors deal with this choice explicitly as a way of seeking generalizable findings (Grossen; Naylor & Cowie; Ivinson; Rojas-Drummond). Most researchers present results of one-time only experiments that are carried out in the classroom. Examples of protocols that result from this procedure are: teachers' utterances towards students (Ireson); small groups of students' verbal and nonverbal behaviour during play (Leseman et al), and during arithmetic (Kumpulainen & Mutanen). Grossen describes contextual features that influence students who participated in psychological tests by presenting experimenters'and students' verbal utterances.

Brown and Renshaw, as well as Rojas-Drummond, Van Boxtel et al., and Wegerif and Mercer carried out pretest-intervention-post test designs in the classroom. All of them describe contextual features in which the experiment was carried out, and where the data were collected. Elbers and Streefland, and Naylor and Cowie presented case studies involving participants from one school. As they identified the specific roles of the participants in their investigation, they analysed the change in relationship between teachers and students (Elbers and Streefland), between peer supporters and users, as well as between and within peer supporters themselves (Naylor and Cowie). Ivinson describes explicitly how she collected data using ethnomethodological methods in schools.

Several contributions in this volume are based on continuous engagement and observation of relevant practice, but not all of them. The more these studies contain descriptions of contextual features the more they enable the reader to visualize the meaning of the discourse fragments that are included. In this way, we see more clearly how the settings of activities contribute to the equality of the process of knowledge construction. It also helps researchers recognize the importance of carrying out research in real-life settings, and sharing the problems of such research that will have to be solved.

Are relevant non-verbal aspects of communication included in the analysis of interactions?

The restriction of analysis to the words spoken by the interacting partners may mean that some important aspects of the process of knowledge construction are lost. Both prosodic elements of the language (pitch, speed, rhythm, and accent) and other non-verbal aspects of communication elements (eye gaze, spatial organization, and kinesics) may be important factors in the encounters of teaching and learning. Particularly in situations where discourse comprehension is heavily and implicitly dependent on shared knowledge, or where non-verbal elements play an important role (e.g. young children, or in practical activities), such information may be vital. But on the other hand, a researcher cannot ever make a comprehensive record of any event. Moreover to gather data in too much detail would be overwhelming and ultimately self-defeating (and may simply defer selectivity to the later analytic stage of research).

Most authors in this volume have used ways of analysing discourse which include, at least to some extent, the consideration of non-verbal aspects of communication; but none explicitly discusses the possibility that leaving non-verbal aspects out may result in an impoverished, incomplete account of the way that knowledge is jointly constructed. We therefore draw particular attention to Rojas-Drummond's contribution, as she describes a series of *dimensions* and *actions* that were used for showing how the process of teaching and learning is enacted. Her analytic scheme deals with both the verbal and non-verbal activity of teachers and students.

Does the research draw on multiple data sources and informants?

Does the research represent the voices of the various partners in the social interactions studied?

Again we have two questions which deal with overlapping concerns — in this case — to do with the extent to which the actions and perspectives of various contributors to any process of learning and instruction are embodied in the research. The use of multiple data sources, e.g. written documents, observation and questioning techniques, brings with it the likelihood that disparate voices or influences will be represented. The exclusive use of one observational source of data (e.g. transcriptions of talk, or outcome measures of problem solving) may easily lead to conclusions that are an artifact of the data source used. Researchers who are dependent on single sources of data may use certain validation techniques as appropriate. For example, inferences from the statements of particular participants may be checked through triangulation or comparisons between observations of different, related events. As it is hard to discover patterns of discourse and conceptions of social identities without qualitative information, a combination of quantitative and qualitative data may be useful.

The researchers included here have responded to this question in a number of ways. Most used the analysis of discourse to show how social learning is pursued through a peer group activity in the classroom (Kumpulainen & Mutanen; Leseman et al.; Van Boxtel et al.; Wegerif & Mercer), between teachers and students (Brown & Renshaw; Elbers & Streefland; Grossen; Naylor & Cowie; Rojas-Drummond), how it is supported by the talk of students (Ivinson), teachers (Ireson). Some authors consider the outcomes of group processes (Brown & Renshaw; Kumpulainen & Mutanen; Rojas-Drummond) while others deal only with individual scores (Ireson; Ivinson; Leseman et al.); a few combine group results with individual scores (Van Boxtel et al.; Wegerif & Mercer).

The use of multiple data sources is achieved in several ways, and to different extents. It is inevitably limited by the ways it is treated as an aspect of the design of methods for data collection. Ivinson's contribution is exceptional as she describes explicitly how the ethnomethodological approach is carried out, and how the learning task has been designed to reveal the relationship of curriculum and classroom talk. Few authors discuss, in detail, the limitations of their chosen research design. Future research would benefit from our engagement, as researchers, in a reflective joint consideration of such matters through peer group discourse — the very process that we commonly advocate in classrooms. This would be a suitable theme for future symposia and workshops.

Does the research provide generalizable findings (and is this generalizability well substantiated)?

The practical relevance of any piece of educational research is obviously limited by its generalizability. On reading a particular study, one usually wishes it to be shown that what has been found can inform a range of perspectives in real-life settings. Careful sampling should of course guide all such research, with the typicality of any case studies being accounted for. It is the task of the researcher to demonstrate the rules that guide a discourse, and to give some information regarding generalizability, both in terms of data gathering and assumptions about the similarity or typicality of events described.

The provision of research findings with a wide generalizability is not claimed to any great extent by the researchers presented here who have used only qualitative, descriptive methods. This sometimes reflects the fact that the studies described are parts of larger investigations in which only the discourse aspect is presented as prototypical or used to describe social learning as part of knowledge construction (Kumpulainen & Mutanen; Brown & Renshaw; Elbers & Streefland; Grossen; Ireson; Leseman et al.; Naylor & Cowie). Those involved in experimental studies, however, do discuss the generalizability of their findings, albeit with limited consideration of design features which affect the validity and reliability of the findings (Ivinson; Rojas-Drummond; Van Boxtel et al.; Wegerif & Mercer).

Do the conclusions drawn properly reflect the theory and methods employed?

It is our view that reports of research should have a certain symmetry, so that hypotheses, issues and theoretical perspectives raised in an introduction, and carried through the accounts of data collection and analyses, should be revisited in conclusion. In this way, an informed reader can engage easily but critically with the concerns of the researcher, and so gain the best appreciation of what their efforts have achieved. In relation to the studies reported here, we offer the following comments.

Several of the contributions in this volume are grounded explicitly in theory, and theoretical issues are related to methodological decisions (e.g. Brown & Renshaw; Elbers & Streefland; Grossen; Ivinson; Leseman et al; Kumpulainen & Mutanen;

Van Boxtel et al.; Rojas-Drummond; Wegerif & Mercer). It would perhaps have been good to see more reflective considerations of the relationship between theoretical and methodological decisions and their implications for future research.

New Perspectives on Discourse: Ways to Emancipate the Meaning of Discourse for Teaching and Learning Regarding Concept and Method

Our review suggests that the studies represented here provide several new and valuable perspectives on the role of discourse in the construction of knowledge. We have tried to provide some evaluation of methods that are currently used for the analysis of the process of the joint construction of knowledge through talk; and we leave it to the reader to consider the extent to which the specific contributions of participants, task and contextualizing environment in the construction of knowledge are adequately handled by these methods. This could be of great significance for future research.

We end with two suggestions that may be helpful for those designing studies of the discursive construction of knowledge. The first is Grossen's explicit warning that social organizations are not homogeneous systems, and that activities in schools may invoke various, and sometimes conflicting, identities of participants. We suggest that researchers who aim to identify elements of social interaction related to the construction of knowledge make explicit, for their own benefit, as well as for the readers' of their research reports, how they deal with this matter. (See Brown, 1994; Dallos, 1992; Grossen, Iannaccone, Liengme Bessire & Perret-Clermont, 1997; Littleton, 1999).

Our second suggestion refers to both the scope of discourse analysis and the particular features of the institutional contexts in which teaching and learning is studied. Discourse analysis need not be confined to the consideration of speech; as some of the chapters in this book show, it can incorporate the consideration of joint activity and non-verbal aspects of communication. We should recognise that in some educational settings (such as schools for children with learning and communicational disorders) the social construction of knowledge may depend heavily on the use of other modes of communication than spoken language.

References

Chapter 2

Bakeman, R., & Gottman, J.M. (1997). *Observing Interaction. An Introduction to Sequential Analysis*. Cambridge: Cambridge University Press.

Bales, R.F. (1968). Interaction process analysis. In D.L. Sills (Ed.). *International Encyclopedia of the Social Sciences. Vol. 7*, New York: Crowell, Collier, Mcmillan.

Bronfenbrenner, U., & Ceci, S.J. (1994). Nature–nurture reconceptualized in developmental perspective: A bioecological model. *Psychological Review, 10*, 568–586.

Bus, A.G., Belsky, J., Van IJzendoorn, M.H., & Crnic, K. (1997). Attachment and bookreading patterns: A study of mothers, fathers, and their toddlers. *Early Childhood Research Quarterly, 12*, 81–98.

Ceci, S.J., Rosenblum, T., de Bruyn, E., & Lee, D.Y. (1997). A bio-ecological model of intellectual development: Moving beyond h2. In R.J. Sternberg & E. Grigorenko (Eds.). *Intelligence, Heredity and Environment* (pp. 303–322). Cambridge: Cambridge University Press.

Chen, (1999).

Creswell, J.W. (1998). *Qualitative Inquiry and Research Design*. London: Sage.

Cronbach, L.J. (1975). Beyond the two disciplines of scientific psychology. *American Psychologist, 30*, 116–127.

Dallos, R. (1992). Creating relationship. In D. Miell, & R. Dallos (Eds.). *Social Interaction and Personal Relationships* (pp. 102–157). Milton Keynes: Butler & Tanner.

Edwards, A.D., & Westgate, D.P.G. (1994). *Investigating Classroom Talk*. London: Palmer Press.

Elbers, E., & Streefland, L. (1997). *Changing Identities in the Classroom*. Paper presented at EARLI Conference, Athens: August 26–30.

Erkens, G. (1997). *Cooperative Problem Solving with Computers in Education*. Utrecht: University Press, dissertation.

Erickson, M.F., Sroufe, L.A., & Egeland, B. (1985). The relationship between quality of attachment and behavior problems in a high-risk sample. In J. Bretherton, & E. Waters (Eds.). *Growing Points of Attachment Theory and Research. Monographs of the Society for Research in Child Development* (pp. 147–166), 50.

Flanders, N.A. (1967). Flanders system of interaction analysis. In E.J. Amidon, & J.B. Hough (Eds.). *Teachers' Influence in the Classroom* (pp. 103–116). Reading Mass: Addison Wesley.

Gee, J.P., & Green, J.L. (1998). Discourse analysis, learning, and social practice: A methodological study. *Review of Research in Education, 23*, 119–169.

Grossen, M. & Perret-Clermont, A.N. (1994). Psycho-social perspective on cognitive development construction of adult–child intersubjectivity in logic tasks. In W. de Graaf & R. Maier (Eds.). *Sociogenesis Reexamined* (pp. 243–260). New York: Springer.

Grossen, M., Iannaccone, A., Liengme Bessire, M-J., & Perret-Clermont, A.-N. (1997). Actual and perceived expertise: The role of social comparison in the mastery of right and left recognition in novice–expert dyads. *Swiss Journal of Psychology, 55,* 176–187.

Guba, E.G. & Lincoln, Y.S. (1983). *Effective Evaluation.* San Francisco: Jossey Bas Publishers.

Gutierrez, K.D., Larson, J., & Kreuter, B. (1995). Cultural tensions in the scripted classroom. The value of the subjugated perspective. *Urban Education, 29,* 410–442. London: Sage Publications, Inc.

Harinck, F.J.H. (1986). Research on the play therapy process. In R. van der Kooij, & J. Hellendoorn (Eds.). *Play, Play Therapy, Play Research* (pp. 205–231). Lisse: Swets & Zeitlinger.

Harinck, F.J.H., & Hellendoorn, J. (1987). *Therapeutisch Spel: Proces en Interactie* [*Therapeutic Play: Process and Interaction*]. Lisse: Swets & Zeitlinger.

Harms, T., & Clifford, R.M. (1980). *Early Childhood Environment Rating Scales.* New York: Teachers College Press.

Hicks, D. (1995). Discourse, learning, and teaching. *Review of Research in Education, 21,* 49–95.

Hill, C. E. (1995). Musings about how to study therapist techniques. In L.T. Hoshmand, & J. Martin (Eds.). *Research as Praxis* (pp. 81–103). New York: Teachers College Press.

Hoogsteder, M., Maier, R., & Elbers, E. (1996). The architecture of adult–child interaction. Joint problem solving and the structure of cooperation. *Learning and Instruction, 6,* 345–358.

Hoshmand, L.T., & Martin, J. (Eds.). (1995). *Research as Praxis.* New York: Teachers College Press.

Howe, K., & Eisenhardt, M. (1990). Standards for qualitative (and quantitative) research: A Prolegomenon. *Educational Researcher, 19,* 2–9.

Karasavvidis, I., Pieters, J.M., & Plomp, T. (1998). *Comparing Frequency Based with Sequential Discourse Analysis: Convergence or Divergence?* Poster at the second International Conference on Methods and Techniques in Behavioural Research. Groningen: 18–21 August.

Kazdin, A.E. (Ed.) (1992). *Methodological Issues and Strategies in Clinical Research.* Washington: APA.

Kiesler, D.J. (Ed.) (1973). *The Process of Psychotherapy: Empirical Foundations and Systems of Analysis.* Chicago: Aldine Publications.

Larson, J. (1995). Talk Matters: The Role of Pivot in the Distribution of Literacy Knowledge among Novice Writers. *Linguistics and Education, 7,* 277–302.

Littleton, K., & Light, P. (Eds.) (1999). *Learning with Computers. Analysing Productive Interaction.* London: Routledge.

Miles, M.B., & Huberman, A.M. (1984). *Qualitative Data Analysis: A Sourcebook of New Methods.* London: Sage Publications.

Orlinsky, D.E., & Howard, K.I. (1975). *Varieties of Psychotherapeutic Experience.* New York: Teachers College Press.

Palincsar, A.S. (1998). Social constructivist perspectives on teaching and learning. *Annual Review Psychology, 49,* 345–375.

Patton, M.Q. (1986). *Utilization Focused Evaluation.* London: Sage Publications.

Riksen-Walraven, J.M., Smeekens, J., & Stapert, G.H.M. (1999). Meten van de kwaliteit van ouder-kind-interactie: is éen keer observeren genoeg? *Nederlands Tijdschrift voor Opvoeding, Vorming en Onderwijs, 15,* 67–81.

Salomon, G., & Perkins, D.N. (1998). Individual and social aspects of learning, *Educational Researcher*, *23*, 1–20.

Sfard, A. (1998). On two metaphors for learning and the danger of choosing just one. *Educational Researcher*, *27*, 4–13.

Shotter, J. (1990). Getting in touch: the metamethodology of a postmodern science of mental life. In J. Shotter (Ed.). *Knowing of the Third Kind* (pp. 35–46). Utrecht: ISOR

Spradley, J.P. (1979). *The Ethnographic Interview*. New York: Holt, Rinehart & Winston.

Van der Aalsvoort, G.M., Meesters, G., & Ruijssenaars, A.J.J.M. (1998). *Improving Competence with Intellectually Disabled Students by Video Feedback on Social Interaction Quality*. Paper presented at the 22nd National Conference of the Australian Association of Special Education: Canberra, 28th September.

Vosnadiou, S. (1996). Towards a revised cognitive psychology for new advances in learning and instruction. *Learning and Instruction*, *6*, 95–109.

Wampold, B.E. (1995). Analysis of behavior sequences in psychotherapy. In J. Siegfried (Ed.). *Therapeutic and Everyday Discourse as Behavior Change: Towards a Micro-analysis in Psychotherapy Process Research* (pp. 189–214). Norwood: Ablex Publishing Corporation.

Chapter 3

Atkinson, J.M., & Heritage, J. (1984). *Structures of Social Action*. Cambridge: Cambridge University Press.

Bacon, F. (1996). *Entretiens*. Paris: Editions Carré.

Budge, G.S., & Katz, B. (1995). Constructing psychological knowledge. Reflections on science, scientists and epistemology in the APA manual. *Theory and Psychology*, *5*(2), 217–231.

Chaiklin, S., & Lave, J. (Eds.) (1993). *Understanding Practice*. Cambridge: Cambridge University Press.

Cole, M. (1996). *Cultural Psychology: A Once and Future Discipline*. Cambridge: The Belknap Press.

Donaldson, M. (1978). *Children's Minds*. Fontana: Glasgow.

Edwards, D., & Mercer, N. (1987). *Common Knowledge: The Development of Understanding in the Classroom*. London: Methuen.

Elbers, E. (1986). Interaction and instruction in the conservation experiment. *European Journal of Psychology of Education*, *1*(1), 77–89.

Elbers, E. (1991). The development of competence and its social context. *Educational Psychology Review*, *3*(2), 73–94.

Engeström, Y., & Middleton, D. (Eds.) (1996). *Cognition and Communication at Work*. Cambridge: Cambridge University Press.

Goodwin, C., & Duranti, A. (1992). Rethinking context: An Introduction. In A. Duranti, & C. Goodwin (Eds.). *Rethinking Context* (pp. 1–42). Cambridge: Cambridge University Press.

Grossen, M. (1988). *L'intersubjectivité en Situation de Test*. Cousset (CH-Fribourg): Delval.

Grossen, M. (1994). Theoretical and methodological consequences of a change in the unit of analysis for the study of peer interactions in a problem-solving situation. *European Journal of Psychology of Education*, *10*(2), 159–173.

Grossen, M., Iannaccone, A., Liengme Bessire, A., & Perret-Clermont, A.-N. (1996). Actual and perceived expertise: the role of social comparison in the mastery of right and left recognition in novice-expert dyads. *Swiss Journal of Psychology*, 55(2–3), 176–187.

Grossen, M., Liengme Bessire, M.-J., Perret-Clermont, A.-N., & Iannaccone, A. (1995). *Learning to Teach and Teaching to Learn in Novice–Expert Interactions.* Paper at the 6th Conference of the European Association for Research on Learning and Instruction (EARLI). Nijmegen, Netherlands, 26–31 août 1995.

Grossen, M., & Perret-Clermont, A.-N. (1994). Psycho-social perspective on cognitive development: construction of adult–child intersubjectivity in logic tasks. In W. de Graaf, & R. Maier (Eds.). *Sociogenesis Reexamined* (pp. 243–260). New York: Springer.

Grossen, M., Perret-Clermont, A.-N., & Liengme Bessire, M.J. (1997). Construction de l'interaction et dynamique socio-cognitives. In M. Grossen, & B. Py (Eds.). *Pratiques Sociales et Médiations Symboliques* (pp. 221–247). Berne: Peter Lang.

Hundeide, K. (1992). The message structure of some Piagetian experiments. In A.H. Wold (Ed.). *The Dialogical Alternative. Towards Theories of Language and Minds* (pp. 139–156). Oslo: Scandinavian University Press.

Latour, B. (1996). *Petite Réflexion sur le Culte Moderne des Dieux Faitiches.* Le Plessis-Robinson: Synthélabo Groupe.

Latour, B. (1994). Une sociologie sans objet? Remarques sur l'interobjectivité. *Sociologie du Travail, 4,* 587–607.

Lave, J., & Wenger, E. (1991). *Situated Learning: Legitimate Peripheral Participation.* Cambridge: Cambridge University Press.

Light, P. (1986). Context, conservation and conversation. In M. Richards, & P. Light (Eds.). *Children of Social Worlds. Development in a Social Context.* Cambridge: Polity Press.

Mercer, N. (1995). *The Guided Construction of Knowledge. Talk Amongst Teachers and Learners.* London: Multilingual Matters.

Monteil, J.-M. (1993). Contextes sociaux et activités cognitives: quelques illustrations exemplaires. In J.-M. Monteil (Ed.). *Soi & le Contexte* (pp. 93–108). Paris: Armand Colin.

Nicolet, M. (1995). *Dynamiques Relationnelles et Processus Cognitifs. Etude du Marquage Social chez des Enfants de 5–7 ans.* Paris et Neuchâtel: Delachaux et Niestlé.

Quelhas, A.C., & Pereira, F. (Eds.) (1998). *Cognition and Context.* Special issue of Analise Psicologica. Lisboa: Instituto Superior de Psicologia Applicada.

Resnick, L., Säljö, R., Pontecorvo, C., & Burge, B. (Eds.) (1997). *Discourse, Tools, and Reasoning: Essays on Situated Cognition.* New York: Springer.

Rochex, J.-Y. (1996). *Le Sens de l'Expérience Scolaire.* Paris: Presses Universitaires de France.

Rogoff, B. (1990). *Apprenticeship in Thinking. Cognitive Development in Social Context.* New York: Oxford University Press.

Rogoff, B. (1995). Observing sociocultural activity on three planes: Participatory appropriation, guided participation, and apprenticeship. In J.V. Wertsch, P. del Rio, P. & A. Alvarez (Eds.). *Sociocultural Studies of Mind* (pp. 139–163). Cambridge: Cambridge University Press.

Rommetveit, R. (1978). On Piagetian cognitive operations, semantic competence, and message structure in adult–child interaction. In I. Marková (Ed.). *The Social Context of Language* (pp. 113–150). Chichester: Wiley.

Rommetveit, R. (1992). Outlines of dialogically based social-cognitive approach to human cognition and communication. In A.H. Wold (Ed.). *The Dialogical Alternative. Towards Theories of Language and Minds* (pp. 19–44). Oslo: Scandinavian University Press.

Säljö, R. (1991). Piagetian controversies, cognitive competence, and assumptions about human communication. *Educational Psychology Review*, 3(2), 117–126.

Schubauer-Leoni, M.L., Bell, N., Grossen, M., & Perret-Clermont, A.-N. (1989). Problems in assessment of learning: The social construction of questions and answers in the scholastic context. *International Journal of Educational Research*, 13(6), 671–668.

Schubauer-Leoni, M.L., & Grossen, M. (1993). Negotiating the meaning of questions in didactic and experimental contracts. *European Journal of Psychology of Education*, 8(4), 451–471.

Tremblay, M. (1994). *Un Ange Cornu avec des Ailes de Tôle*. Paris: Actes Sud.

Valsiner, J. (1997). Subjective construction of intersubjectivity. Semiotic mediation as a process of preadaptation. In M. Grossen, & B. Py (Eds.). *Pratiques Sociales et Médiations Symboliques* (pp. 46–60). Bern: Peter Lang.

Wertsch, J.V. (1991). *Voices of the Mind: A Socio-cultural Approach to Mediated Action*. London: Harvester Wheatsheaf.

Chapter 4

Antaki, C., & Widdicombe, S. (1998). Identity as an achievement and as a tool. In C. Antaki, & S. Widdicombe (Eds.). *Identities in Talk* (pp. 1–14). London: Sage.

Barnard, A. (1996). Emic and etic. In A. Barnard and J. Spencer (Eds.). *Encyclopedia of Social and Cultural Anthropology* (pp. 180–183). London: Routledge.

Bennett, N., & Dunne, E. (1991). The nature and quality of talk in co-operative classroom groups. *Learning and Instruction*, 1, 103–118.

Brown, A., & Campione, J. (1994). Guided discovery in a community of learners. In K. McGilly (Ed.). *Classroom Lessons. Integrating Cognitive Theory and Classroom Practice* (pp. 229–270). Cambridge: MIT press.

Cowie, H., Smith, P., Boulton, M., & Laver, R. (1994). *Cooperation in the Multi-Ethnic Classroom*. London: Fulton.

Edwards, D., & Mercer, N. (1987). *Common Knowledge. The Development of Understanding in the Classroom*. London: Routledge.

Elbers, E. (1996). Citizenship in the making. Themes of citizenship in children's pretend play. *Childhood*, 3, 499–514.

Elbers, E., Derks, A., & Streefland (1995). *Learning in a Community of Inquiry: Teacher's Strategies and Children's Participation in the Construction of Mathematical Knowledge*. Paper presented to the EARLI conference, Nijmegen (August 26–31).

Elbers, E., & Kelderman, A. (1995). Ground rules for testing: Expectations and misunderstandings in test situations. *European Journal of Psychology of Education*, 9, 11–120.

Elbers, E., & Streefland, L. (1997). *Learning by Participation in a Community of Inquiry*. Paper presented at the EARLI conference, Athens (August 26–30).

Elbers, E., & Streefland, L. (1998). *Collaborative Learning and the Social Construction of Knowledge in the Classroom*. Paper presented at the ISCRAT conference, Aarhus (June 7–11).

Freudenthal, H. (1991). *Revisiting Mathematics Education*. Dordrecht: Kluwer.

Goffree, F. (1993). HF: Working on mathematics education. *Educational Studies in Mathematics*, 25, 21–49.

Gumperz, J., & Cook-Gumperz, J. (1982). Language and the communication of social identity. In J. Gumperz (Ed.). *Language and Social Identity* (pp. 1–21). Cambridge: Cambridge University Press.

Maybin, J. (1993). Children's voices. Talk, knowledge and identity. In D. Graddol, J. Maybin & B. Stierer (Eds.). *Researching Language and Literacy in Social Context* (pp. 131–150). Clevedon: Multilingual Matters.

Mercer, N. (1995). *The Guided Construction of Knowledge*. Clevedon: Multilingual Matters.

Muller, N., & Perret-Clermont, A.-N. (in press). Negotiating identities and meanings in the transmission of knowledge: analysis of interactions in the context of a knowledge exchange network. In J. Bliss, P. Light, & R. Säljö (Eds.). *Learning Sites. Social and Technological Contexts for Learning*. Amsterdam: Elsevier.

Orellana, M. (1996). Negotiating power through language in classroom meetings. *Linguistics and Education, 8*, 335–365.

Potter, J., & Wetherell, M. (1987). *Discourse and Social Psychology: Beyond Attitudes and Behaviour*. London: Sage.

Rogoff, B. (1994). Developing understanding of the idea of communities of learners. *Mind, Culture and Activity, 1*, 209–229.

Rojas-Drummond, S., Hernández, G., Vélez, M., & Villagrán, G. (1998). Cooperative learning and the appropriation of procedural knowledge by primary school children. *Learning and Instruction, 8*, 37–61.

Saville-Troike, M. (1989). *The Ethnography of Communication*. Oxford: Blackwell (second edition).

Seixas, P. (1993). The community of inquiry as a basis for knowledge and learning: the case of history. *American Educational Research Journal, 30*, 305–324.

Streefland, L. (1993). The design of a mathematics course. A theoretical reflection. *Educational Studies in Mathematics, 25*, 109–135.

Taconis, R., & Holleman, W. (1998). *Van VWO naar WO: Aansluitprocessen en Problemen in de Propedeuse* (From secondary school to university: processes and problems in the first year at university). Utrecht: Utrecht University.

Wells, G. (1983). Talking with children. The complementary roles of parents and teachers. In M. Donaldson, R. Grieve, & C. Pratt (Eds.). *Early Childhood Development and Education* (pp. 127–150). Oxford: Blackwell.

Widdicombe, S. (1998). Identity as an analysts' and a participants' resource. In C. Antaki, & S. Widdicombe (Eds.). *Identities in Talk* (pp. 191–206). London: Sage.

Wood, D. (1988). *How Children Think and Learn*. London: Blackwell, 1988.

Chapter 5

Bakhtin, M. (1981). *The Dialogic Imagination: Four Essays*. Michael Holquist (Ed.). Austin, Texas: University of Texas Press.

Bereiter, C. (1994). Implications of postmodernism for science, or, science as progressive discourse. *Educational Psychologist, 29*(1) 3–12.

Bruner, J. (1996). *The Culture of Education*. Cambridge: Harvard University Press.

Brown, R.A.J. (1994). *Collective Mathematical Thinking in the Primary Classroom: A Conceptual and Empirical Analysis Within a Sociocultural Framework*. Bachelor of Educational Studies (Hons.) Thesis, University of Queensland.

Brown, R.A.J. (1997). "You can't explain infinity!": Collective argumentation discourse across primary school subject domains. In M. Goos, K. Moni, & J. Knight (Eds.). *Scholars in Context: Prospects and Transitions* (pp. 17–22). Brisbane: Post Pressed.

Brown, R.A.J. (1998). "Where do you people get your ideas from?": Negotiating zones of collaborative learning within an upper primary classroom. In B. Baker, M. Tucker, & C. Ng (Eds.). *Education's New Timespace: Visions from the Present* (pp. 107–112.). Brisbane: Post Pressed.

Brown, R.A.J., & Renshaw, P.D. (1995). Developing collective mathematical thinking within the primary classroom. In B. Attache, & S. Flavel (Eds.). *Proceedings of the Eighteenth Annual Conference of the Mathematics Education Research Group of Australasia (MERGA)* (pp. 128–134). Darwin: Mathematics Education Research Group of Australasia.

Brown, R.A.J., & Renshaw, P.D. (1996). Collective argumentation in the primary mathematics classroom: Towards a community of practice. In P.C. Clarkson (Ed.). *Technology in Mathematics Education: Proceedings of the Nineteenth Annual Conference of the Mathematics Education Research Group of Australasia (MERGA)* (pp. 85–92). Melbourne: Mathematics Education Research Group of Australasia.

Edwards, C., & Mercer, N. (1987). *Common Knowledge: The Development of Understanding in the Classroom*. New York: Routledge.

Forman, E., Stein, M.K., Brown, C., & Larreamendy-Joerns, J. (1995). *The Socialization of Mathematical Thinking: The Role of Institutional, Interpersonal, and Discursive Contexts*. Paper presented at the annual meeting of the American Educational Research Association, San Francisco, CA, April.

Kruger, A.C., & Tomasello, M. (1986). Transactive discussions with peers and adults. *Developmental Psychology*, *22*(5), 681–685.

Kutz, E. (1990). Authority and voice in student ethnographic writing. *Anthropology and Education Quarterly*, *21*, 340–357.

Lampert, M. (1990). When the problem is not the question and the solution is not the answer: Mathematical knowing and teaching. *American Educational Research Journal*, *27*(1), 29–63.

Mercer, N. (1995) *The Guided Construction of Knowledge: Talk Amongst Teachers and Learners*. Clevedon: Multilingual Matters.

Miller, M. (1987). Argumentation and cognition. In M. Hickmann (Ed.). *Social and Functional Approaches to Language and Thought* (pp. 225–249). London: Academic Press.

O'Connor, M.C., & Michaels, S. (1996). Shifting participant frameworks: Orchestrating thinking practices in group discussions. In D. Hicks (Ed.). *Discourse, Learning and Schooling* (pp. 63–103). Cambridge: Cambridge University Press.

Renshaw, P.D. (1998). Sociocultural pedagogy for New Times: Reframing the ZPD and community of learners. *Australian Educational Researcher*, *25*(3), 83–100.

Renshaw P.D., & Brown, R.A.J. (1997). Learning partnerships: The role of teachers in a community of learners. In L. Logan, & J. Sachs (Eds.). *Meeting the Challenges of Primary Schools* (pp. 200–211). London: Routledge.

Renshaw, P.D., & Brown, R.A.J. (1998a). Orchestrating different voices in student talk about infinity: Theoretical and empirical analyses. In C. Kanes, M. Goos, & E. Warren (Eds.). *Teaching Mathematics in New Times: Proceedings of the Twenty-first Annual Conference of the Mathematics Education Research Group of Australasia*, Volume 2, (pp. 468–475). Gold Coast, Australia: MERGA.

Renshaw, P.D., & Brown, R.A.J. (1998b). Voices in classroom talk: Author(ity) and identity. Paper presented at the Annual Conference of the Australian Association for Research in Education, Adelaide, November 1998.

Siegler, R.S. (1976). Three aspects of cognitive development. *Cognitive Psychology*, *4*, 481–520.

Siegler, R.S. (1978). The origins of scientific reasoning. In R.S. Siegler (Ed.). *Children's Thinking: What Develops?* (pp. 109–149). Hillsdale, N.J.: Erlbaum.

Vice, S. (1997). *Introducing Bakhtin.* Manchester: Manchester University Press.

Vygotsky, L.S. (1987). *The Collected Works of L.S Vygotsky, Volume 1: Problems of General Psychology.* New York: Plenum Press.

Wertsch, J.V. (1998). *Mind as action.* New York: Oxford University Press.

Chapter 6

Bernstein, B. (1971). On the classification and framing of educational knowledge. In M.F.D. Young (Ed.). *Knowledge and Control,* pp. 47–69. London: Collier-Macmillan.

Bernstein, B. (1974). *Class, Codes and Control. Theoretical Studies Towards a Sociology of Language.* Second (revised) edition. London: Routledge.

Bernstein, B. (1981). Codes, modalities and the process of cultural reproduction: a model. *Language and Society, 10,* 327–363 [reprinted with some expansion in *Class, Codes and Control,* Vol. IV: *The Structuring of Pedagogic Discourse.* London and New York: Routledge].

Bernstein, B. (1990). *The Structuring of Pedagogic Discourse.* London and New York: Routledge.

Bernstein, B (1996). *Pedagogy Symbolic Control and Identity Theory, Research, Critique.* London and Bristol: Taylor and Francis.

Daniels, H.R.J. (1989). Visual displays as tacit relays of the structure of pedagogic practice. *British Journal of Sociology of Education, 10*(2), 123–140.

Diaz, M. (1984). *A Model of Pedagogic Discourse with Special Application to Colombian Primary Level.* University of London: Unpublished PhD thesis.

Duveen, G., & Lloyd, B. (1986). The significance of social identities. *British Journal of Social Psychology, 25,* 219–230.

Duveen, G., & Lloyd, B. (1990). Introduction. In G. Duveen, & B. Lloyd (Eds.). *Social Representations and the Development of Knowledge,* pp. 1–10. Cambridge: Cambridge University Press.

Duveen, G., & Lloyd, B. (1993). An ethnographic approach to social representations. In G.M. Breakwell, & D.V. Canter (Eds.). *Empirical Approaches to Social Representations,* pp. 90–108. Oxford: Oxford University Press.

Duveen, G. (1994). Criancas enquanto atores sociais. In S. Jovchelovitch and P. Guareschi (Eds.). *Textos em Representacoes Sociais.* Petropolis, Brazil: Vozes.

Duveen, G. (1997). Psychological development as a social process. In L. Smith, J. Dockrell, & P. Tomlinson (Eds.). *Piaget, Vygotsky and Beyond.* London: Routledge.

Ivinson, G. (1998a). *The Construction of the Curriculum.* University of Cambridge: Unpublished PhD thesis.

Ivinson, G. (1998b). The child's construction of the curriculum. *Papers in Social Representation: Threads and Discussions. Special Issue: The Development of Knowledge,* 7(1–2), 21–40.

Jovchelovitch, S. (1995). Social representations in and of the public sphere: Towards a theoretical articulation, *Journal for the Theory of Social Behaviour, 25*(1), 81–102.

Kelly, G.A. (1955). *The Psychology of Personal Constructs.* New York: W.N. Norton and Company Inc.

Lloyd, B., & Duveen, G. (1989). The construction of social knowledge in the transition from sensorimotor to conceptual activity: the gender systems. In A. Gellatly, D. Rogers, & J. Sloboda (Eds.). *Cognition and Social Worlds*, pp. 83–98. Oxford: Oxford University Press.

Lloyd, B., & Duveen, G. (1990). A semiotic analysis of the development of social representations of gender. In G. Duveen & B. Lloyd (Eds.). *Social Representations and the Development of Knowledge*, pp. 27–46. Cambridge: Cambridge University Press.

Lloyd, B., & Duveen, G. (1992). *Gender Identities and Education. The Impact of Starting School*. Hemel Hempstead: Harvester Wheatsheaf.

Morias, A.M., Fontinhas, F., & Neve, I.P. (1993). Recognition and realisation rules in acquiring school science: Contribution of pedagogy and social background of pupils. *British Journal of the Sociology of Education*, 13(2), 247–270.

Moscovici, S. (1976). *La Psychanalyse, son Image et son Public*, 2nd edn. Paris: Presses Universitaires de France.

Moscovici, S. (1981). On social representation. In J. Forgas (Ed.). *Social Cognition*, pp. 181–203. London: Academic Press.

Moscovici, S. (1984). The phenomenon of social representations. In R.M. Farr, & S. Moscovici (Eds.). *Social Representations*, pp. 3–69. Cambridge: Cambridge University Press.

Moscovici, S. (1990). Social psychology and developmental psychology: extending the conversation. In G. Duveen, & B. Lloyd (Eds.). *Social Representations and the Development of Knowledge*, pp. 164–185. Cambridge: Cambridge University Press.

Moscovici, S. (1998). The history and actuality of social representations. In U. Flick (Ed.). *Psychology of the Social*, pp. 209–247. Cambridge: Cambridge University Press.

Mugny, G., De Paolis, P., & Carugati, F. (1984). Social regulation in cognitive development. In W. Doise, & A. Palmonari (Eds.). *Social Interaction in Individual Development*, pp. 127–144. Cambridge: Cambridge University Press.

Piaget, J. (1932). *The Moral Judgement of the Child*. London: Routledge.

Piaget, J. (1951). *Play, Dreams and Imitation in Childhood*. London: Routledge and Kegan Paul (Original edition: 1946).

Ravenette, A.T. (1975). Grid techniques for children. *Journal of Child Psychology and Psychiatry*, 6, 79–83.

Shweder, R. (1990). Cultural psychology: What is it? In J.W. Stigler, R. Shweder, & G. Herdt (Eds.). *Cultural Psychology*, pp. 1–43. Cambridge: Cambridge University Press.

Singh, P. (1993). Instructional discourse: a case study of the social construction of technical competence in the primary school classroom. *British Journal of Sociology of Education*, 14(1), 39–58.

Smith, M. (1986). INGRID program. Manchester: UMIST.

Walkerdine, V. (1988). *The Mastery of Reason*. London, New York: Routledge.

Wallon, H. (1970). *De l'Acte a la Pensee*. Paris: Flammarion.

Wertsch, J.V. (1985). *Vygotsky and the Social Formation of Mind*. Cambridge, MA: Harvard University Press.

Whitty, G., Rowe, G., & Aggleton, P. (1994a). Discourse in cross-curricular contexts: Limits to empowerment. *International Studies in the Sociology of Education*, 4(1), 25–41.

Whitty, G., Rowe, G., & Aggleton, P. (1994b). Subjects and themes in secondary school curriculum. *Research Papers in Education*, 9(2), 159–181.

Wood, D., Bruner, J.S., & Ross, G. (1976). The role of tutoring in problem solving. *Journal of Child Psychology and Psychiatry*, 17, 89–100.

Chapter 7

Carr, R. (1994). Peer helping in Canada. *Peer Counseling Journal, 11*(1), 6–9.

Cowie, H. (2000) Bystanding or standing by: gender issues in coping with bullying, *Aggressive Behavior, 26*, 85–97.

Cowie, H. (1998). Perspectives of teachers and pupils on the experience of peer support against bullying. *Educational Research and Evaluation, 4*, 108–125.

Cowie, H., & Olafsson, R. (2000). The role of peer support in helping victims of bullying. *School Psychology International, 20*(2), 25–41.

Cowie, H., & Sharp, S. (1996). *Peer Counselling in Schools: A Time to Listen.* London: David Fulton.

Craig, W., & Pepler, D. (1996). Peer processes in bullying and victimisation: An observational study. *Exceptionality Education Canada, 5*, 81–95.

Cunningham, C., Cunningham, L., Martorelli, V., Tran, A., Young, J., & Zacharias, R. (1998). The effects of primary division, student-mediated conflict resolution programs on playground aggression. *Journal of Child Psychology and Psychiatry, 39*(5), 653–662.

Dalrymple, J., and Hough, J. (1995). *Having a Voice: An Exploration of Children's Rights and Advocacy.* Birmingham: Venture Press.

Department for Education and Science. (1989). *Discipline in Schools: Report of the Committee Chaired by Lord Elton.* London: HMSO.

Department for Education and Employment. (1999). *Secondary Schools' Performance Tables 1998.* London: Department for Education and Employment. Retrieved January 20th 1999 from the World Wide Web: http://www.dfee.gov.uk/cgi bin/shlea_98?lea=891&type=b.

Gilligan, C. (1982). *In a Different Voice: Psychological Theory and Women's Development.* Cambridge, MA: Harvard University Press.

Hazler, R. (1996). Bystanders: an overlooked factor in peer on peer abuse. *The Journal for the Professional Counsellor, 11*, 11–21.

MacLeod, M., & Morris, S. (1996). *Why Me?* London: ChildLine.

Naylor, P., & Cowie, H. (1999). The effectiveness of peer support systems in challenging school bullying: the perspectives and experiences of teachers and pupils. *Journal of Adolescence, 22*, 467–479.

Office for Standards in Education (1998). *Inspection Report: Elliott Durham School, Nottingham.* Contract number: 930/S5/700210. London: Office for Standards in Education.

Rigby, K., & Slee, P. (1991). Bullying among Australian school children: Reported behaviour and attitudes to victims. *Journal of Social Psychology, 131*, 615–627.

Salmivalli, C., Lagerspetz, K., Björkvist, K., Österman, K., & Kaukiainen, A. (1996). Bullying as a group process: Participant roles and their relations to social status within the group. *Aggressive Behavior, 22*, 1–15.

Tharp, R., & Gallimore, R. (1988). *Rousing Minds to Life: Teaching, Learning and Schooling in Social Context.* Cambridge: Cambridge University Press.

Tinker, R. (1998). ABC: Peer Counselling at Elliott Durham School. *Peer Support Networker, 8*, Spring.

Vygotsky, L.S. (1978). *Mind in Society: The Development of Higher Psychological Processes.* Cambridge, MA: Harvard University Press.

Wood, D. (1988). *How Children Learn and Think.* Oxford: Basil Blackwell.

Chapter 8

Aureli, T., & Colecchia, N. (1996). Day care experience and free play behavior in preschool children. *Journal of Applied Developmental Psychology, 17*, 1–17.

Bourdieu, P., & Passeron, J.C. (1977). *Reproduction in Education, Society and Culture.* London: Sage.

Bruner, J.S. (1983). *Child's Talk: Learning to Use Language.* New York: Norton.

Bullock, J.R. (1993). Children's temperament: How can teachers and classrooms be more responsive? *Early Child Development and Care, 88*, 53–59.

Bus, A.G., Van IJzendoorn, M.H., & Pellegrini, A.D. (1995). Joint book reading makes for success in learning to read. A meta-analysis on intergenerational transmission of literacy. *Review of Educational Research, 65*, 1–21.

Case, R. (1998). Changing views of knowledge and their impact on educational research and practice. In D.R. Olson, & N. Torrance (Eds.). *The Handbook of Education and Human Development. New Models of Learning, Teaching, and Schooling* (pp. 73–99). Cambridge, Massachusetts: Blackwell Publishers.

Cocking, R.R., & Renninger, K.A. (1993). Psychological distance as a unifying theory of development. In R.R. Cocking, & K.A. Renninger (Eds.). *The Development and Meaning of Psychological Distance* (pp. 3–18). Hillsdale, New Jersey: Erlbaum.

Cohen, E.G., & Lotan, R.A. (1995). Producing equal-status interaction in the heterogeneous classroom. *American Educational Research Journal, 32*(1), 99–120.

de Beaugrande, R., & Dressler, W. (1981). *Introduction to Text Linguistics.* London: Longman.

Dickinson, D.K., & Smith, M.W. (1991). Preschool talk: Patterns of teacher-child interaction in early childhood classrooms. *Journal of Research in Childhood Education, 6*(1), 20–29.

Fabes, R.A., Eisenberg, N., & Eisenbud, L. (1993). Behavioral and physiological correlates of children's reactions to others in distress. *Developmental Psychology, 29*(4), 655–663.

Fodor, J.A. (1975). *The Language of Thought.* Cambridge, Massachusetts: Harvard University Press.

Garvey, C. (1993). Diversity in the conversational repertoire: The case of conflicts and social pretending. *Cognition and Instruction, 11*(3 & 4), 251–264.

Gillies, R.M. (1997, March). *Interaction of children in classroom-based workgroups.* Paper presented at the Annual Meeting of the American Educational Research Association. Chicago, Illinois.

Greenwood, C.R., Todd, N.M., Hops, H., & Walker, H.M. (1982). Behavior change targets in assessment and treatment of socially withdrawn preschool children. *Behavioral Assessment, 4*(3), 273–297.

Grice, H.P. (1975). Logic and conversation. In P. Cole, & J.L. Morgan (Eds.). *Syntax and Semantics 3: Speech Acts* (pp. 41–58). London: Academic Press.

Howes, C. (1988). Peer interaction of young children. *Monographs of the Society for Research in Child Development, 53*, 1.

Johnson-Laird, P.N. (1983). *Mental Models.* Cambridge: Cambridge University Press.

Keogh, B.K. (1986). Temperament and schooling: Meaning of Goodness-of-Fit? In J.V. Lerner, & R.M. Lerner (Eds.). Temperament and social interaction in infants and children. *New Directions for Child Development, 31*, 89–108.

Keogh, B.K. (1989). Applying temperament research to school. In G.A. Kohnstamm, J.E.Bates, & M.K.Rothbart (Eds.). *Temperament in Childhood* (pp. 437–450). Chichester, England: Wiley.

Kintsch, W. (1998). *Comprehension: A Paradigm for Cognition*. Cambridge: Cambridge University Press.

Leseman, P.P.M., & F.F. Sijsling (1996). Cooperation and instruction in practical problem-solving: Differences in interaction styles of mother–child dyads as related to socioeconomic background and cognitive development. *Learning and Instruction*, 6(4), 307–323.

Leseman, P.P.M., & de Jong, P.F. (1998). Home literacy: opportunity, instruction, co-operation, and social-emotional quality predicting early reading achievement. *Reading Research Quarterly*, 33(3), 294–318.

Leseman, P.P.M., & van den Boom, D.C. (1999). Effects of quantity and quality of home proximal processes on Dutch, Surinamese-Dutch, and Turkish-Dutch preschoolers' cognitive development. *Infant and Child Development*, 8, 19–38.

Lewis, M. (1977). Early socioemotional development and its relevance for curriculum. *Merill Palmer Quarterly*, 23(4), 279–286.

Martin, R.P. (1989). Temperament and education: implications for underachievement and learning disabilities. In G.A. Kohnstamm, J.E. Bates, & M.K.Rothbart (Eds.). *Temperament in Childhood* (pp. 451–461). Chichester, England: Wiley.

Mercer, N. (1996). The quality of talk in children's collaborative activity in the classroom. *Learning and Instruction*, 6(4), 359–377.

Musatti, T. (1993). Meaning between peers: The meaning of the peer. *Cognition and Instruction*, 11(3–4), 241–250.

Ninio, A., & Snow, C.E. (1996). *Pragmatic Development*. Boulder, Colorado: Westview Press.

Pellegrini, A.D. (1991). *Applied Child Study. A Developmental Approach*. Hillsdale, New Jersey: Erlbaum.

Renshaw, P.D., & Gardner, R. (1990). Process versus product task interpretation and parental teaching practices. *International Journal of Behavioral Development*, 13, 489–506.

Rogoff, B. (1990). *Apprenticeship in Thinking. Cognitive Development in Social Context*. New York: Oxford University Press.

Rogoff, B. (1998). Cognition as a collaborative process. In W. Damon, D. Kuhn & R.S. Siegler (Eds.). *Handbook of Child Psychology* (pp. 674–744). New York: Wiley.

Rollenberg, L., & Leseman, P.P.M. (1997). *Handleiding voor het Coderen van Videoobservaties*. Amsterdam: University of Amsterdam, Department of Education (unpublished coding manual).

Rubin, S.S. (1982). Expressive language deficits and treatment of socially withdrawn preschool children. *American Journal of Orthopsychiatry*, 52(1), 58–64.

Schonewille, B., & van der Leij, A. (1995). De rol van de leerkracht voor allochtone en autochtone leerlingen in het eerste jaar van het bassonderwijs. *Pedagogische Studiën*, 72, 242–257.

Searle, J.R. (1965). What is a speech act? In M. Black (Ed.). *Philosophy in America* (pp. 221–239). London: Allen & Unwin.

Serpell, R. (1999). Theoretical conceptions of human development. In L. Eldering, & P.P.M. Leseman (Eds.). *Effective Early Education: Cross-cultural Perspectives* (pp. 41–66). New York: Falmer Press.

Sigel, I.E., Stinson, E.T., & Kim, K.(1993). Socialization of cognition: the distancing model. In R.H. Wozniak, & K.W. Fischer (Eds.). *Development in Context. Acting and Thinking in Specific Environments* (pp. 211–224). New York: Erlbaum.

Smilansky, S. (1968). *The Effect of Socio-Dramatic Play on Disadvantaged Preschool Children*. New York: Wiley.

van Dijk, T.A. (1987). Episodic models in discourse processing. In R. Horowitz, & S.J. Samuels (Eds.). *Comprehending Oral and Written Language* (pp. 161–196). San Diego, California: Academic Press.

van Kuyk, J.J. (1996). *Leerlingvolgsysteem Ordenen* [Ordering. A student achievement monitoring system]. Arnhem, Netherlands: CITO National Educational Testing Service.

Verba, M. (1993). Cooperative formats in pretend play among young children. *Cognition and Instruction, 11*(3 & 4), 265–280.

Verba, M. (1994). The beginnings of collaboration in peer interaction. *Human Development, 37*, 125–139.

Webb, N.M. (1991). Task-related verbal interaction and mathematics learning in small groups. *Journal for Research in Mathematics Education, 22*, 366–389.

Wegerif, R. & Mercer, N. (2000). Language for thinking: A Study of children showing reasoning test problems together (this volume).

Wertsch, J.V., & Bivens, J.A. (1993). The social origins of individual mental functioning: Alternatives and perspectives. In R.R. Cocking, & K.A. Renninger (Eds.). *The development and Meaning of Psychological Distance* (pp. 203–218). Hillsdale, New Jersey: Erlbaum.

Wood, D., & Wood, H. (1996). Contingency in tutoring and learning. *Learning and Instruction, 6*(4), 391–397.

Chapter 9

Barr, R., & Dreeben, R. (1991). Grouping students for reading instruction. In R. Barr, M. Kamil, P. Mosenthal, & P.D. Pearson (Eds.). *Handbook of Reading Research* Vol. 2, pp. 885–910. New York: Longman.

Bronfenbrenner, U. (1979). *The Ecology of Human Development*, London: Harvard.

Ceci, S.J., & Bronfenbrenner, U. (1985). Don't forget to take the cupcakes out of the oven: strategic time-monitoring, prospective memory and context. *Child Development, 56*, 175–190.

Bruner, J.S. (1983). *Child's Talk: Learning to Use Language*. New York: Norton.

Clay, M.M. (1985). *The Early Detection of Reading Difficulties: A Diagnostic Survey with Recovery Procedures* (3rd ed.). Auckland: Heinemann.

Clay, M.M., & Cazden, C.B. (1990). A Vygotskian interpretation of Reading Recovery. In L.C. Moll (Ed.). *Vygotsky and Education: Instructional Implications and Applications of Socio-Historical Psychology* (pp. 206–222) New York: Cambridge University Press.

Fox, B. (1993). *The Human Tutorial Dialogue Project: Issues in the Design of Instructional Systems* London: Lawrence Erlbaum Associates.

Gonzalez, M.-M. (1996). Tasks and activities: a parent–child interaction analysis. *Learning and Instruction, 6*(4), 287–306.

Goodnow, J.J. (1990). The socialization of cognition: What's involved? In J. Stigler, R. Schweder, & G. Herdt (Eds.). *Cultural Psychology* (259–286) Chicago: University of Chicago Press.

Greenfield, P. (1984). A theory of the teacher in the learning activities of everyday life. In B. Rogoff, & J. Lave (Eds.). *Everyday Cognition* London: Harvard University Press.

Guskey, T.R. (1986). Staff development and the process of teacher change. *Educational researcher, 15*(5), 5–12.

Hickey, K. (1977). Dyslexia: a language course for teachers and learners. Private publication.

Hornsby, B., & Shear, F. (1993). *Alpha to Omega*. Fourth edition. Oxford: Heinemann Educational.

Ireson, J. (1997). Cultural contexts for learning to read: a case of conflicting pedagogies? *Paper presented at an International Symposium Integrating Research and Practice in Literacy*, Institute of Education, University of London, December 1997.

Ireson, J., Blatchford, P., & Joscelyne, T. (1995). What do teachers do? Classroom activities in the teaching of reading. *Educational Psychology, 15*(3), 245–256.

Ireson, J., & Blay, J. (1999). Constructing activity: Participation by adults and children *Learning and Instruction, 9*, 19–36.

Lave, J., & Wenger, E. (1991). *Situated Learning: Legitimate Peripheral Participation*. Cambridge: Cambridge University Press.

Levin, I., & Korat, O. (1997). Social effects on maternal role in child's literacy: maternal beliefs and interaction with her child. *Paper presented at an International Symposium Integrating Research and Practice in Literacy*, Institute of Education, University of London, December 1997.

Nilholm, C., & Saljo, R. (1996). Co-action, situation definition and sociocultural experience: an empirical study of problem solving in mother–child interaction. *Learning and Instruction, 6*(4), 325–344.

McArthur, D., Stasz, C., & Zmuidzinas, M. (1990). Tutoring techniques in algebra. *Cognition and Instruction, 7*(3), 197–244.

Paradise, R. (1996). Passivity of tacit collaboration: Mazahua interaction in cultural context. *Learning and Instruction, 6*(4), 379–390.

Rogoff, B. (1990). *Apprenticeship in Thinking*. Oxford: Oxford University Press.

Rogoff, B. (1995). Sociocultural activity on three planes, In J.V. Wertsch, P. del Rio, & A. Alvarez (Eds.). *Sociocultural Studies of Mind* (pp. 56–74). Cambridge: Cambridge University Press.

Rogoff, B., Mistry, J., Goncu, A., & Mosier, C. (1993). Guided participation in cultural activity by toddlers and caregivers. *Monographs of the Society for Research in Child Development, 58*(8).

Saljo, R., & Wyndham, J. (1993). Solving problems in the formal setting: an empirical study of the school as a context for thought. In S. Chaiklin, & J. Lave (Eds.). *Understanding Practice*. Cambridge University Press.

Stanovich, K. (1994). Constructivism in reading education. *The Journal of Special Education, 28*(3), 259–274.

Vygotsky, L. (1978). *Mind in Society*. Cambridge: Harvard University Press.

Wertsch, J.V. (1995). The need for action in sociocultural research. In J.V. Wertsch, P. del Rio, & A. Alvarez (Eds.). *Sociocultural Studies of Mind* (pp. 56–74). Cambridge: Cambridge University Press.

Wertsch, J.V., Minick, N., & Arns, F.J. (1984). The creation of context in joint problem solving. In B. Rogoff & J. Lave (Eds.). *Everyday Cognition: Its Development in Social Context*. London: Harvard University Press.

Wood, D., Bruner, J.S., & Ross, G. (1976). The role of tutoring in problem solving. *Journal of Child Psychology and Psychiatry, 17*, 98–100.

Chapter 10

Austin, J.L. (1962). *How to do Things with Words*. Oxford: Clarendon Press.

Anderson, J.F., Reder, L.M., & Simon, H.A. (1997). Situative versus cognitive perspectives: Form versus substance. *Educational Researcher, 26*, 18–21.

Barnes, D., & Todd, F. (1977). *Communication and Learning in Small Groups*. London: Routledge and Kegan Paul Ltd.

Barnes, D., & Todd, F. (1995). *Communication and Learning Revisited, Making Meaning Through Talk*. Portsmouth, NH: Boynton/Cook Publishers Heinemann.

Bergqvist, K., & Säljö, R. (1995, August). *Social Languages in Classroom Discourse — Identifying and Appropriating Knowledge*. Paper presented at the 6th European Association for Research on Learning and Instruction conference. Nijmegen, the Netherlands.

Brown, J.S., Collins, A., & Duguid, P. (1989). Situated cognition and the culture of learning. *Educational Researcher, 18*, 32–42.

Bruner, J. (1990). *Acts of Meaning*. Cambridge: Harvard University Press.

Cazden, C. (1988). *Classroom Discourse, the Language of Teaching and Learning*. Portsmouth, NH: Heinemann Educational Books Inc.

Cohen, E. (1994). Restructuring the classroom: Conditions for productive small groups. *Review of Educational Research, 64*(1), 1–35.

Cole, M., & Wertsch, J. (1997). "Beyond individual-social antimony in discussions of Piaget and Vygotksy" [http://www.massey.ac.nz/~ALock/virtual/colevyg.htm]. 6 March 1997.

Delamont, S. (1976). *Interaction in the Classroom. Contemporary Sociology of the School*. Suffolk: Richard Clay Ltd.

Doise, W., & Mugny, G. (1984). *The Social Development of the Intellect*. Oxford: Pergamon Press.

Edwards, D. (1993). Concepts, memory, and the organization of pedagogic discourse: A case study. *Educational Research, 19*, 205–225.

Edwards, D., & Mercer, N. (1987). *Common Knowledge*. London: Methuen.

Edwards, D., & Potter, J. (1992). *Discursive Psychology*. Newbury Park, CA: Sage.

Edwards, D., & Westgate, D. (1994). *Investigating Classroom Talk* (2nd ed.). Basingstoke: Falmer Press.

Fisher, E. (1993). Distinctive features of pupil–pupil classroom talk and their relationship to learning: How discursive exploration might be encouraged. *Language and Education, 7*(4), 239–257.

Fisher, E. (1996). Identifying effective educational talk. *Language and Education, 10*, 237–253.

Forman, E. (1989). The role of peer interaction in the social construction of mathematical knowledge. *International Journal of Educational Research, 13*, 55–70.

Forman, E., & Cazden, C. (1985). Exploring Vygotskian perspectives in education: the cognitive value of peer interaction. In J. Wertsch (Ed.). *Culture, Communication and Cognition: Vygotskian Perspectives* (pp. 323–347). Cambridge, MA: Cambridge University Press.

Fourlas, G., & Wray, D. (1990). Children's oral language: A comparison of two classroom organisational systems. In D. Wray (Ed.). *Emerging Partnerships, Current Research in Language and Literacy* (pp. 76–86). Clevedon: Multilingual Matters Ltd.

Green, J., & Mayer, L. (1991). The embeddedness of reading in classroom life: Reading as a situated process. In C. Baker, & A. Luke (Eds.). *Toward a Critical Sociology of Reading Pedagogy* (pp. 141–160). Amsterdam: Benjamins Publishing Company.

Green, J., & Wallat, C. (1981). Mapping instructional conversations — a sociolinguistic ethnography. In J. Green, & C. Wallat (Eds.). *Ethnography and Language in Educational Settings* (pp. 161–228). Norwood: Ablex Publishing Corporation.

Greeno, J.G. (1997). On claims that answer the wrong questions. *Educational Researcher, 26*, 5–17.

Greeno, J.G., Smith, D.R., & Moore, J.L. (1993). Transfer of situated learning. In D.K. Detterman, & R.J. Sternberg (Eds.). *Transfer on Trial: Intelligence, Cognition, and Instruction* (pp. 99–167). Norwood, NJ: Ablex.

Grossen, M. (1994). Theoretical and methodological consequences of a change in the unit of analysis for the study of peer interactions in a problem solving situation. *European Journal of Psychology of Education, 11*(1), 159–173.

Halliday, M.A.K., & Hasan, R. (1989). *Language, Context, and Text*. London: Oxford University press.

Harré, R., & Gillett, G. (1994). *The Discursive Mind*. London: Sage Publications.

John-Steiner, V., & Mahn, H. (1996). Sociocultural approaches to learning and development: A Vygotskian framework. *Educational Psychologist, 31*, 191–206.

Kumpulainen, K. (1996). The nature of peer interaction in the social context created by the use of word processors. *Learning and Instruction, 6*, 243–261.

Kumpulainen, K. (1997). Learning interactions during collaborative group work. A research project [http://koklweb1.oulu.fi/kokl/facct/enfacct.htm]. 3 Nov 1997.

Kumpulainen, K., Kaartinen, S., & Mutanen, M. (1998, September). *Constructing Joint Understanding of Solids in a Collaborative Design Task*. A paper presented at the Annual conference of the European Educational Research Association, Ljubljana, Slovenia.

Kumpulainen, K., & Mutanen, M. (1998). Collaborative practice of science construction in a computer-based multimedia environment. *Computers and Education, 30*, 75–85.

Kumpulainen, K., & Mutanen, M. (1999). The situated dynamics of peer group interaction: An introduction to an analytic framework. *Learning and Instruction, 9*, 448–474.

Lave, J., & Wenger, E. (1991). *Situated Learning. Legitimate Peripheral Participation*. Cambridge: Cambridge University Press.

Lemke, J.L. (1990). *Talking Science: Language, Learning and Values*. Norwood, NJ: Ablex.

Light, P., & Perret-Clermont, A.-N. (1991). Social context effects in learning and testing. In P. Light, S. Sheldon, & M. Woodhead (Eds.). *Learning to Think, Child Development in Social Context 2* (pp. 136–150). London: Routledge

Light, P., Littleton, K., Messer, D., & Joiner, R. (1994). Social and communicative processes in computer-based problem solving. *European Journal of Psychology of Education, 11*(1), 93–109.

Mercer, N. (1994). The quality of talk in children's joint activity at the computer. *Journal of Computer Assisted Learning, 10*, 24–32.

Mercer, N. (1995). *The Guided Construction of Knowledge: Talk Among Teachers and Learners*. Clevedon: Multilingual Matters.

Mercer, N. (1996). The quality of talk in children's collaborative activity in the classroom. *Learning and Instruction, 6*, 359–377.

Palincsar, A.S. (1986). The role of dialogue in providing scaffolded instruction. *Educational Psychologist, 21*, 73–98.

Perret-Clermont, A.-N., Perret, J.-F., & Bell, N. (1991). The social construction of meaning and cognitive activity in elementary school children. In L.B. Resnick, J.M. Levine & S.D.Teasley (Eds.). *Perspectives on Socially Shared Cognition* (pp. 41–62). Washington: American Psychological Association.

Phelan, P., Davidson, A.L., & Cao, H.T. (1991). Students' multiple worlds: Negotiating the boundaries of family, peer, and school cultures. *Anthropology & Education Quarterly, 22,* 224–250.

Piaget, J. (1970). *Structuralism.* New York: Basic Books.

Resnick, L.B. (1989). *Knowing. Learning and Instruction: Essays in Honour of Robert Glaser.* Hillsdale, NJ: Lawrence Erlbaum Associates.

Resnick, L.B., Levine, J.M., & Teasley, S.D. (1991) (Eds.). *Perspectives on Socially Shared Cognition.* Washington: American Psychological Association.

Rogoff, B. (1990). *Apprenticeship in Thinking: Cognitive Development in Social Context.* New York: Oxford University Press.

Rosenshine, B.R., & Meister, C. (1994). Reciprocal teaching: A review of research. *Review of Educational Research, 64,* 479–530.

Salomon, G. (1997, August) *Novel Constructivist Learning Environments and Novel Technologies: Some Issues to be Concerned With.* Paper presented at the 7th European Conference for Research on Learning and Instruction (EARLI), Athens, Greece.

Salomon, G., & Perkins, D.N. (1998). Individual and social aspects of learning. *Review of Research in Education, 23,* 1–24.

Schwandt, T. (1998). Constructivist, interpretivist approaches to human inquiry. In N.K. Denzin & Y.S. Lincoln (Eds.). *The Landscape of Qualitative Research, Theories and Issues* (pp. 221–259). London: Sage Publications.

Schubauer-Leoni, M.L., & Grossen, M. (1993). Negotiating the meaning of questions in didactic and experimental contratcs. *European Journal of Psychology of Education, 8,* 451–471.

Schwartz, D.L. (1995). The emergence of abstract representations in dyad problem solving. *The Journal of the Learning Sciences, 4,* 321–354.

Sharan, S., & Shachar, H. (1988). *Language and Learning in the Cooperative Classroom.* New York: Springer-Verlag.

Suortti, J., & Atjonen, P. (1995). The teaching_learning laboratory. A learning environment with a challenge, *Aktuumi, 4,* 42–45.

Teasley, S., & Roschelle, J. (1993). Constructing a joint problem space: The computer as a tool for sharing knowledge. In S.P. Lajoie & S.J. Derry (Eds.). *Computers as Cognitive Tools* (pp. 229–257). Hillsdale, NJ: Lawrence Erlbaum Associates.

Teasley, S. (1995). The role of talk in children's peer collaborations. *Developmental Psychology, 31,* 207–220.

Tharp, R., & Gallimore, R. (1988). *Rousing Minds to Life.* Cambridge: Cambridge University Press.

Tudge, J., & Rogoff, B. (1989). Peer influences on cognitive development: Piagetian and Vygotskian perspectives. In M. Bornstein & J. Bruner (Eds.). *Interaction in Cognitive Development* (pp. 17–40). Hillsdale, NJ: Erlbaum.

Tuyay, S., Jennings, L., & Dixon, C. (1995). Classroom discourse and opportunities to learn: An ethnographic study of knowledge construction in a bilingual third grade classroom. In R. Durán (Ed.). *Discourse Processes (Literacy Among Latinos: Focus on School Contexts), 19,* 75–110.

Van der Veer, R., & Valsiner, J. (Eds.). (1994). *The Vygotsky Reader.* Oxford: Blackwell Publishers.

Vion, R. (1992). *La Communication Verbale. Analyse des Interactions.* Paris: Hachette.

Vygotsky, L.S. (1962). *Thought and Language* (E. Hanfmann, & G. Vakar, Eds. and Trans.). Cambridge, MA: MIT Press.

Vygotsky, L. S. (1978). *Mind in Society: The Development of Higher Mental Processes* (M.

Cole, V. John-Steiner, & E. Souberman (Eds.). Cambridge, MA: Harvard University Press.

Webb, N.M., Troper, J.D., & Fall, R. (1995). Constructive activity and learning in collaborative small groups. *Journal of Educational Psychology*, *87*(3), 406–423.

Wells, G., & Chang-Wells, G.L. (1992). *Constructing Knowledge Together: Classrooms as Centers of Inquiry and Literacy*. Portsmouth, NH: Heinemann.

Wertsch, J. (1985). *Vygotsky and the Social Formation of Mind*. Cambridge, MA: Harvard University Press.

Wertsch, J. (1991). *Voices of the Mind: A Sociocultural Approach to Mediated Action*. Cambridge, MA: Harvard University Press.

Wertsch, J., & Stone, A. (1985). The concept of internalization in Vygotsky's account of the genesis of higher mental functions. In J. Wertsch (Ed.). *Culture, Communication, and Cognition: Vygotskian Perspectives* (pp. 162–179). New York: Cambridge University press.

Westgate, D., & Hughes, M. (1997). Identifying "quality" in classroom talk: An enduring research task. *Language and Education*, *11*, 125–139.

Chapter 11

Alexander, P.A., & Kulikowich, J.M. (1994). Learning from physics text: a synthesis of recent research. *Journal of Research in Science Teaching*, *31*(9), 895–911.

Bennett, N., & Dunne, E. (1991). The nature and quality of talk in co-operative classroom groups. *Learning and Instruction*, *1*, 103–118.

Biemans, H.J.A. (1997). *Fostering Activation of Prior Knowledge and Conceptual Change*. Arnhem: H.J.A. Biemans: Dissertation.

Brown, A.L., & Palincsar, A.S. (1989). Guided cooperative learning and individual knowledge acquisition. In L.B. Resnick (Ed.). *Knowing, Learning and Instruction, Essays in Honor of Robert Glaser* (pp. 395–451). Hillsdale, New Jersey: Lawrence Erlbaum.

Caravita, S., & Halldén, O. (1994). Re-framing the problem of conceptual change. *Learning and Instruction*, *4*, 89–111.

Carter, G., & Gail Jones, M. (1994). Verbal and nonverbal behavior of ability-grouped dyads. *Journal of Research in Science Teaching*, *31*(6), 603–619.

Centraal Instituut voor Toets Ontwikkeling (1987). *Belevingsschaal voor Wiskunde*. Arnhem: Cito.

Chinn, C.A., & Brewer, W.F. (1993). The role of anomalous data in knowledge acquisition: a theoretical framework and implications for science instruction. *Review of Educational Research*, *63*(1), 1–49.

Cohen, E.G. (1986). *Designing Groupwork. Strategies for the Heterogeneous Classrooms*. New York: Teachers College Press.

Cohen, E.G. (1994). Restructuring the classroom: Conditions for productive small groups. *Review of Educational Research*, *64*, 1–35.

Damon, W., & Phelps, E. (1989). Critical distinctions among three methods of peer education. *International Journal of Educational Research*, *13*, 9–19.

Dillenbourg, P., Baker, M., Blay, A., & O'Malley, C. (1995). The evolution of research on collaborative learning. In H. Spada, & P. Reimann (Eds.). *Learning in Humans and Machines. Towards an Interdisciplinary Learning Science* (pp. 189–211). Oxford: Pergamon.

Doise, W., & Mugny, G. (1984). *The Social Development of the Intellect*. Oxford: Pergamon Press.

Elshout-Mohr, M., & Hout-Wolters, B. van (1995). Actief leren en studeren: acht scenario's. *Pedagogische Studiën*, 72, 273–300.

Erkens, G. (1997). *Coöperatief Probleemoplossen met Computers in het Onderwijs. Het Modelleren van Coöperatieve Dialogen voor de Ontwikkeling van Intelligente Onderwijssystemen*. Utrecht: Brouwer Uithof.

Eylon, B., & Linn, M.C. (1988). Learning and instruction: an examination of four research perspectives in science education. *Review of Educational Research*, 58(3), 251–301.

Ferguson-Hessler, M.G.M., & De Jong, T. (1993). Het leren van exacte vakken. In W. Tomic, & P. Span (Eds.). *Onderwijspsychologie. Benvloeding, Verloop en Resultaten van Leerprocessen* (pp. 331–351). Utrecht: Lemma BV.

Graesser, A.C., Person, N.K., & Huber, J. (1993). Question asking during tutoring and in the design of educational software. In M. Rabinowitz (Ed.). *Cognitive Science Foundations of Instruction* (pp. 149–172). Hillsdale, New Jersey: Erlbaum.

Grossen, M. (1994). Theoretical and methodological consequences of a change in the unit of analysis for the study of peer interactions in a problem solving situation. *European Journal of Psychology of Education*, 9, 159–173.

Hidi, S. (1990). Interest and its contribution as a mental resource for learning. *Review of Educational Research*, 60, 549–571.

Joshua, S., & Dupin, J.J. (1987). Taking into account student conceptions in instructional strategy: an example in physics. *Cognition and Instruction*, 4(2), 117–135.

King, A. (1990). Enhancing peer interaction and learning in the classroom through reciprocal questioning. *American Educational Research Journal*, 27(4), 664–687.

Krapp, A., Hidi, S., & Renninger, K.A. (1996). Interest, learning and development. In R.M. Sorrentino, & E.T. Higgins (Eds.). *Handbook of Motivation and Cognition*. Volume 3. *The Interpersonal Context* (pp. 3–26). New York/London: The Guilford Press.

Kumpulainen, K. (1996). The nature of peer interaction in the social context created by the use of word processors. *Learning and Instruction*, 6, 243–261.

Lemke, J.L. (1990). *Talking Science. Language, Learning and Values*. Norwood, New Jersey: Ablex Publishing Corporation.

Licht, P. (1990). A microscopic model for a better understanding of the concepts of voltage and current. In P.L. Lijnse, P. Licht, W. de Vos, & A.J. Waarlo (Eds.). *Relating Macroscopic Phenomena to Microscopic Particles* (pp. 316–327). Utrecht: CD-B Press.

Lijnse, P.L., & De Vos, W. (1990). *Didactiek in Perspectief. Het Centrum voor Didactiek van Wiskunde en Natuurwetenschappen Geopend*. Utrecht: CD-B Press, Centrum voor B-didactiek.

O'Donnell, A.M., Dansereau, D.F., Hall, R.H., & Rocklin, T.R. (1987). Cognitive, social/affective, and metacognitive outcomes of scripted cooperative learning. *Journal of Educational Psychology*, 79, 431–437.

Palincsar, A.S., Anderson, C., & David, Y.M. (1993). Pursuing scientific literacy in the middle grades through collaborative problem solving. *The Elementary School Journal*, 93, 643–658.

Perkins, D.N., & Unger, C. (1994). A new look in representations for mathematics and science learning. *Instructional Science*, 22, 1–37.

Pintrich, P.R., Marx, W., & Boyle, R.A. (1993). Beyond cold conceptual change: the role of motivational beliefs and classroom contextual factors in the process of conceptual change. *Review of Educational Research*, 63(2), 167–199.

Roschelle, J. (1992). Learning by collaborating. Convergent conceptual change. *The Journal of the Learning Sciences*, *2*(3), 235–276.

Roth, W-M., & Roychoudhury, A. (1993). The concept map as a tool for the collaborative construction of knowledge: A microanalysis of high school physics students. *Journal of Research in Science Teaching*, *30*, 503–534.

Roth, W-M., & Roychoudhury, A. (1994). Science discourse through collaborative concept mapping: new perspectives for the teacher. *International Journal of Science Education*, *6*(4), 437–455.

Rumelhart, D.E., & Orthony, A. (1978). The representation of knowledge in memory. In R.C. Anderson, R.J. Spiro & W.E. Montague (Eds.). *Schooling and the Acquisition of Knowledge* (pp. 99–135). Hillsdale, New Jersey: Erlbaum.

Schmidt, H.G., De Volder, M.L., De Grave, W.S., Moust, J.H.C., & Patel, V.L. (1989). Explanatory models in the processing of science text: the role of prior knowledge activation through small-group discussion. *Journal of Educational Psychology*, *81*(4), 610–619.

Salomon, G., & Globerson, T. (1989). When teams do not function the way they ought to. *International Journal of Educational Research*, *13*, 89–99.

Salomon, G., & Perkins, D.N. (1998). Individual and social aspects of learning. In P.D. Pearson, & A. Iran-Nejad (Eds.). *Review of Research in Education* (pp. 1–24). Washington: American Educational Research Association.

Sizmur, S., & Osborne, J., (1997). Learning processes and collaborative concept mapping. *International Journal of Science Education*, *19*(10), 1117–1135.

Tobias, S. (1994). Interest, prior knowledge, and learning. *Review of Educational Research*, *64*(1), 37–54.

Van Boxtel, C. (1997). Samenwerkend leren: begripsontwikkeling in interactie. In L. Meeuwesen, & H. Houtkoop-Steenstra (Eds.). *Sociale Interactie in Nederland* (pp. 205–224). Utrecht: ISOR.

Van Boxtel, C., Van der Linden, J., & Kanselaar, G. (1998). Collaborative construction of conceptual understanding: interaction processes and learning outcomes emerging from a concept mapping and a poster task. *Journal of Interactive Learning Research*, *8*(3/4), 341–362.

Webb, N. M., & Palincsar, A.S., (1996). Group processes in the classroom. In D.C. Berliner, & R.C. Calfee (Eds.). *Handbook of Educational Psychology* (pp. 841–873). New York: Simon & Schuster Macmillan.

Webb, N. (1991). Task-related verbal interaction and mathematics learning in small groups. *Journal of Research in Mathematics Education*, *22*, 366–389.

Webb, N.M. (1989). Peer interaction and learning in small groups. *International Journal of Educational Research*, *13*, 21–39.

Yager, S., Johnson, D., & Johnson, R. (1985). Oral discussion, group-to-individual transfer and achievement in cooperative learning groups. *Journal of Educational Psychology*, *77*, 60–66.

Chapter 12

Burbules, N., & Rice, S. (1991). Dialogue across differences: continuing the conversation. *Harvard Educational Review*, *61*(4), pp. 393–416.

Dawes, L. (1997). Teaching talk. In *Computers and Talk in the Primary Classroom*. R. Wegerif, & P. Scrimshaw (Eds.). Clevedon: Multi-lingual Matters.

Donaldson, M. (1992). *Human Minds*. London: Allen Lane.

Edwards, D., & Mercer, N. (1987). *Common Knowledge: The Development of Understanding in the Classroom.* London: Methuen/Routledge.

Habermas, J. (1990). *Moral Consciousness and Communicative Action.* Cambridge: Polity Press.

Habermas, J. (1991). *The Theory of Communicative Action,* Vol. 1. Cambridge: Polity Press.

Habermas, J. (1995). The unity of reason in the diversity of its voices. In J. Habermas (Ed.). *Postmetaphysical Thinking* (pp. 112–148). Cambridge: Cambridge University Press.

Halliday, M.A.K. (1987). *Spoken and Written Modes of Meaning in Comprehending Oral and Written Language.* London: Academic Press.

Howe, C., Tolmie, A., Anderson, A., & Mackenzie, M. (1992). Conceptual knowledge in physics: The role of group interaction in computer-supported teaching. *Learning and Instruction, 2,* 161–183.

Kruger, A.C. (1993). Peer collaboration: conflict, co-operation, or both? *Social Development, 23,* 165–182.

Mercer N., Wegerif, R., & Dawes (1999). Children's talk and the development of reasoning in the classroom. *British Educational Research Journal, 25*(1), 95–111.

Mercer, N. (1995). *The Guided Construction of Knowledge: Talk Amongst Teachers and Learners.* Clevedon: Multilingual Matters.

Mercer, N. (1996a). The quality of talk in children's collaborative activity in the classroom. *Learning and Instruction, 64,* 359–379.

Mercer, N. (1996b). Socio-cultural perspectives and the study of classroom discourse. In C. Coll, & D. Edwards (Eds.). *Teaching, Learning and Classroom Discourse.* Madrid: Infancia and Aprendizaje, pp. 13–23.

Mercer, N., & Fisher, E. (1993). How do teachers help children to learn? An analysis of teachers' interventions in computer-based activities. *Learning and Instruction, 2,* 339–355.

Olson, D. (1986). *Mind, Media and Memory: the Archival and Epistemic Functions of Written Text.* McLuhan Program in Culture and Technology, University of Toronto.

Piaget, J. (1971/47). *The Psychology of Intelligence.* London: Routledge.

Raven, J., Raven, C., & Court, J. (1995). *Manual for Raven's Progressive Matrices and Vocabulary Scales.* Section I: General Overview. Oxford: Oxford Psychologists Press.

Rorty, R. (1991). *Objectivity, Relativism, and Truth: Philosophical Papers,* Vol. 1. Cambridge: Cambridge University Press.

Wegerif, R. (1999). Two images of reason in educational theory. *The School Field, 9*(3), 77–105.

Wegerif, R., & Mercer, N. (1997a). A dialogical framework for researching peer talk. In R. Wegerif, & P. Scrimshaw (Eds.). *Computers and Talk in the Primary Classroom* (pp. 49–61). Clevedon: Multi-lingual Matters.

Wegerif, R., & Mercer, N. (1997b). Using computer-based text analysis to integrate quantitative and qualitative methods in the investigation of collaborative learning. *Language and Education, 11*(3), 271–286.

Wegerif, R., Mercer, N., & Dawes, L. (1999). From social interaction to individual reasoning: an empirical investigation of a possible socio-cultural model of cognitive development. *Learning and Instruction, 9*(5), 493–516.

White, S. (1988). *The Later Work of Jurgen Habermas.* Cambridge, MA: Harvard University Press.

Wood, D. (1988). *How Children Think and Learn.* Oxford: Basil Blackwell.

Chapter 13

Blanton, W., Moorman, G., Hayes, B., & Warner, M. (1996). Effects of participation in the Fifth Dimension on school achievement. Technical Report 3. Fifth Dimension Project. Presented at the 2nd Conference of Socio-Cultural research: Vygotsky-Piaget, Geneva, Switzerland.

Bronckart, J.P. (1992). El discurso como acción. Por nuevo paradigma psicolongüístico. *Anuario de Psicologa*, Universidad de Barcelona, *54*, 3–48.

Brown, A.L., & Campione, J.C. (1996). Psychological theory and the design of innovative learning environments: on procedures, principles and systems. In L. Schauble, & R. Glaser (Eds.). *Innovations in Learning: New Environments for Education* (pp. 289–325). Mahwah, NJ: Lawrence Erlbaum Associates, Inc.

Brown, A.L., & Reeve, R. (1987). Bandwidths of competence: the role of supportive contexts in learning and development. In L.S. Liben (Ed.). *Development and Learning: Conflict or Congruence?* (pp. 173–223). Hillsdale, NJ: Lawrence Erlbaum.

Brown, A.L., & Palincsar A.S. (1989). Guided, co-operative learning and individual knowledge acquisition. In L. Resnick (Ed.). *Knowing, Learning and Instruction* (pp. 393–451). New York: Lawrence Erlbaum.

Bruner, J. (1990). *Acts of Meaning*. London: Harvard University Press.

Cole, M. (1996). *Cultural Psychology. A Once and Future Discipline*. Cambridge, MA: Harvard University Press.

Cole, M. (1998). Can Cultural Psychology help us think about diversity? *Mind, Culture and Activity*, *5*(4), 291–304.

Cole, M., & Brown, C. (1996–1997). Using new information technologies in the creation of sustainable afterschool literacy activities. *Third Year Report to A.M. Foundation*. Laboratory of Comparative Human Cognition, University of California, San Diego.

Coll, C., & Edwards, D. (Eds.). (1996). *Teaching, Learning and Classroom Discourse*. Madrid: Infancia y Aprendizaje.

Cowie, E., Smith, P., Boulton, M., & Laver, R. (1994). *Cooperation in the Multi-Ethnic Classroom: The Impact of Cooperative Group Work on Social Relationships in Middle Schools*. London: David Fulton.

Edwards, D., & Mercer, N. (1987). *Common Knowledge: The Development of Understanding in the Classroom*. London: Methuen/Routledge.

Elbers, E., Maier, R., Hoekstra, T., & Hoogsteder, M. (1992). Internalisation and adult-child interaction. *Learning and Instruction*, *2*, 101–118.

Hammersley, M. (1994). Questioning the qualitative and quantitative divide. Paper presented at the 1994 Annual Conference of the British Psychological Society.

Hedegaard, M. (1996). The zone of proximal development as basis for instruction. In H. Daniels (Ed.). *An Introduction to Vygotsky* (pp. 171–195). London: Routledge.

Hicks, D. (Ed.). (1996). *Discourse, Learning and Schooling*. Cambridge: Cambridge University Press.

Hohmann, J., Banet, J., & Weikart, D. (1979). *Young Children In Action*. Ypsilanti, the High/Scope Press.

Lave, J., & Wenger, E. (1991). *Situated Learning. Legitimate Peripheral Participation*. Cambridge: Cambridge University Press.

Mercado, R. (1997). El habla en el aula como vehiculo del proceso de ensenanza-aprendizaje en una escuela primaria de Mexico. Doctoral Thesis, Autonomous University of Madrid, Spain.

Mercado, R., Rojas-Drummond, S.M., Mercer, N., Dabrowski, E., & Huerta, A. (1997). La interacción maestro-alumno como vehículo del proceso de enseñanza-aprendizaje en la escuela primaria. *Morphé, 8–9*(15/16), July 1996–June 1997.

Mercer, N. (1995). *The Guided Construction of Knowledge: Talk Amongst Teachers and Learners.* Clevedon: Multilingual Matters.

Moll, L. (1990). *Vygotsky and Education: Instructional Implications and Applications of Socio-Historical Psychology.* Cambridge: Cambridge University Press.

Newman, D., Griffin, P., & Cole, M. (1989). *The Construction Zone. Working for Cognitive Change in School.* Cambridge: Cambridge University Press.

Nicolopolou, A., & Cole, M. (1993). The Fifth Dimension, its play-world, and its institutional contexts: The generation and transmission of shared knowledge in the culture of collaborative learning. In E.A. Forman, N. Minnick, & C.A. Stone (Eds.). *Contexts for Learning. Sociocultural Dynamics in Children's Development.* New York: Oxford University Press.

Renshaw, P., & Brown R. (1999). Appropriation and resistance within collaborative learning activities. Analyses of teacher-student and student-student interaction based on Bakhtin's theory of voice. Paper presented at the European Association for Research on Learning and Development Conference, Göteberg, Sweden, 1999.

Rogoff, B. (1994). Developing understanding of the idea of communities of learners. *Mind, Culture and Activitiy, 1*(4), 209–229.

Rogoff, B., & Lave, J. (1984). *Everyday Cognition: Its Development in Social Context.* Cambridge, MA: Harvard University Press.

Rogoff, B., & Wertsch, J. (Eds.). (1984). Children's learning in the zone of proximal development. *New Directions for Child Development.* No. 23, San Francisco: Jossey Bass.

Rogoff, B. (1990). *Apprenticeship in Thinking. Cognitive Development in Social Context.* New York: Oxford University Press.

Rojas-Drummond, S., & Alatorre, J. (1994). The development of independent problem solving in pre-school children. In N. Mercer, & C. Coll (Eds.). *Explorations in Socio-cultural Studies, Vol. 3: Teaching, Learning and Interaction* (pp. 161–175). Madrid: Infancia y Aprendizaje.

Rojas-Drummond, S., Dabrowski, E., & Gomez, L. (1998). Functional literacy in Mexican primary schools: A research review. *Center for Language and Communications Occasional Papers, 55,* November. Milton Keynes: The Open University.

Rojas-Drummond, S., Hernandez, G., Velez, M., & Villagran, G. (1998). Cooperative learning and the appropriation of procedural knowledge by primary school children. *Learning and Instruction, 8*(1), 37–62.

Rojas-Drummond, S., & Laboratorio de Cognicion y Comunicacion (1998). Creando comunidades de aprendizaje en escuelas primarias en Mexico: Una perspectiva Sociocultural. *Educar, 9.* Guadalajara, Jalisco: Secretaria de Educacion Publica Mexico, pp. 29–40.

Rojas-Drummond, S., Mercer, N., & Dabrowski, E. (in press). Teacher-student interaction and the development of problem solving in Mexican classrooms. *British Journal of Educational Psychology.*

Rojas-Drummond, S., Marquez, A., Rios, R., & Velez, M. (1999). The social construction of knowledge in learning communities: analysing and promoting adult-child and child-child interactions. Paper presented at the European Association for Research on Learning and Development Conference, Göteberg, Sweden, 1999.

Rojas-Drummond, S., Mercer, N., Velez, M., & Rios, R. (in press). Interaction, discourse and the promotion of functional literacy in the classroom. *Center for Language and Communications Occasional Papers.* Milton Keynes: The Open University.

Saxe, J. Guberman, S., & Gearhart, M. (1987). Social processes in early number development. *Monographs of the Society for Research in Child Development.* (216), *52*(2).

Vygotsky, L.S. (1962). *Thought and Language.* Cambridge, MA: MIT Press.

Vygotsky, L.S. (1978). *Mind in Society.* Cambridge, MA: Harvard University Press.

Wegerif, R., & Mercer, N. (1997). Using computer-based text analysis to integrate qualitative
and quantitative methods in research on collaborative learning. *Language and Education,*
11(3), 271–286.

Wegerif, R., & Scrimshaw, P. (Eds.). (1997). *Computers and Talk in the Primary Classroom.*
Clevedon: Multilingual Matters.

Wegerif, R., Rojas-Drummond, S., & Mercer, N. (1999). Language for the social construction
of knowledge: comparing classroom talk in Mexican preschools. *Language and Education,*
13(2), 133–151.

Wertsch, J. (1991). *Voices of the Mind.* London: Harvester.

Wertsch, J. (1998). *Mind as Action.* New York: Oxford University Press.

Wertsch, J., Del Rio, P., & Alvarez, A. (Eds.). (1995). *Sociocultural Studies of Mind.*
Cambridge: Cambridge University Press.

Wertsch, J., McNamee, G., McLane J., & Budwing, N. (1980). The adult-child dyad as a
problem-solving system. *Child Development, 51,* 1215–1221.

Wood, D., Bruner, J., & Ross, G. (1976). The role of tutoring in problem-solving. *Journal of
Child Psychology and Psychiatry, 17,* 89–100.

Chapter 14

Brown, A. (1994). The advancement of learning. *Educational Researcher, 23,* 4–12.

Creswell, J.W. (1998). *Qualitative Inquiry and Research Design.* London: Sage.

Dallos, R. (1992). Creating relationship. In D. Miell, & R. Dallos (Eds.). *Social Interaction
and Personal Relationships* (pp. 102–157). Milton Keynes: Butler & Tanner.

Gee, J.P., & Green, J.L. (1998). Discourse analysis, learning, and social practice: A
methodological study. *Review of Research in Education, 23,* 119–169.

Grossen, M., Iannaccone, A., Liengme Bessire, M-J., & Perret-Clermont, A-N. (1997).
Actual and perceived expertise: the role of social comparison in the mastery of right and
left recognition in novice-expert dyads. *Swiss Journal of Psychology, 55,* 176–187.

Kazdin, A.E. (Ed.) (1992). *Methodological Issues and Strategies in Clinical Research.*
Washington: APA.

Littleton, K., & Light, P. (Eds.) (1999). *Learning with Computers. Analysing Productive
Interaction.* London: Routledge.

Littleton, K. (1999). Productivity through interaction. In K. Littleton, & P. Light (Eds.).
Learning with Computers. Analysing Productive Interaction (pp. 179–194). London:
Routledge.

Index